THE
DACHSHUND

Anna Katherine Nicholas and Marcia A. Foy
With a special section on Dachshund Field Trials
by Patricia Nance

Title page: Fleming's Bronze Benedictine, double granddam of Fleming's Cherry Genevieve who, bred to Red Locket Racketeer (Dorward) produced Ch. Fleming's Cherry Carmela. Genevieve's grandsires were Ch. Flair of Gera and Ch. Lance of Heying-Teckel. Mrs. Polly Fleming, Los Angeles, California.

Distributed in the UNITED STATES by T.F.H. Publications, Inc., 211 West Sylvania Avenue, Neptune City, NJ 07753; in CANADA to the Pet Trade by H & L Pet Supplies Inc., 27 Kingston Crescent, Kitchener, Ontario N2B 2T6; Rolf C. Hagen Ltd., 3225 Sartelon Street, Montreal 382 Quebec; in CANADA to the Book Trade by Macmillan of Canada (A Division of Canada Publishing Corporation), 164 Commander Boulevard, Agincourt, Ontario M1S 3C7; in ENGLAND by T.F.H. Publications Limited, 4 Kier Park, Ascot, Berkshire SL5 7DS; in AUSTRALIA AND THE SOUTH PACIFIC by T.F.H. (Australia) Pty. Ltd., Box 149, Brookvale 2100 N.S.W., Australia; in NEW ZEALAND by Ross Haines & Son, Ltd., 18 Monmouth Street, Grey Lynn, Auckland 2 New Zealand; in SINGAPORE AND MALAYSIA by MPH Distributors (S) Pte., Ltd., 601 Sims Drive, #03/07/21, Singapore 1438; in the PHILIPPINES by Bio-Research, 5 Lippay Street, San Lorenzo Village, Makati Rizal; in SOUTH AFRICA by Multipet Pty. Ltd., 30 Turners Avenue, Durban 4001. Published by T.F.H. Publications Inc. Manufactured in the United States of America by T.F.H. Publications, Inc.

Contents

In Appreciation

To all of the fanciers who have responded so promptly and generously to our requests for material for this book, our deepest gratitude. We are thrilled with the support we have received and proud of the results in adding interest and value to this book.

We gratefully acknowledge, the special features some of our leading authorities have enabled us to present. John R. Hart's American Dachshund Club Honor Roll gives you a complete resumé of pertinent facts about the ADC Specialties from the beginning until time of writing. Dee Hutchinson has given us a marvelous section on grooming the longhaired dachshund. Denny Mounce has shared with us her secrets for superb presentation of the Wirehaired Dachshund in her feature "Grooming the Wire Coat," this being a very difficult matter for many to understand! Muriel Newhauser has permitted us to share her research on Miniature Dachshunds, and it is on her notes, and some from Jeanne Rice, that the Miniature section is based. Many long-time fanciers have shared with us pictures of early "greats" to augment our own.

To each of you, our heartfelt thanks.

About the Authors

Anna Katherine Nicholas

Since early childhood, Anna Katherine Nicholas has been involved with dogs. Her first pets were a Boston Terrier, an Airedale, and a German Shepherd Dog. Then, in 1925, came the first of the Pekingese, a gift from a friend who raised them. Now her home is shared with two Miniature Poodles and numerous Beagles.

Miss Nicholas is best known throughout the Dog Fancy as a writer and as a judge. Her first magazine article, published in *Dog News* magazine around 1930, was about Pekingese, and this was followed by a widely acclaimed breed column, "Peeking at the Pekingese," which appeared for at least two decades, originally in *Dogdom* then, following the demise of that publication, in *Popular Dogs*. During the 1940's she was a Boxer columnist for *Pure-Bred Dogs/American Kennel Gazette* and for *Boxer Briefs*. More recently many of her articles, geared to interest fanciers of every breed, have appeared in *Popular Dogs, Pure-Bred Dogs/American Kennel Gazette, Show Dogs, Dog Fancy*, and *The World of the Working Dog*, and for both the Canadian publications, *The Dog Fancier* and *Dogs in Canada*. Her *Dog World* column, "Here, There and Everywhere" was the Dog Writers' Association of America winner of the Best Series in a Dog Magazine Award for 1979. Also a feature article of hers, "Faster Is Not Better," published in *Canine Chronicle*, received Honorable Mention on another occasion.

In 1970 Miss Nicholas won the Dog Writers' Association Award for the Best Technical Book of the Year with her *Nicholas Guide to Dog Judging*. In 1979 the revision of this book again won this award, the first time ever that a revision has been so honored by this organization. Other important dog writer awards which Miss Nicholas has gained over the years have been the Gaines "Fido" on two occasions and the *Kennel Review* "Winkies" also on two occasions, these both in the Dog Writer of the Year category.

It was during the 1930's that Miss Nicholas's first book, *The Pekingese*, appeared in print, published by the Judy Publishing Company. This book, and its second edition, sold out quickly and is now a collector's item, as is her *The Skye Terrier Book* which was published during the 1960's by the Skye Terrier Club of America.

During recent years, Miss Nicholas has been writing books consistently for T.F.H. These include *Successful Dog Show Exhibiting, The Book of the Rottweiler, The Book of the Poodle, The Book of the Labrador Retriever, The Book of the English Springer Spaniel, The Book of the Golden Retriever, The Book of the German Shepherd Dog, The Book of the Shetland Sheepdog, The Book of the Miniature Schnauzer, The World of the Doberman Pinscher* and *The World of the Rottweiler.* Plus, in the newest T.F.H. series, *The Maltese, The Keeshond, The Chow Chow, The Poodle, The Boxer, The Beagle, The Basset Hound,* (the latter two co-authored with Marcia A. Foy), *The German Pointer, The Collie, The Weimaraner,* and numerous other titles. In the KW series she has done *Rottweilers, Weimaraners* and *Norwegian Elkhounds.* And she has written American chapters for two popular English books purchased and published in the United States by T.F.H., *The Staffordshire Bull Terrier,* and *The Jack Russell Terrier.*

Miss Nicholas's association with T.F.H. began in the early 1970's when she co-authored for them five books with Joan Brearley. These are *The Wonderful World of Beagles and Beagling* (also honored by the Dog Writers Association), *This is the Bichon Frise, The Book of the Pekingese, The Book of the Boxer,* and *This is the Skye Terrier.*

Since 1934 Miss Nicholas has been a popular dog show judge, officiating at prestigious events throughout the United States and Canada. She is presently approved for all Hounds, all Terriers, all Toys and all Non-Sporting; plus all Pointers, English and Gordon Setters, Vizslas, Weimaraners, and Wirehaired Pointing Griffons in the Sporting Group and Boxers and Dobermans in Working. In 1970 she became only the third woman ever to have judged Best in Show at the famous Westminster Kennel Club event at Madison Square Garden in New York City, where she has officiated as well on some sixteen other occasions over the years. She has also officiated at such events as Santa Barbara, Chicago International, Morris and Essex, Trenton, Westchester, etc., in the United States; the Sportsman's and the Metropolitan among numerous others in Canada; and Specialty shows in several dozen breeds in both countries. She has judged in almost every one of the United States and in four of the Canadian Provinces. Her dislike of air travel has caused her to refrain from acceptance of the constant invitations to officiate in other parts of the world.

Marcia A. Foy

Marcia A. Foy was born in Chicago and raised in the suburbs of the North Shore. From early childhood she loved dogs and had many breeds at one time or another as pets, including Pekes, a Basset, a Gordon Setter, and Miniature Poodles.

Her first show dog was a Kerry Blue Terrier, That's Dundel of Delwin, who came from the noted Delwin Kennels of Ed Sayres, Sr. She showed this dog for the first time in 1945, when she was eleven years old.

Marcia moved East in 1960, at which time she acquired her first Beagles. Among those she has owned and shown are the unforgettable Champion Kings Creek Triple Threat; his son Champion Rocka-plenty's Wild Oats (who now belongs to A.K.N.); the magnificent bitch, Trippe's daughter, Champion Foyscroft Triple Lena Wor Lo; the multi-Group winners Champion Junior's Foyscroft Wild Kid and the 13" Champion Jo Mar's Repeat Performance; and many others. Although she raised only a limited number of litters, she has bred a goodly number of champions, among them dogs who have provided foundation stock for other successful kennels.

Interest in Beagles is shared by a very special love of Poodles, a breed which has long been one of her favorites.

It was in 1976 that Marcia officiated for the first time as a judge, an experience which she has grown to thoroughly enjoy. Her first breeds were Beagles and Dachshunds. Currently she is approved for all Hounds and the Hound Group, the majority of the Terriers, and Best in Show. Her judging assignments take her on a wide course of travel each year, and she has officiated at leading shows throughout the United States and in most of Canada. One of her earliest assignments was that of the National Beagle Club Sweepstakes at Aldie, and she has also judged the Blossom Valley Beagle Club Specialty in California, along with dozens of all-breed shows.

Marcia has been largely instrumental in having persuaded the Southern New York Beagle Club, of which she is an Honorary Member, to hold an annual conformation Specialty, which it now does in conjunction with the Westchester Kennel Club each September—most successfully, we might add!

Ch. Fritz Forst, also from the early 1900's, owned by Mr. Sinnott, Philadelphia, Pennsylvania.

This is another famous early Dachshund, Ch. Drickes owned by Mrs. Hungerford.

Chapter 1

Origin and Early History of the Dachshund

The Dachshund, or Teckel as he is affectionately known in Germany, is a breed of dog developed in Germany over a period of several hundred years for the specific purpose of hunting badger. That the progenitors of these dogs may well have been among the long bodied-short legged dogs depicted with fair frequency on medieval Egyptian woodcuts and other forms of artwork from as far back as the middle 1500's would seem fairly certain. But somewhere along the way migration to Germany took place, where the dogs were bred and adapted to the German peoples' own specific needs as "earth dogs" or "badger dogs."

It is felt that prior to the mid-1700's, the smooth haired Dachshund was derived from crossing the Bracke (Miniature French Pointer) with the Pinscher (German identification of Terrier), the hoped-for result being a dog strong enough to handle badger, built along lines enabling him to "go to ground" in pursuit of his quarry, and with a good nose for trailing. A strong dog was needed, weighing on average between 30-35 pounds for expeditious handling of a badger. At this period, the Dachshund was felt to be primarily a Terrier in type and inclinations. Then came the French Revolution in the mid-1700's, leading to great numbers of emigrants leaving France hastily, accompanied in at least some cases, by their French Basset dogs. The resemblance between the Dachshund and the Basset was obvious, although in those days, contrary to the present, the Dachshund was the larger, stronger and heavier breed. Inter-breeding took place, producing puppies of two quite different types: on the one hand the short-legged puppies with shorter ears and pointed forefaces (more of terrier type) which were called Dachshunds; on the other hand, longer-legged specimens from these litters were called Dachsbracks.

The name "Dachshund" has often led to misconception since many people have felt it indicates that the dog is a hound. Let us remember that the breed was originally named in Germany, where Dachshund correctly translates Badger-dog, Dachs being the German word for badger as is Hund for dog. It is this misunderstanding that originally led the Dachshund to be officially classified as a Hound in English-speaking countries, but actually the tendencies of the breed are more inclined to terrier.

The Longhaired Dachshund is thought to have been created from the original Smooth Dachshunds by the process of selective breeding. It has been noted that from earliest times there was a variance in the amount and texture of Dachshund coats, leading to the theory that those inclined towards long hair were bred to others of similar tendency to produce the Longhaired variety. The other theory we have read on this subject is that a Spaniel cross was introduced to create the Longhaired, but as has been pointed out before now, there is no visible sign of any Spaniel characteristics in the Longhaired Dachshund which would give credibility to this conjecture. One authority has stated that the two types of coat were in evidence long before the breed was officially recognized.

The Wirehaired Dachshund is a comparatively recent development as compared to the smooths and longcoats. Dogs similar to Dachshunds in type with wire coats are known to have existed in earlier centuries, but as a separate breed, or variety of breed; the first reference we have found to a rough-coated Dachshund was in the late 1790's. Early in the 1800's a Wirehaired Dachshund has been described as taller in leg than the smooth variety with forelegs curved but less bent than in the smooth. We understand that during the late 19th century these dogs were bred for working purposes only, and that no pictures or pedigrees of them are to be found today. It is believed that the Wirehaired Dachshund was derived from the smooth Dachshund and the rough coated Pinscher, with a Dandie Dinmont Terrier outcross eventually for more depth of body and greater length.

The German Dachshund Club was founded in 1888, seven years later than the Dachshund Club in Great Britain.

Chapter 2

The Dachshund in Great Britain

It has been speculated that the first Dachshund to arrive in England was probably one brought over by Prince Albert, Queen Victoria's consort, about 1845, a painting of which, done by the famous artist Landseer, hangs in the gallery at Windsor. Prince Albert is credited with having imported several others of these dogs as well from Prince Edward of Saxe-Weimar. We have read that these first importations were to be seen frequently in Windsor Forest accompanying the Prince on pheasant shooting expeditions.

Both Queen Victoria and Prince Albert were keenly interested in the little Dachshund dogs, and of course their patronage of them made Dachshunds immediately fashionable in social circles.

The descendants of the Dachshunds originally brought to England were bred throughout Queen Victoria's reign; and during the latter part of their lifetime by the Prince of Wales, who later became King Edward VII. Queen Victoria had always been interested in showing her dogs, and the Dachshunds were no exception. King Edward VII also carried on this tradition with a team of his own. Dog show records of the past include the fact that at the famed Crystal Palace Dog Show in 1875, Edward had four Dachshunds in competition, winning first prize in the class of black and tans where the second place award was to a bitch bred by Queen Victoria. Queen Alexandra, wife of King Edward, also loved the Dachshunds.

Show Dachshunds as a recognized breed did not reach England until about 1870. Previously, those few which were exhibited were shown in the class for foreign breeds, and as late as 1874 they were classified as "German badger hounds" until such time as the explanation of the noted authorities on the subject, Dr. Caius and George R. Krehl had persuaded the public that what in Germany

Ch. Imber Coffee Bean at age 10½ years, bred and owned by Mrs. K. M. Raine, can well be called "the father of the modern British long haired Dachshund." Born in 1954, he sired a record 15 British Champions and was Top Sire ten times.

is a "hund" is in England a "dog," and that correctly the breed is "Badger dog."

As already noted, the Dachshund Club of England was founded more than half a dozen years earlier than the one in Germany. This occasion took place on January 7, 1881 in London, attended by a group of England's leading Dachshund breeders of the day. Mr. A. M. Arkwright had been breeding extensively since the late 1870's, raising such notable early champions as Maximus, Superbus, Olympian, Ozone and Senta. Major Harry Jones was breeder of, or had owned at one time or another, during the major portion of the late 1800's most prominent winners, including Champions Jackdaw, Pterodactyl, Joan of Arc, Wiseacre, Jabin and Jude to name only a few. Mr. Montague Wootten was breeder of Champions Zigzag, Hagar, Jezebel, Zedkiel, Zeyn and Zulemus. These gentlemen, along with one or two others, became the officers of the new club, Mr. Wootten serving as secretary.

Strange as it may seem, this being a German breed, the first "conception of the ideal specimen" or "standard of points" as we now call it, was drawn up not in Germany but by the English Club since it was organized ahead of the German one. Since this was probably drawn up after the appearance of the dogs of that day, and is actually the original breed standard for Dachshunds, we reprint it here for the attention of our readers.

HEAD AND SKULL — Long, level and narrow; peak well developed, no stop, eyes intelligent and somewhat small, following the body in colour.   12 points

EARS — Long, broad and soft; set on low and well back; carried close to the head.   6½ points.

JAWS — Strong, level and square to the muzzle; canines recurrent.   5 points

CHEST — Deep and narrow; breast bone prominent. 7 points

LEGS AND FEET — Forelegs very short and strong in bone, well crooked, not standing over; elbows well clothed with muscle, neither in nor out; feet large, round and strong, with thick pads and strong nails. Hind legs smaller in bone and higher, hind feet smaller. The dog must stand true, i.e., equally on all parts of its foot.   20 points

SKIN AND COAT — Skin thick, loose, supple and in great quantity; coat dense, short and strong.   13 points

LOIN — Well arched, long and muscular.

STERN — Long and strong, flat at root, tapering to the tip; hair on underside coarse; carried low except when excited. Quarters very muscular.5 points

BODY — Length from back of head to root of stern two and a half times the height at shoulder. Fore-ribs well sprung; back ribs very short.   13½ points

COLOUR — Any colour; nose to follow body colour; much white objectionable.

SYMMETRY AND QUALITY — The Dachshund should be long, low and graceful — not cloddy.

WEIGHT — Dogs about 21 lbs.; bitches about 18 lbs.

What a very different standard this is from those which have followed! In looking at it, please bear in mind that the dog it describes was the Badger Hunting Hound as in those days in the British Isles Dachshunds were still considered to be *hounds*.

Needless to say, in 1888 when the German Dachshund Club prepared its own standard, requisites were quite different! Called for here was a dog far more in keeping with the modern version of the breed, cleaner in outline, compact although long and low, with well ribbed body, very little crook in the forelegs, and a sounder dog without exaggeration. We understand that both standards existed until 1907 when the British Dachshund Club set up a committee to review their standard and revise it more in keeping with that of the German Club.

The majority of the early fanciers were no longer active by the close of World War I, almost the only exception having been Major P.C.G. Hayward. He had some excellent dogs and bitches descended from his Honey strain which he had started some 25 years earlier, based on the first Dachshund he had purchased in 1893 from Major Jones. She was named Honey, a chocolate bitch by a son of Champion Jackdaw from a daughter of Champion Pterodactyl. Also from the pre-war years Miss F.E. Dixon still had a few with which to carry on as did Mr. E.W. Ricks, Mrs. R. Saunders and Lord Wrottesley. Under the leadership of Major Hayward and the veteran Dachshund owner John F. Sayer, these people formed a group to push the Dachshund to the fore, which they did admirably.

Many important Dachshund kennels were active in England during the period between World War I and World War II, and, happily, it was found at the close of the latter that breeders had somehow managed to hold on to representatives of the splendid bloodlines established during the between-wars years. Thus it was that many postwar champions were produced from these same strains to carry on the quality which they had previously attained.

Currently in Great Britain Mrs. M.E. Davies is breeding Standard and Miniature Smooths at her Topthorne Kennels in Suffolk; Mrs. S.M. Clarke is breeding Standard Smooths and Standard and Miniature Longhairs under the Hilmar prefix at Quinton, Wilts. (She speaks with pride of Hilmar Royal Celebrity, son of Champion Phaeland Phreeranger who has many Best of Variety and Best Dachshund wins to his credit); and Tanya Dovey, at Tancegems Kennels in Cornwall, co-owns that area's top winning Miniature Wire Dachshund with Jenny Harvey: Tancegems Larry Lickerish, unbeaten at all open shows attended in Cornwall during 1984.

Joan Danvers breeds Miniature Wires and Miniature Smooths at Danverly Kennels, Halstead, Essex. Among her dogs are the Wirehaired champions, Drakesleaf Rough Stuff and Cannobio Teddy Bear. She also has Danverly Top of the Bill, a homebred son of Champion Drakesleat Komma, among her Wires, plus a Smooth son of Champion Jubilee Gift of Wingcrest, Kabardin Black Diamond.

At Great Harwood, Blackburn, one finds the Loretto Kennels of Mrs. J. Hallett, where Minature Wirehairs are featured. Pride of place here goes to Champion Loretto Fred Flintstone, the winner of seven Challenge Certificates and five reserves, whose wins include the C.C. and Best of Breed at Crufts, another C.C. at South Wales, and yet another at the Lancashire and Cheshire Championship show along with two reserves during 1984 despite the fact that his owner's indisposition has necessitated his being shown only occasionally. Mrs. Hallet is also pleased with Fred's young son, Loretto Pay the Piper, who has won all his six classes at three championship shows during this same period.

Shalfleet Kennels owned by Mrs. Barbara Wilton-Clark at Reading, Berkshire, so famous in the world of Whippets, are now breeding Minature Longhair Dachshunds as well.

Primrose Patch has long been a kennel identification famous in the Dachshund world. Mrs. Sidgwick continues to breed Miniature Longhairs at Mundesley, and has the lovely Champion Primrose Patch Valentine (Champion Woodreed Neddie ex Primrose Patch Lady Perdita) representing her at present.

Bellbar is another kennel featuring handsome mini-longs, this one owned by Mrs. Elliott Wilson at Suffolk. Two good litters being watched with interest at this kennel as we write are by Champion Southcliff Starsky ex Bellbar Victoria; and from Victoria's little sister, Bellbar Virginia by Champion Southcliff Sonosash.

Sidegate Dachshunds, established by Doris Groom in 1939, still are active and located at Ipswich, with some splendid dogs who are winning and siring well.

A large and busy kennel featuring Longhaired Dachshunds is Africandawns, owned by Tony and Jacqueline Johnson, Huntington, Cambs. Among the English Champions one finds on the credit list for this kennel are Africandawns Wagon Master, Boobs of Loggeta, Liberty Bodis, Yang Go Home, Beau Louie, Beau

Top: English Ch. Truanbru Beau Brummel of Africandawns as a puppy. T. L. Johnson, owner, Africandawns Dachshunds, Huntington, Cambs, England. **Bottom:** Africandawns Blond Mystery, winner of 2 Challenge Certificates, also belongs to Mr. Johnson.

Would Be, Susan's Touch of Africandawns, and Murrumbidgee Paganini and Isabella along with Truanbru Beau Brummel of Africandawns. The Johnsons, along with all these champions at home, point with pride to numerous others from their kennel in South Africa, Australia and the United States. Among these are South African Champions Africandawns Bra, Tasty Tart, Big Dick and So He's Erotic; Australian Champions Africandawns Night Quinton, Night Panter, Night Arrow; and American Champion Africandawns So Be Erotic.

Other exports from this kennel include several not yet finished in the States and in South Africa where they have gone quite recently.

Although work and other interests prevent the Johnsons from showing as often as they would enjoy doing, they do breed some very excellent stock and are pleased that numerous of today's well-known kennels have purchased their foundation stock from them while others have used their stud dogs. The young bitch, Champion Susan's Touch of Africandawns, gained her title at Birmingham during 1984 and won her fourth Challenge Certificate at the Club Championship Show. She was campaigned for the Johnsons by Audrey Bishop.

HILMAR

Hilmar Dachshunds, specializing in both Standards and Miniatures, are owned by Mrs. S.M. Clarke at Wiltshire, England. Ever since childhood she has loved the breed, but unfortunately did not get to owning one until about the mid-1970's.

Mrs. Clarke's first Dachshund was a black and tan Standard Longhair dog. Some years later she acquired her first bitch, and the two of them stimulated her interest in showing and breeding. The bitch qualified for Crufts in her first year.

Since that time, Mrs. Clarke has bred and shown on a regular basis with a number of successes.

Early in the 1980's, Mrs. Clarke purchased some property with about two acres of land, and is now establishing a sound breeding program with the prime objective temperament, followed closely by quality. The dog currently being shown is Hilmar Royal Celebrity, a homebred born in 1981. He is a golden red Standard Longhair of super quality, sired by Champion Phaeland Phreeranger from Berkara Benina.

The Hilmar strain is based on Phaeland lineage. Another of the current winners is Hilmar Scarlet Ruby, also homebred, who qualified twice for Crufts, and has numerous wins at Open and Championship shows.

Mrs. Clarke is interested in breeding Standard Smooths and Miniature Longhairs at the present time, with several litters planned around the time that we are going to press. She also is intrigued with the various colors in the minis, and owns silver dapples, red, and black and tan, hoping to bring cream in later.

IMBER

Imber is the kennel identification of one of the world's most dominant strains of Longhaired Dachshunds, owned by Miss Katherine M. "Molly" Raine, who purchased her first Dachshund, a Smooth, in England during 1938, soon after her return there from ten years spent in Canada and New York.

Miss Raine owned and bred champions in all three coats. But it was in Longhairs that her greatest success was achieved. Imber dogs in that variety are admired wherever Dachshunds are known, especially through her dominant force of stud dogs who have sired the record total of 40 British champions in that variety, and who won the Top Sire Award on 16 occasions.

The homebred Champion Imber Coffee Bean is referred to by many as "the father of the modern British Longhaired Dachshund". His own champion progeny included a record 15 British title-holders. He was a prepotent stud, and we are told that he gave the breed the length of head and neck and the correct angulation both front and rear which were sadly lacking at that period.

Coffee Bean was sired by Imber Black Coffee, a recessive Longhair bred from two Smooth parents. His dam, Liza von Holzner, was by a pure Longhair-bred dog from an imported German Longhair bitch.

Apart from his British progeny, Coffee Bean had a tremendous influence on the breed in Australia through his son, Australian Champion Simeon Coffee Bean, owned by Mrs. Ruth Simon.

We are indebted to Jeff Crawford for the information on Miss Raine and the Imber dogs. His own kennel prefix is Voryn, and his own first Longhair was a gift to him from Miss Raine in appreciation of Mr. Crawford's having finished his sire for her. From 1963 onward, Mr. Crawford handled all of Miss Raine's dogs. In

Hilmar Scarlet Ruby, one of the excellent Longhairs owned by Mrs. S. M. Clarke, Hilmar Kennels, Wiltshire, England.

Hilmar Royal Celebrity, born in 1981, is among the handsome Longhair Standard Dachshunds to be found at Hilmar Kennels, Mrs. S. M. Clarke, Wiltshire, England.

speaking of Coffee Bean, Mr. Crawford remarks that he is "behind all of the Longhairs in England many, many times."

Champion Imber Hot Coffee was bred by Miss Raine and is co-owned by her with Mr. Crawford. A son of Champion Albany's Red Rheinhart from Imber Kaffa Moka, he was born in January 1973. He is still with Mr. Crawford as a gray and dignified old gentleman. Hot Coffee has also been highly influential as a stud dog. He is the last of the great Imber sires, and the most successful of them all as a show dog.

Hot Coffee won 24 Challenge Certificates in a long show career that spread over six years. He came out of retirement at Crufts in 1982 and won his 25th C.C. on that occasion at the age of nine years. His earlier wins included three Hound Group 1sts, he was the Top-winning Longhair for 1975 and 1977, Top Sire in 1980 and 1981, and has so far sired seven champions, a number which should be increased as at the present time Mr. Crawford is showing two ten-month-old dog puppies by him from his last litter.

He, too, in addition to his British progeny has had a strong influence on Australian Longhairs, through his son Australian Champion Imber Irish Coffee, owned there by Mrs. Rhonda Phillips of the Lohengrin prefix.

SEVORG

Sevorg Dachshunds are owned by Mr. and Mrs. Ray Groves at Blackwood in Gwent. Theirs is a small kennel operation which prides itself on quality and soundness with, above all, good temperaments.

The Standard Smooth bitch, Hydax Encounter Of Sevorg, belongs to Mr. and Mrs. Groves, and represents leading American bloodlines, her sire being Carrakot Crackerjack of Hydax, who is a grandson of the American import Clarion Call Von Westphalen. Encounter's dam is Hydax Comet, a Challenge Certificate winner with several reserves and four Bests in Show.

Encounter is the winner of many first prizes at open and championship shows, including the Dachshund Club Specialty judged by Mrs. Muriel Newhauser from the United States. She was Best Dachshund at Royal Welsh Agricultural Society in 1983, and Top Winning Standard Dachshund in Wales that year; also Best in Show at the West of England Dachshund Association in October 1984 under judge Mrs. Rene Gale, owner of Womack Dachshunds.

Then there is the Miniature Wire bitch Gaygait Lovable Lily of Sevorg, born in 1981, by Gaygait O'Grady ex Gaygait Miss Groucho. She is a consistent winner at championship shows and was a Best of Breed winner when only eight months of age. She qualified and placed at Crufts in 1982 and 1983.

Ch. Dachsland Forever Yours taking a Best in Show during 1963. Handled by Elaine Rigden for owner, Mrs. Juanita R. Brown.

Ch. White Gables Ristocrat winning Best of Variety at Westminster in 1961. Owner-handled by Ramona (Mrs. Albert E.) Van Court.

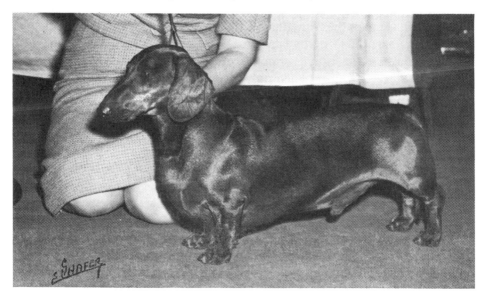

Chapter 3

Dachshunds in the United States

The Dachshund Club of America was founded in 1895. Far earlier than that, however, Dachshunds were enjoying popularity here, and, doing research, we find frequent references to a Dr. Twadell, from Philadelphia, and to a friend of his, Dr. Downie, from Maryland, both of whom had imported some of these dogs using them successfully for "rabbiting."

It was in 1880 that William Loeffler started to exhibit his German imports. This gentleman remained loyal to and involved with showing the breed until the beginning of World War I in 1914. His foundation stock came from Germany, where he visited in 1897. In his search for some quality dogs, he found what he had been seeking at the kennels of the Duke of Coburg, and had the good fortune to acquire a pair from there. The dog was Waldmann, who became famous as a truly outstanding example of the breed. The bitch did not really please Mr. Loeffler; therefore before returning to America he selected what he considered to be a more suitable bitch as a mate for Waldmann; she was Helba bei Meiningen. Upon his return here, Mr. Loeffler exhibited his importations, who did well for themselves, always being in first or second place.

From the breeding of Waldmann and Helba a litter of three puppies was born. Sad to relate, Waldmann was killed in an accident, leaving with Mr. Loeffler a bitch, his daughter, with whom to carry on. Finding a dog to whom she could be bred was not easy. Finally, however, a red dog was located, Unser Fritz, at the kennel of Dr. Twadell—an interesting dog who was a first prize winner at Philadelphia in 1876, whom Dr. Twadell had received as a gift from the Duke of Baden. This alliance produced another litter of three for Mr. Loeffler, who around this time moved from

Ch. Richmond's Flambeau winning at Suffolk County in 1967. Owner-handled by Paul Richmond of Long Island.

Opposite page:
(Top) Ch. Antje von Lichtenstein, from the early 1900's, owned by Mrs. Hungerford of Bayshore, New York. *(Center)* Int'l. Ch. Mighty Fine von Walder, leading imported Miniature Longhair owned by Nancy Onthank, is behind almost all Miniature Longhairs to-day in the United States. Rose Farm Kennels, Pound Ridge, New York. *(Bottom)* Ch. Cavalier v Marienlust, by Ch. Leutnant v Marienlust ex Moya v Marienlust, was one of the great Dachshunds owned by the White Gables Kennels of Mrs. Miriam Van Court, Canoga Park, California. Photo Courtesy of Mrs. Catherine Burg.

Ch. Herman VI, one of the great show Dachsunds of 1963 as a youngster. A multiple Best in Show and consistent Hound Group winner. Owned by Mr. and Mrs. W. Seward Webb, Jr., North Hollywood, California, and handled by Woodie Dorward.

St. Louis, Missouri to Preston, Minnesota, taking along the dogs and continuing breeding there. As time progressed, outcrosses were introduced in the form of a pair imported from the kennels of Count Bismarck with several other purchases from kennels in the United States owned by Charles Klocke at Pittsburgh, Pennsylvania; William Korb, Milwaukee, Wisconsin, and B.F. Seitner, Dayton, Ohio. The pair from Count Bismarck were not what Mr. Loeffler sought, since he found them to be sharp-bitten, bad tempered and quite small; therefore he did not use those in his breeding program. The next purchase was that of Hundesports Bergman and Hundesports Zanker from Herr Ernst von Otto-Kreckwitz, who owned the widely admired Hundesports Waldmann, (not to be confused with the aforementioned) whom we have read of as "the best dog in Germany at the time." Now he felt that he was set with a splendid foundation for breeding, an idea widely shared as he sold many dogs for breeding purposes to all parts of the country.

Among the most important of all early Dachshund breeders was Dr. Montebacher, who was a chemist and a doctor living in New York City. It was this gentleman and another whose name is well-known to fanciers of many breeds, with an interest in early art involving dogs, the great artist G. Muss-Arnolt, who were involved with the foundation of the Dachshund Club of America.

Eventually Harry Peters, who was President of the Dachshund Club of America over all the early years, inherited Dr. Montebacher's dogs. It is interesting to note the association through Dachshunds of Mr. Peters and Mr. Muss-Arnolt, for Mr. Peters was one of the most appreciative fanciers of this artist's tremendous talent, and when Harry Peters, Jr., died a few years back, among the canine memorabilia treasures of his estate were innumerable Muss-Arnolt paintings and drawings of the Windholme Beagles, Greyhounds, and other breeds synonymous with this record-making hound kennel! A great many other fanciers over the years also availed themselves of the opportunity to enjoy Muss-Arnolt's ability to so perfectly depict their dogs, and his popularity, as well as the present value of his work, attest to his success.

Eventually Harry Peters sold the Dachshunds to Mrs. Hungerford of Bayshore, New York, who used them well and at one time had a total of 16 champions in her kennel, which was an especially remarkable record in those days. Half of her dogs were black and tan, the other half red. Two of her particular favorites were Champion Antje v Lichtenstein and Champion Drickes.

The Keller Kennel in Massachusetts also was known for good Dachshunds of that day; and shortly thereafter Mr. Sinnott of Philadelphia was an important force in the breed.

During the first decade of this century, one of the leading Dachshund kennels was that of Mr. George Semler of New York City. As one of the really early Dachshund breeders, Mr. Semler had imported Lutz-Erdmannsheim and Nelly Erdmannsheim in 1898, but the kennel did not reach its full potential until around 1906. Mr. Semler systematically went about purchasing the cream of top quality from Germany. These included the noted Drickes (we assume the same one mentioned above as a favorite of Mrs. Hungerford's), Ramsch v Seelberg, Tell v d Bergsteig, Gugeline Isarlust, and Laufamholz bei Nurnberg among many others. With a system like this, who possibly could fail to succeed? These dogs were identified mostly by the affix "von Lichtenstein" to which Mr. Semler was in the habit of adding his own identification, "West End" on those imported by him. Bonnie v Lichtenstein

West End was said to be especially outstanding among them. Mr. Semler's list of importations continued to grow even beyond this point.

The best part of all this is that these Dachshunds were put to good use here in the United States, and they and their bloodlines provided influential backgrounds behind many succeeding generations. For example, Mr. Semler was the breeder of Champion Plum West End and Champion Brunhilde v Lichtenstein who became the parents of Champion Voewood Frieda and Voewood Alma, two names from the past who influenced the future, and the Voewoods, owned by Mrs. C. Davies Tainter at White Plains, New York, played an important role in furthering Dachshund quality here in the East.

Several of Mr. Semler's dogs also joined the Windholme Kennels of Harry Peters, but mainly they went to Mrs. Hungerford. A side note in speaking of Mr. Peters is that he is credited with having been the earliest exhibitor of dapples, having shown the several who were among the dogs taken over by him when Dr. Montebacher died.

Back in the beginning, when Dachshunds first were accepted for registration by the American Kennel Club, only 11 appeared in the stud books between 1879 and 1885. In reviewing available historical information, it would seem that the breed has prospered well since that time, marking a steady increase during each decade until the present registration total keeps the Dachshunds consistently among the ten most popular breeds of dog in the United States.

During World War I, we have read that three Dachshund kennels of prominence in the United States remained active. These were Isartar, Cleveland, and Allendale. Mrs. Justus Erhardt of Boston, Massachusetts, was breeding prior to that time and continued to do so for many years thereafter.

In the period following World War I, many dogs from leading German kennels were imported by American breeders.

A tremendously active kennel which started in the post-war period (WWI) was Ellenbert Farm belonging to Mr. and Mrs. Herbert Bertrand at Greenwich, Connecticut. Most of their foundation stock came from Flottenberg lines, and included such famed Dachshund names as Champions Heini Flottenberg and Feri Flottenberg and Hela Flottenberg. The kennel produced many splen-

Ch. Voewood Freda, from Mrs. C. Davis Tainter's famous kennels, later owned by Mrs. Rubino of Bayshore, New York, in the early 1900's.

Jerry Rigden's famous Ch. Guyman's Long Deal, one of the numerous outstandingly successful winners with whom this noted Dachshund breeder and all-breed professional handler has been associated.

Am. and Can. Ch. Cid Junior of Lakelands, by Ch. Cid v Werderhavel-strand ex Ch. Harriet v Stalhaus, was one of the "greats" owned by Miriam Van Court, White Gables Kennels, California.

Ch. Derbydachs Schatze, a very famous top winning Dachshund of the 1950's and dam of three champions in one litter (Chs. Badger Hill Nobby, Nox and New Deal). Owned by Jerry Rigden, Wadsworth, Ohio.

did champions from its importations, and was an important one in the Dachshund world of the Eastern United States.

No Dachshund book would be complete which did not pay tribute to the gentleman who to many fanciers was "Mr. Dachshund," Laurence Alden Horswell of Elmhurst, New York. Born in 1892, Mr. Horswell started breeding Dachshunds during the 1920's. He was for many years a Director of the Dachshund Club of America, also holding various terms as President and Secretary. He did a tremendous job as Chairman of the Information Committee; was an Honorary Member of the Dachshund Club of America and 12 of the regional clubs, and a judge of all Hounds starting in the mid-1930's. He was a prolific writer about his favorite breed, holding long tenures as columnist for the *Gazette* and for *Popular Dogs*. He was loved, respected and admired not only in the Dachshund world but by the Dog Fancy in general, and his death was deeply mourned. His wife, Dorothy Allison Horswell, shared his Dachshund interest with him as a Dachshund breeder and judge.

Probably the most influential kennel in all American Dachshund history was von Marienlust owned by Mr. and Mrs. Josef Mehrer, West Hempstead, New York. Here were bred such fantastic dogs as Champion Leutnant v Marienlust (Champion Zep v Marienlust–Champion Denta v Luitpoldsheim), Champion Gunther v Marienlust (Leutant's son from Moya v Marienlust), Champion Herzville v Marienlust (Champion Hertzrumpf v Teckelhof–Veni v Marienlust), Champion Aristo v Marienlust (Bruce v Marienlust–Freda O'Redbairn), Champion Zep v Marienlust, Champion Superman v Marienlust, and so many, many more.

If you will check back in your pedigrees, you will be impressed with the dominance, some generations back, of the von Marienlust dogs; and now in the present day of their descendants. From coast to coast these great dogs made their presence felt, and are to be found in the background, from the mid-1900's and earlier, of some of the leading names in our modern Dachshund history.

We have saved the most famous of these dogs until the end of our comments on this kennel. Rather like frosting on the cake! For where do words even begin to describe the magnificent Smooth Standard whose name was Champion Favorite v Marienlust?? Bred by the Mehrers and owned by Rose and Fred Heying, he became an International Champion, an all-breed Best in Show winner with 35 Group firsts to his credit plus 67 Bests of Variety.

And he founded a dynasty of his own as the sire of about 100 champions (I think that is a conservative count, believing there to be even more), among them the almost equally proficient Champion Falcon of Heying-Teckel, bred by the Heyings, winner of six all-breed Best in Show, 30 Hound Group Firsts, 70 Bests of Variety, and the sire of more than 80 champions! Thus this father and son duo, with a total of close to 180 champions between them, became the two top siring Dachshunds of all time; and other Favorite sons have long lists to their own credit, as do some of Falcon's. On this branch of the family alone, von Marienlust can take a well deserved bow. But then there are, as well, all the other important successful dogs from there, and *their* future generations of progeny!

In 1947 Favorite was Best Smooth Dachshund at Westminster. In 1952, his son Lance won it. In 1954 another son, Livewire, was Best Wire Dachshund there; and in 1956 Falcon was Best Smooth there with his son, Champion Caseway of Firebird, taking Best Smooth there in 1958. The Favorite line is a most notable Dachshund family indeed. Champion Favorite v Marienlust was by Bruce v Marienlust ex Belinda v Marienlust. His son, Champion Falcon of Heying-Teckel, was from Lana of Geran, by Champion White Gables Basil ex Jessy of Gera.

It is interesting to note that Favorite was a half brother to Champion Aristo v Marienlust, owned by Mrs. Lancaster Andrews who later became Mrs. Albert E. Van Court and then Mrs. John Marshall Jones. Aristo made a memorable show record of his own as a Best in Show and Group winner and was a very widely admired little dog.

We wish that this was one of our big books, as there are many other people and dogs influential to the progress of Dachshunds in the first half of the 1900's of whom we would like to write at length. But space simply does not permit. The first Dachshund I knew personally, back in the early 1930's, was Champion Elsa Cinders owned by James Walker Trullinger who became a famous all-breed judge but who always retained a special affection for this breed, I am sure largely due to that gorgeous bitch!

What a lot of truly superb dogs were shown in those days by both Mrs. Maude Daniels Smith and Mrs. Leila Du Bois (who later became Mrs. Richard V. Pell). Maude was a big exhibitor on the East Coast, always represented with a sizeable entry, and al-

Ch. Falcon of Heying-Teckel during his show career in the early 1960's earned 6 Bests in Show, 13 Specialties, and 29 Group Firsts. Sire of more than 60 champions, a son of Ch. Favorite v Marienlust who surely followed in the footsteps of his famous sire. Bred and owned by Mr. and Mrs. Fred Heying, Heying-Teckel Kennels. Photo courtesy of Mrs. Catherine Burg.

The incomparable Int'l. Ch. Favorite v Marienlust in 1958 at the age of 13 years, pictured with two of his grandsons. Photo courtesy of Mrs. Catherine (Katay) Burg.

ways with *good* dogs. Especially successful were Champion Cinnamon v Dachshafen 2nd and Champion Cinnamon v Dachshafen 3rd, father and son as one would surmise. Champion Voewood's Dago v Dachshafen (Champion Vodegel's Raecher–Champion Ren Lak Cilly) was a homebred. Champion Sungold of White Gables was by Champion Cid Junior of Lakelands ex Champion Cornhill Goldie and was bred by Miriam Van Court. Champion Arnette v Dachshafen was by Champion Arno v Hildesheim ex Elsa of Balred, homebred. And there were many more. Both Maude and Leila Pell were very much "into" the Wires, too, especially Mrs. Pell who owned the well-known Champion Arno v Hildesheim, a homebred by Champion Achat v Werderhavelstrand ex Champion Mimosa v Hildesheim. Both of these ladies were temendously good friends to the Dachshund.

Whenever I think of Longhairs from the early days, it is immediately Miss Laura F. Delano who comes to mind. This lady bred Longhairs and Irish Setters at her Knocknagree Kennels, and hers were among the very finest of the mid-1900's. As for de Sangpur, and Gracie Hill (Mrs. William Burr), one could write volumes

Mrs. Winifred Heckmann handling her own famous Standard Smooth, Ch. Sherlitt's Dr. Hank, born July 1958 by Ch. Dalton's Hilary ex Connie v Sigmaringen, bred by Marjorie and Robert Frazier. Pictured at the Dachshund Club of New Jersey 1959 Specialty.

The famous
Standard Smooth
dog, Ch. Venture
of Hardway, bred
and owned by
Nancy Onthank
was an important
Best in Show
winner of his day.
By Ch. Hardway
Welcome Stranger
ex Ch. Red Velvet
of Fre-Delsa.

Ch. Hardway
Welcome Stranger
winning the Hound
Group at Ladies
Kennel Ass'n in
1953. Owned and
handled by
Jeannette W.
Cross, Bennington,
Vermont and
Delray Beach,
Floria. A. K.
Nicholas judging.

The famous Ch. Aristo v Marienlust in the late 1940's winning Best in Show. Owner-handled by Ramona Van Court.

Ch. Celloyd's Daniel, the famous winner of the late 1950's, making one of his many important wins. A multi-Best in Show and Group dog, this son of Daniel v Benmarden ex Celloyd Trinket was a tremendous favorite in his day. Pictured winning the Hound Group at Newtown K.C. in 1958. Owner-handled by Loyd M. Case.

Ch. Holmdachs Consrant Favorite in September 1962. An important Eastern winner owner-handled by Mrs. Betty Holmberg, Holmdachs Kennels.

about this kennel and its owner's various contributions to the breeds. You will find many references to her in the pages of this book, especially in the kennel stories.

John Cook, busy nowadays as a judge, was another breeder who always had the best representing him at Eastern shows. His winners included Champion Kleetal's Delight, Champion Kleetal's Rhapsody, Champion Kleetal's Enchantress, and very many more.

A lady still very active in our dog show world is Katherina Lehfeldt of Westwood, New Jersey. She is a tremendous enthusiast still for the Dachshund although no longer exhibiting, and keeps in touch with her many friends in the Fancy through her activities in the Kennel Club of Northern New Jersey and some of the other New Jersey dog clubs. Her Teckeldorf Kennels were represented in the ring at leading Eastern events over at least several decades.

There are so many dogs and so many people to whom we would like to pay tribute, but present space does not permit. For now I shall turn our readers over to the kennel stories, which will bring you abreast of what is taking place currently in the Dachshund breed. You will find famous long established kennels along with new ones just getting started which we consider to be of promise for the future.

Mrs. Betty Holberg with her handsome winner Ch. Happy Go Lucky of Willow Creek taking Best Wirehair at the Dachshund Club of New Jersey Specialty in May 1962.

Ch. Hainheim's Olinda. By Ch. Hainheim's Lance ex Adora von Marienlust, winning Best of Breed at Westminster in 1955. Handled by Lorraine Heichel Masley under judge Jeanette Cross.

Chapter 4

Dachshund Kennels in the United States

APOTHECARY

Apothecary Dachshunds are owned by Waldemar Rivera at Guaynabo, Puerto Rico, and are fast becoming known for quality and for success in the show ring.

Waldemar is a pharmacist by profession (hence the selection of "Apothecary" as his kennel name), and is a marketing representative for Smith, Kline and French Laboratories.

The first association for Waldemar with Dachshunds came about through the purchase of a pet in 1976, which led to an interest in acquiring a nice bitch from whom to breed. His first attempt, as happens to so many of us, was not what he had hoped for, but his interest continued to grow and he purchased a very nice dog whom Ed Barringer handled to the title for him, Champion Carramoll's Call Be Mathias, who had been bred by Clara Jean Davis and was Winners Dog at the National Specialty in 1979.

While campaigning Mathias, Ed Barringer saw a bitch whom he felt would be exactly what Waldemar should have as a foundation to his breeding program. Thus Tom-Mar's Lyra Nick was purchased. After finishing title (she was a 1981 Group winner and Best of Variety at the Mid-West Dachshund Club Specialty) she was bred to Champion Boondox Chuckie Bunyan and produced a red dog and a black and tan bitch who have certainly made their presence felt in keenest competition. The dog became Champion Apothecary The Say Hey Kid who finished his championship on the strongly competitive Florida Circuit, winning among other awards Best of Variety at the Florida East Coast Dachshund Specialty. The bitch, now Champion Apothecary Black Rosey Rose and co-owned by Waldemar Rivera with Ivelisse Seda, has among her ring credits Best of Variety at the American Kennel Club Centennial Dog Show, November 1984; 17 times Best of Variety in less than three months of showing; and Best of Opposite Sex to Best of Breed at the Sooner Dachshund Club of Oklahoma, both of these young homebreds handled by Hannelore Heller.

Needless to say, no time was lost in breeding Lyra Nick for the second time, on this occasion to Waldemar's own first champion dog, Mathias. There is a lovely litter as the result, with puppies maturing for it is hoped, future show careers.

Champion Abbadare Smooth Jonny, bred by Dick Vaughn, is another of the Dachshunds at Apothecary.

BADGER LAND

Badger Land Dachshunds, owned by Maurice Klinke at Madison, Wisconsin, specialize in Miniature Smooth red and black and

Ch. Barhar Pickwick at two years of age. This handsome Wirehaired Dachshund owned by Charles A. Baris and John R. Hart, Barhar Kennels, Montrose, New York. Charles Baris handling. "Pippin," by Ch. Westphal's Shillalah ex Ch. Midernoch's Wild Card W, sired 5 champions and was No. 1 Wire, *Dachshund Variety System*, in 1975.

tans. Mr. Klinke started with the breed in about 1970, and takes great pleasure in his dogs.

His breeding stock is founded mostly on that from Jeanne Rice's kennel and that of the late Gracie Hill, to both of whom he gives credit for starting him on the road to success. A good Smooth Miniature Dachshund is one of the most difficult little dogs to come by; Mr. Klinke remarks, "I learned years ago that it takes dedication and stick- to-it-iveness to overcome some of the disappointments that accompany trying to breed a better Miniature."

Among the winners in which Mr. Klinke takes pride are Champion Tori-Jarice's Wee Robyn MS, by Tori's Russet Prince MS ex De Sangpur Jarice's Tamara MS, bred by Jeanne Rice and born in September 1977.

The black and tan Champion Badgerlands Wee Bo Jangles, by Tori- Jarice's Wee Thaddeus MS ex Boes Badgerland Wee Robyn, was bred by Sylvia J. Ayen and born in 1981. He has some excellent wins, including at Specialty shows, to his credit.

Champion Rose Farms Sally of Trebor MS is a red miniature by Champion Rose Farms Timothy MS ex Champion Rose Farms Elsie MS. Born in 1982, she was bred by Robert A. Hauslohner. Mr. Klinke's Miniatures are all most capably handled by Hannelore Heller.

BARHAR

Barhar Dachshunds began in 1964 when John Hart decided that he would like to breed and moderately show some wirehaired Dachshunds. Soon he and Charles Baris (the kennel identification is a combination of their two names, BARis and HARt) found their mutual interest in Dachshunds growing steadily until, in 1970, the first Barhar litter was born. Just to start them off right, two of this litter gained championships. In 1971, "the Barhar Boys" began showing on an infrequent but reasonably steady basis.

Then, in 1973, came the now famous Barhar five Wire champion litter which included Champion Barhar Pickwick W, Champion Barhar's Minnie's Boy W, Champion Barhar New Girl in Town W, Champion Barhar Gingerbread Lady W, and Champion Barhar Dulcinea W.

Pickwick, better known as "Pippin," and brother "Buzz"

(Champion Barhar Minnie's Boy W) went on to become the leading standard Wire winners in the country during the mid-1970's owner-handled. "Pippin" earned a show record which included ten Hound Group placements, twice was Best in Specialty Shows, won Best of Variety on 52 occasions at all-breed shows, and ten times Best of Opposite Sex to Best of Variety. "Buzz" (Minnie's Boy) was the #1 Standard Wire in America for 1976. He had two Bests in Show at all-breed events, twice won Best in Specialty Show, had 29 Hound Group placements, and 125 times Best of Variety including 14 Specialties. "Pippin" and "Buzz" were sired by Champion Westphal's Shillalah ex Champion Midernoch's Wild Card W. In 1975, "Buzz" completed his championship by going Best of Variety from the classes at the Dachshund Club of America National Specialty, repeating for Best of Variety there the following year. In 1977 "Pippin" beat his brother for the honor. In 1982 the Dachshund Club of America Best of Variety in Wires went to his son, Champion Lauterdach's Dukat W. In 1983 the Best of Variety award there went to his grandson, Champion Mareldach's Heinzelman; In 1984 to another grandson, Champion Be Patient Buccaneer W. All told, "Buzz" sired a total of 14 champions.

In 1975, Barhar started to actively show and campaign on a weekly basis, which continued to be their practice during the next eight or nine years, specialing some very impressive dogs. During this time they bred some 25 litters of Dachshunds in all three coats.

The background of this breeding program was, of course, the wonderful Wirehair bitch Champion Midernoch's Wild Card W, daughter of Champion Villa Rose's Tenor v Midernoch ex Holmdach's Honey v Midernock. She became the dam of ten champions, which made her the #2 all-time dam for Wire Dachshunds. She is the famous "Minnie" to whom John and Charles owe such deep gratitude for all her contributions, not only to their own kennel but to quality generally in the breed.

Champion Fairmeadow Light Up The Sky was born in May 1974 and died in May 1984. This magnificent Standard Smooth dog was by Champion Dunkeldorf's Gunther ex Champion Farmeadow Fairest Rose, bred by Augusta M. Schneider. The sire of 55 champions, Sky was himself an unforgettable show dog who earned the honor of #1 Smooth Dachshund, all systems, in 1976.

He was Best of Variety Smooth Dachshund at the National Specialty in 1976, 1977 and 1978, and at Dachshund Club of America in 1978 his son was Winners Dog, his daughter was Winners Bitch, and Sky himself was Best Stud Dog. In 1980, again at the Dachshund Club of America National Specialty another son, Champion Doxhaus Accolade, was Best of Variety. Sky was the Top Smooth Dachshund sire in 1978, 1979, 1980, 1981 and 1982. He was a Specialty and an all-breed Best in Show winner with 73 Hound Group placements to his credit of which 14 were Firsts; and his 165 times Best of Variety included 17 times at Specialty Shows.

Following Sky, John and Charles tried their hand with the lovely Longhair, Champion Kemper Dachs Bad Habits. This greatly admired standard dog was by Champion Bayard le Jourdan ex Champion Kemper Dachs Rainy Jane, and he was born May 1976 bred by Patricia P. and James S. Kemper III, Patricia remaining co-owner on him along with John and Charles. "Timmy" is the sire of 18 champions, a multiple Best in Show and Specialty Best in Show winner, has 18 Hound Group Firsts on his record, plus 73 Group placements. His 215 Bests of Variety include 19 Specialties.

Champion Doxhaus Starmaker of Barhar is a daughter of Sky who was bred by Elizabeth and Philip Haus. She won multiple Hound Group Firsts during the early 1980's, building up a nice record.

Barhar Dachshunds are located at Montrose, New York, a small kennel of bitches whose owners are proud of their record as breeders of 30 champions. These are in addition to dogs they have owned or co-owned which when added in bring the total to 42. Thirty-two of these they finished and campaigned themselves—four with the help of professional handlers early on, the balance shown by Charles Baris.

Barhar has shown three dogs (Minnie's Boy, Sky, and Bad Habits), who represent all three varieties of Dachshund; and one bitch (Starmaker) to Best in Show awards. They believe that they are the only Dachshund kennel to have shown all three varieties to all-breed Best in Show honors, with Charles the only owner-handler to accomplish this feat.

Barhar is the only kennel ever to have won the Dachshund Club of America Specialty seven times. In fact in two consecutive years,

1976 and 1977, they had the honor of winning *both* the Smooth and the Wire Best of Variety awards, plus several other Bests of Variety at this prestigious National Specialty over the years.

In retrospect, as John and Charles reflect on the past, it was well worth the "run for the roses."

BEVERLY KELLY DODDS

Beverly Kelly Dodds is the owner of the very distinguished winner Champion Han-Jo's Candyman with whom she did a notable amount of winning in the late 1970's.

Candyman was born on November 23, 1974, bred by Hannelore Heller and owner-handled by Beverly to his exciting ring successes. This handsome Longhaired Standard was sired by Champion Han Jo's Flaming Flare ex Han Jo's Yum Yum, thus he was a member of the famous "C" litter of seven from which all became champions.

#1 Dachshund, all coats under all systems for 1978 - 1979, Candyman stands as well in the distinguished Top Five producing studs of the decade along with his sire, Champion Han-Jo's Flaming Flare, and his grandsire Champion Robert de Bayard.

Candyman came to Beverly Kelly as a two-year-old champion in August of 1976. Always owner-handled, his Specialty Bests of Breed total 26 including the National at Kansas City in 1978 and the National host club Specialties in 1978 and 1979. He had, additionally, multiple Group wins and a consistent record of Group placements from New York to Florida to California and then to the state of Washington.

Candyman is retired now and enjoying life with his obedient friend Beverly Kelly Dodds in California.

BOONDOX

Dan Harrison, owner of Boondox Dachshunds, finished his first champion in March of 1978, since which time he has bred a total of more than 40 champions in all three coats. Boondox is located at Mecca, Indiana.

The first of Dan's champions was Rose Farms Choo Choo who was in the Top Ten Smooths for two years and was a Top Producer as well, the dam of two Group winners and two Specialty Show winners. A daughter of Champion Karlstaft's Lionel ex Champion Rose Farms Impatiens, she was bred by Dee Hutchin-

Ch. Moffett's Oona v Boondox, by Ch. Moffett's Boondox Crockett ex Ch. Moffett's Miss Flint, multiple Specialty and Best of Breed winner. Bred by Thelma Moffett who co-owned with Dan Harrison.

son and Judy Anderson, co-owned by Dan with Dee.

In Longs, the foundation was Rose Farms Blackberry Buff, the dam of ten champions and closing in on the all-time Top Longhair producer mark. She is a daughter of Champion Trailblazer Red Baron ex Delldachs Blackberry Girl, was bred by Dee Hutchinson and Sheila Ledbetter and is owned by Dan with Dee Hutchinson.

Since 1980, Dan Harrison and Dee Hutchinson have won the points in Longhairs nine times at the shows over Dachshund Club of America weekend, a fact in which Dan takes particular pride for, as he remarks, "D.C.A. is where everyone comes with their best prospects."

Other dogs from this kennel include Champion Boondox Chuckie Bunyan, by Champion Moffett's George ex Champion Rose Farms Choo Choo, a Group winner, a multiple Specialty winner, and the Top Smooth Sire of 1984. Bred by Dan with Dee Hutchinson, Chuckie now is owned by John Thompson and Terry Snyder.

Champion Moffett's Oona of Boondox, by Champion Moffett's Boondox Crockett ex Champion Moffett's Miss Flint, is a multiple Specialty Best of Breed winner and a granddaughter of Choo Choo. She was bred by Thelma Moffett who co-owns her with Dan Harrison.

Champion Rose Farms Zesabel of Boondox, by Champion B's Javelin de Bayard ex Rose Farms Blackberry Buff, is a Group winner, a multiple Specialty winner, and was Best of Winners at the Dachshund Club of America in 1980 and dam of the Winners Dog there in 1984. Dan Harrison co-owns her with Mr. and Mrs. Walt Jones.

Champion Rose Farm Dolly v Boondox is a multiple Specialty winner by Champion B's Javelin de Bayard ex Rose Farms Blackberry Buff. She is one of her mother's ten champions.

Champion Rose Farms Hannelore Boondox is by Champion B's Javelin de Bayard ex Champion Rose Farms Country Girl. She finished at the Dachshund Club of America in 1984.

Dan Harrison feels that his success is due largely to the excellence of the foundation bloodlines with which he has been working, Rose Farm, the Moffetts, Hannelore Heller's dogs and Mary Howell's. Virtually all of his Dachshunds go back to these kennels.

BRISTLEKNOLL

Bristleknoll Dachshunds, at Murfreesboro, Tennessee, are owned by Lucille (Lucy) Moden, who despite the fact that she has been a devoted Dachshund owner for more than 25 years, did not begin breeding and showing until about 1970.

Lucy's first Dachshund was a purebred red Standard Smooth whom she adopted from the Delaware Humane Association. Dearly loved, this little fellow lived five months past his 18th birthday, and was a source of pleasure to his owner throughout his long lifetime.

The first show quality Dachshund which Lucy acquired was a puppy purchased in 1970, a bewhiskered little wild boar fellow who won her heart on sight. This pup grew up to become Champion Tag Along's Bad Boy, sired by Champion Holmdach's Tag Along W, a grandson of the great Champion Pondwick's Hobgoblin and Champion Tubac's Abner. The famous and widely acclaimed English dog, Champion Gisbourne Inca W was a great-grandfather.

Bad Boy finished in short order with some good wins, after which a bitch was added to the family. From these two came Lucy's first home-bred champion. This was Mo-Dachs Wile E Wire, who finished easily including two back to back 4-point majors on the summer Carolina circuit. Not being interested in specialing a dog at that time, Lucy gave Wile E to some "really super people," and believes that he is still alive and well.

A bitch puppy from Wile E's same litter, Mo-Dach's Sunday Smile W, gave Lucy her second Dachshund litter, five pups of which two were lost early on. The others were not show quality convincing Lucy that she had to go another way for future breeding. Thus started the search for that most difficult of all commodities to acquire: a top quality show/brood bitch.

During her prospecting efforts, Lucy became acquainted with John Hart and Charles Baris, of Barhar Kennels. They did not have a bitch available, but offered her a young male. This was not what she really wanted, but when Lucy saw the dog at Atlanta in the spring of 1975, she was unable to resist him. This was Barhar Take Me Along, and Lucy made him a champion in six shows. This young fellow became known as "Sherman," and his new owner took him out on the specials trail. He did some creditable winning, considering that he was being handled by an unknown amateur.

The search for exactly the right bitch continued, during which time Lucy finished several more dogs, including some very good Standard Longhairs, and she was learning her way out of what she describes as "Noviceitis."

Then Lady Luck smiled in her direction, and Lucy learned that a lady named Joan Darnell at Kingsport, Tennessee, had bought out the entire Standard Wirehair kennel of Richard and Marcia Tharp. One of the bitches, Tharp's Bonnie Boom W, a Champion Tharp's Boom Boom daughter, had a litter of puppies, and Joan asked Lucy to look at the only one she had left, a red bitch, to see if she was show potential. Lucy peered into the crate in the back of Joan's station wagon and there she was, the show/brood bitch prospect for which Lucy had searched so long. This was Hollydach's Betsy Ross W.

Lucy's first move was to get her new acquisition tidied up for the show ring, and to enter her in Puppy Sweepstakes and the 6-9 month puppy bitch class at the Dachshund Club of Alabama Specialty. She was Best Puppy in Sweeps over 27 pups awarded by judge Joyce Osburn; and Winners Bitch and Best of Winners under John H. Cook. Then came a 5-point major under Garland Bell, and a third major, this time from judge Pat Hastings.

The Bristleknoll kennel prefix, rather new in comparison to the length of time Lucy has been "in" Dachshunds, was selected when it came time to register Holly's first puppies. These were sired by Champion Midernoch's Sextus Wire who was winning impressively at the time, including Best in Show, and whose pedigree looked as though it should be compatible with Holly's. There were seven puppies, two red males, one wild boar male, two red bitches, and two wild boar bitches. The first to finish, Champion Bristleknoll Big Hug W, was co-owned with a couple fairly new to showing dogs. "Huggie's" record was six shows; one major reserve, four majors (5, 4, 4, 3) and two points. A dog and bitch, Champion Bristleknoll Beardsley W and Champion Bristleknoll Ballyhoo W were Winners Dog and Winners Bitch at the Dachshund Club of America Annual National Specialty at Jacksonville, Florida, in 1979. A fourth member of the litter, now Champion Bristleknoll Brass Buttons W, won Best of Opposite Sex to Best of Variety at Columbine Dachshund Club on Dachshund Club of America weekend 1980 in Denver; and Best of Variety and Best of Opposite Sex to Best of Breed at the Dachshund Club of America in Houston in 1981. There were multiple Hound Group firsts, Specialty Bests of Breed, etc., to her credit, adding up to her finishing 1981 as the #2 Wire in America.

A fifth puppy from this litter, Champion Bristleknoll Banana, was maturing slowly and Lucy sold him to a veterinarian friend. The others in the litter were a smooth red male and a wheaten pet bitch. Holly's second litter produced Champion Bristleknoll Baddie's Boy W.

Holly's third litter was by Champion Barhar's Take Me Along. It consisted of eight pups: seven males and one bitch—all of them red! Seven of these puppies completed titles, becoming Champion Bristleknoll Bonus O'Barhar W, Best Puppy in Sweepstakes, Dachshund Club of America 1980, over 97 puppies, #2 Wire in the nation in 1982 and #5 in 1984 while under lease to Mrs. Alan Robson; a multiple Group and Specialty winner, sire to date of

Lucy Moden's beloved Ch. Tag Along's Bad Boy, by Ch. Holmdachs Tag Along, her first show wire and favorite dog. Bristleknoll Kennels, Murfreesboro, Tennessee.

more than 15 champions; Champion Bristleknoll Brass Tacky W, finished over top winning specials; Champion Bristleknoll Brimful W, finished from Bred-by Class, #7 Wire in 1982; Champion Bristleknoll Brawny Lad W, finished with five majors in just over two-and-a-half weeks; American and Canadian Champion Bristleknoll Barbarian W, shown to title by his Junior Handler, including Group placements from the classes; Champion Bristleknoll Brass Ring W, who, in addition to his championship, has one leg on a C.D. degree and currently is learning tracking; and Champion Bristleknoll Best December W, now owned by Stanley and Martha Hess in Greeley, Colorado, the dam of champions in her first litter.

Lucy was extremely well pleased with the results of the Champion Barhar Take Me Along (Sherman)—Champion Hollydach's Betsy Ross W (Holly) litter, so has repeated the combination twice since these first were born. A litter of five, born in February 1980, produced Champion Bristleknoll Bedwarmer W, an extremely showy wild boar bitch who finished as a puppy and has been a consistent winner as a very lightly shown special, including a Specialty Best of Breed and a Hound Group first. The others were Champion Bristleknoll Brass Belle W; Champion Bristleknoll Bedbug W; Champion Bristleknoll Bohemian W; and Champion Bristleknoll Banshee W.

When Banshee completed her title, her doing so qualified Champion Hollydoch's Betsy Ross W as Top Producing Dachshund Dam of all coats. The former Top Producing dam had been the great Smooth bitch, Champion Moffett's Roseanne.

Holly whelped her final litter on December 23, 1982. Eight pups, evenly divided between dogs and bitches. Three are already finished: Champion Bristleknoll Beauty Spot W, owned by James Grinder, New Canaan, Connecticut; Champion Bristleknoll Bedroom Eyes W, co-owned by Lucy with Larry J. Smith, Wilmington, North Carolina; and Champion Bristleknoll Beau Jeste W, co-owned by Lucy with Tacy Adams, Sacramento, California. Two more are very close to title. Another has just started.

Lucy tells us, "At the least, Holly will soon be the dam of 24 champions, including numerous very successful Specials. Add to this the title of Top Producing Hound Dam (1982) and Top Producing Dam all breeds, *Kennel Review* System 1982, and one can easily understand why Lucy Moden takes such pride in this fantastic bitch.

Holly has thus become the first Dachshund ever to achieve #1 Hound Dam, much less #1 All-Breed Top Producing Dam. Lucy also is proud of the more than 20 second and third generation champion offshoots of the Standard Wires of Bristleknoll, plus many more heavily pointed which should have added still others by the time this book appears in print.

Champion Hollydachs Betsy Ross W was Best Brood Bitch in Show at the Dachshund Club of America in Denver 1980, Houston 1981, Washington, D.C. 1982, and Philadelphia 1984. She could not compete in 1983 as Lucy was Chairperson that year for the Golden Anniversary Independent Specialty Show.

The Bristleknoll story could not be complete without mention of the co-bred Bristleknoll/Solong Standard Longhairs. Using the Java/Flare cross, Kathy Meyer of Athens, Tennessee, and Lucy have come up with some very nice dogs. Four champions to date include Champion Solong Squire v Bristleknoll, who was Best of Breed from Bred-by Exhibitor Class at the Birmingham Specialty among other nice wins, and currently being specialed by new owner Sidney Stafford, Stony Brook, N.Y.

During the summer of 1984, Lucy became very ill and required heart surgery. The Bristleknoll Dachshund population since then has necessarily been greatly reduced. But there is a truly lovely youngster coming along, Bristleknoll I Love Lucy W.

CANDACHS

Candachs Dachshunds, specializing in Smooths, are owned by Carl and Candy Holder at Lumberton, Texas. This is the home of the noted conformation and obedience winner, Champion Dachsborough Nedrum, C.D.X.

Ned is a son of Champion Bigdrum Close Call v Westphal, who was the #1 Dachshund in all three coats in 1981 and the #1 Hound that same year. His dam is Champion Nedra of Dachsborough. In 1979 she became a fourth generation Top Producer.

In conformation, Ned finished his title with two four-point majors and one three-point major being owner-handled. He has numerous honors gained in obedience during the earning of his C.D. and C.D.X. and should have added a Utility Degree by the time you are reading this book.

CANEBRAKE

Canebrake Dachshunds, now in their 15th year, was established by Frank and Monica Canestrini of Wheat Ridge, Colorado, with foundation stock from Marie Mehan's Ski-Hi Kennel of Woodside, California. Now they soon will be on their fifth generation of homebred Wire Dachshund champions.

Of all their dogs, the Canestrinis feel that Champion Canebrake Diamond Lil Wire and Champion Canebrake Pandora Wire best illustrate the Canebrake style and type.

Champion Canebrake Diamond Lil Wire was born in May 1974, daughter of Champion Sky-Hi Diamond Jim Wire ex Canebrake Zelda Wire. She completed her championship at under two years' age, winning Best of Variety on numerous occasions as well as a Specialty Best of Breed and an occasional Group placement. She was ranked in the top Wire Dachshund listing for 1976 and 1977, Dachshund Variety System.

Champion Canebrake Pandora Wire was born in January 1978, by Ch. None Such Maestro Wolfgang ex Canebrake Zelda Wire. A great favorite with breeder-judges, Pandora had numerous Group placements and Specialty Best of Breed wins, and was ranked in the top Wire Dachshunds for 1980, Dachshund Variety System and in *Canine Chronicle's* Top Ten for 1981 and 1982. Owner-handled by her breeders-owners, Pandora scored many an exciting win over dog specials, not always an easy accomplishment for the bitches. Additionally she produced three champions from her one and only litter.

One must not forget a word of mention of the lovely producing bitch, Canebrake Zelda, the dam of both Diamond Lil and Pandora. Zelda, a daughter of Champion Pondwicks Hobgoblin, has given her owners a total of five champions, thus has been an important part of their successful breeding program.

CHRIS HARBOR

Chris Harbor Kennels, owned by Betty and Jim Christian at Panama City, Florida, whelped its first litter of Smooths in 1973, to quote Betty, "strictly pet quality." The start of their success story came when they bred Melody Run's Kiss of Fire-MS (red Smooth Miniature bitch) to Champion Melody Run's Vagabond Lover-MW which produced their first Wire Champion Chris Harbor's Jezebel-MW in 1976.

Jezebel and Champion Hericher's Prime Candidate-MW took it from there and produced 16 offspring, of which ten have completed championships and three puppies will be starting their careers in mid-1985.

Since starting out, the Christians have bred 13 Wire and two Smooth champions, and one C.D. Twelve of these were owner-handled by Betty and Jim. And of course the most exciting production to date has been the highly successful Champion Chris Harbor's Urban Cowboy-MW, noted Best in Show and Group winner.

Champion Chris Harbor's Jezebel is a granddaughter of Champion Wyndel's Michelob MW (Champion Wilheen's Mighty Mike

MW–Champion Wyndel's Katiedid MW, the latter a daughter of Holmdach's Bit O'Whiskers MW); Champion Brunswig's Xenobia MW (Champion Wilheen's Knight Wire MW–Champion Brunswig's Indian Love Call); Champion Tallavast Shiloh–MS (Champion Tallavast Eddie-MS–Tallavast Rite); and Tallmar Sandi-MS (Champion Tallavast's Mistaken Speck MS–Tallamar Frank's Maid Missy- MS. She is the all-time Top Producing Miniature Wirehaired Dachshund Dam, and in 1982 she was #2 Top Producer in the Hound Group and #3 Top Producer All Breeds among producing bitches.

Champion Hericher's Prime Candidate-MS, the sire of Cowboy, in 1982 was #4 Top Producing Wirehaired Dachshund Sire with four champions; and #1 in 1983 with eight champions. He was sired by Lamdach's Chester of Hericher (Champion Melody Runs Vagabond Lover-MW–Lamdach Spirit of Melody Run-MW) from Hericher's Winzig Amanda-MW (Tori-Jarice's Wee Thaddeus-MS, son of Canadian Champion Tori Jarice's Wee Angus-MS–Mar-Betti's Wee Samantha-MW).

The first Jezebel daughter to finish was Champion Chris Harbor's Wire Strudel-MW, sired, as were all of Jezebel's champions to date, by Prime Candidate. Born in 1981, Jezebel finished at ten months of age, and she is a litter sister to Cowboy and Wendy. She is the dam of the Christians' latest champion at time of writing, Chris Harbor's Stardom-MW, born in 1983 who completed title in September 1984. Stardom, for whom the Christians have high hopes as a special of the future, is the third generation of Chris Harbor champions, being Jezebel's granddaughter and Strudel's daugher. Her sire is an importation, English and American Champion Drakesleat Komma-MW, is by English Champion Drakesleat Rough Stuff (English Champion Silvae Rubbermouse–English Champion Drakesleat Riff Raff) from English Champion Drakesleat Klose Encounter (English Champion Klunk Klick of Andyc–English Champion Drakesleat Silver Moon, the latter by English and New Zealand Champion Silvae Handymouse.)

Needless to say, the Christians take tremendous pride in the handsome record winner Champion Chris Harbor's Urban Cowboy-MW has made as a multiple Best in Show and Group. In addition to his successes in the ring, he is carrying on the family producing tradition as already can be seen in Dachshund rings around the country!

CROSSWYNDS

Crosswynd Dachshunds were owned by Mr. and Mrs. Ralph Lovering in Massachusetts where they produced many splendid winning dogs. One of the most representative of the Loverings' breeding program was Champion Crosswynd's Cracker Jack, one of the truly important winners in the breed during the late 1960's.

Jack's record in the ring was outstanding from the start. At the age of 11 months, Barbara Lovering personally handled him to Best of Breed at the Dachshund Club of America Specialty in New York in 1966. He repeated this remarkable victory the next two years. Jack became Dachshund of the year, all coats, and fourth among all Hounds of the year. Two years successively he was awarded first in the Hound Group at Westminster and also won several all-breed Bests in Show.

The lineage behind Jack began when Barbara Lovering purchased a bitch of Marienlust breeding and then bred her to Champion Saber of Gera. This union produced Kenneth of Crosswynds, who sired not only Cracker Jack but 13 additional champions as well. His dam, Crosswynd's Moon Glow, was a daughter of Champion White Gables Ristocrat from the Loverings' Champion Willo-Mar's Night and Day. Moon Glow was the litter sister of two Group winning bitches, the Loverings' Champion Crosswynd Cathy and Champion Constance of Crosswynd, the latter acquired from the Loverings by Ramona Van Court Jones. In the background behind Night and Day was the British breeding from Ashdown Kennels owned by Mary and Bob Pilkington, whom Barbara Lovering met and visited during an English judging engagement in 1969.

Jack was one of nine living puppies, five of whom became champions. These were Champion Victor of Crosswynd, Champion Crosswynd Victoria, Champion Charlotte of Crosswynd, Champion Caroline of Crosswynd, and, of course, Jack. The late Dachshund and Scottie enthusiasts Mr. and Mrs. Charles C. Stalter acquired Jack, who certainly did credit for everyone connected with him, including siring some 30 champions during his short span of eight years.

A repeat breeding of Jack's parents produced another fine puppy, Champion Crosswynd's Firecracker. At 11 months he was shown by Barbara Lovering from the puppy class to second in the Hound Group at Old Dominion Kennel Club. Firecracker was

Ch. Crosswynd's Cracker Jack winning Best in Show at Monmouth County Kennel Club. Frank Hardy handled for Mrs. Barbara Lovering, his breeder and then owner. Crakerjack later was sold to Mr. and Mrs. Charles Stalter for whom he amassed an imposing show record.

purchased by the Willo-Mar Kennel to be their re-start following an absence of five years. He went on to win ten Specialty shows and produced many champions, to the pleasure of the Loverings and to Marcia Wheeler at Willo-Mar.

Following Jack's show career, he returned to the Loverings to spend his remaining years at Crosswynd. Losing him at so young an age was a sad blow; but the legacy he left has made the Loverings justifiably very proud of their very real contribution to the Dachshund world.

DE SANGPUR – GRACE B. HILL

Grace B. Hill was born in Bardin, Florida, 1902. After graduating from high school Gracie entered the business world and traveled around the country selling encyclopedias, textbooks and graduation caps and gowns. In New York she met and married William Burr Hill, Jr. whose father had been a banker-lawyer who was admitted to the United States Supreme Court Bar in the late 1890's.

Grace became involved with dog clubs with membership in the Dachshund Club of America, Inc. in May of 1946. In 1951 she became a director of the DCA and was its Secretary in 1952-53 and from 1955 until her death. In 1950 she was one of the charter members who founded the Dachshund Association of Long Island, Inc. She was the backbone of its specialty shows from the first one in 1952 until she moved to Florida in 1968. The preceding year DALI had become the largest specialty show in the United States and from 1959 through 1968 the DALI Specialty Shows were held on Grace's beautifully landscaped front lawn in Hicksville, Long Island.

In 1952 she was one of the founders of the National Miniature Dachshund Club, Inc. which began to publish a newsletter to keep breeders and owners of miniatures all over the country in touch with one another. The mimeographed Newsletter grew to be a magazine and the Club has had as many as 700 members at one time. In 1977 to celebrate the 25th year of NMDC, Grace was instrumental in organizing the NMDC Annual Miniature Exposition which has had as many as 111 entries—all miniatures! The Expo is run according to AKC regulations, with classes offered as with any AKC point show. There are no points awarded at this exposition, but it has come to be as important as the title "Champion" to miniature breeders. She served NMDC variously as its President, Secretary, Treasurer and Editor of its NMDC Digest. The NMDC is the only active miniature club in the United States as of this writing.

She also helped to found the Sunshine Dachshund Club of Jacksonville (Florida) and served as its President. Her other club affiliations included Brookhaven KC, Suffolk County KC, and Queensboro KC in New York and the Jacksonville Dog Fanciers Association in Florida.

The first Longhaired Dachshund had been registered with the

Gracie Hill with Penelope de Sangpur, her first Dachshund.

Ch. Midas Fancy Decision, Top Winning Longhair, 1968 and 1969. Owned by Grace B. Hill and T. R. Dunk, Jr. The last Dachshund Grace campaigned widely.

American Kennel Club in 1931. Grace B. Hill was an early pioneer in Standard Longhaired Dachshunds beginning in the early 1940's. The Longhaired variety was almost unknown in this country at the time. When they were shown, they had to compete in a division of the Open Class. It was not until 1938 that the Longhaired and the Wirehaired varieties competed with the Smooth in the hound group. Around 1940 Heinz L. Karger of New York City imported Achat v.d. Walleck whose sire was World and Derby Champion Winnetou v. Zinnowitz. Achat earned his American Championship in 1941. Mr. Karger also imported Susi v. Waldenau who was already in whelp to Ferro v. Abtsdorf and the litter was born in the United States. A red Longhaired female from this litter was acquired by Berthold J. D'Alexandre and named Ruby de Sangpur. Ruby was bred to Ch. Achat v.d. Walleck and on January 6, 1942 a litter of four pups was born. A red female named Penelope de Sangpur was purchased by Grace on June 23, 1942.

William Hill kept a journal in the early years relating the various characteristics, coats, dispositions of the dogs and their litters, their show records, and even the occasional bouts with distemper which plagued breeders in those days. This is William's first entry in the journal: "Gracie fell in love with Penny, Penelope de Sangpur, when she first saw her and after considerable argument with William and Alec (Berthold J. D'Alexandre), she purchased her and thereafter was seen constantly at her bridge games with Penny in tow. Penny was devoted to Gracie and was never entirely happy out of her sight."

Mr. D'Alexandre repeated this breeding and another litter of four was born on April 27, 1943. William wrote: "When Gracie saw them, she wanted one as a companion for Penelope (Penny) de Sangpur...Alec was somewhat reluctant to sell, but finally agreed and decided he would let go of Billy, which he considered the poorest dog in the litter. Here he made an error, because Billy turned out to be the best one of them all." The Hills purchased Billy on June 10, 1943 at six weeks and two days of age.

These two litters were the only ones on which Mr. D'Alexandre used 'de Sangpur'; his succeeding litters were registered under 'Golden Paw' and Gracie was given the name 'de Sangpur' which means 'of pure blood'. The Hills began their breeding program in May of 1944 with Penny. Billy was first used at stud in May of 1945.

Billy became Champion William de Sangpur in April of 1946, earning his title with five majors. He did his greatest winning the year he was five years old and became the top winning Longhair of the 40's, a record which stood for many years. At over nine years of age he took Best of Variety at the DALI Specialty Show over a large entry - 33 Longhairs - and went on to third in the Hound Group. A little less than three months before his death on September 21, 1956 at the age of 13 plus, Ch. William placed first in a competitive Veterans Class. Ch. William de Sangpur attained a show record of 65 BOV's, including the Dachshund Club of America Parent Specialty in 1946 and 1948; Morris and Essex in 1946, '47 and '48; and Westminster Kennel Club in 1948.

Champion William de Sangpur was the sire of 38 Champions including several multiple BOV winners and Champion Saqui de Sangpur who went Best in Show at Mount Ogden in 1949. Saqui was the foundation Longhair stud of Donia Cline's Crespi Kennels in California.

Grace and William moved from their apartment in New York City to Massapequa, Long Island in October of 1946. Although William referred to the Massapequa home as "the Hill estate," they moved again in early 1949 to their home in Hicksville, Long Island.

From the very first litter sired by Champion William, Grace chose a bitch puppy, Lolli, who was bred to Seppel v Sollinge III and produced Nancy de Sangpur. Nancy was bred back to her grandfather Champion William and produced Shantee Linda de Sangpur. In January of 1950 Grace purchased a black and tan Miniature Longhair, Tinyteckel Black Silk from Avis Mary Earle of California and later bred him to Shantee Linda. This breeding produced a litter of six including a lovely black and tan bitch that she kept. In 1954 this bitch became the first American-bred Longhair Miniature Champion—De Sangpur Wee Allene. Allene followed in her grandfather Williams' footsteps by accumulating 27 BOV's, six Group placings including an Hound Group First, and Bests of Varieties at the DCA Parent Specialty in 1956 where she went on to Hound Group Third.

Grace and William purchased their first Smooth Dachshund in 1946—a six-week-old black and tan standard named Little Bit of Gulnare from Mrs. Stanley Woodward of Princeton, New Jersey. William's journal lists Little Bit as weighing 22½ pounds at only five-and-a-half months of age! Later they acquired Burrhill Donna, a red Standard Smooth bitch whose sire was Champion Dachshafen II, the paternal grandsire of Little Bit, and both Little Bit and Donna had the Marienlust lines behind them. Grace bred these two and produced Burrhill Annie, a red Smooth. In the first few years of her Smooth breeding program she used 'Burrhill' when registering the Smooths, but eventually all of her Dachshunds were registered with the De Sangpur prefix. Burrhill Annie was bred to Rottfink von Kargollheim III and produced De Sangpur Impchen. Impchen was then bred to Chota's Achilles and produced De Sangpur Wee Impchen. Wee Impchen was mated with Fritz and Ida Kroeff's Jeetzel von Osterholz and this breeding produced the first Smooth red miniature male Champion—De Sangpur Wee Lancelot. Lance was an eight-pound red who reached his title in 1958 with five majors, two BOV's and a Hound Group Fourth. Grace was also the breeder of the third Smooth Miniature (first red) to become a Champion De Sangpur Wee Memmy owned by Mr. and Mrs. James Bell.

The Hill's first Wirehair Dachshund was Georgette Fanelle, whelped April 7, 1947. Georgette was a standard brindle who traced back to the original Marienlust Smooths and Champion Lumpacious Hubertus on her sire's side. On her dam's side she went back to the Swedish brindle Standard Wirehair, Champion Sports Buster. In 1955 Georgette was bred to Fant v. Osterholz co-owned by Grace and Ida Kroeff. This breeding produced De Sangpur Adela who was bred to Champion Tubac's Hornet MW and produced Champion De Sangpur Wee Ad-Lib MW. Ad-Lib's championship in 1964 put Grace Hill into the record books by making her the first in this country to have bred and shown standards and miniatures in all three coats to Championship. She had succeeded in breeding miniature champions who were descendents of her original standard stock.

Over the years, Mary Gore, Gracie's sister, was an integral part of De Sangpur, always being there to help care for the dogs, assist in whelpings and to socialize the puppies. Mary's love for Dachshunds was as great as her sister's. She helped Grace to continue after William Burr Hill, Jr.'s sudden death on March 5, 1957.

Champion Midas Fancy Decision was born in 1964 and was owned by Gracie. After her move to Jacksonville, Florida in 1968, he was co-owned with Thomas R. Dunk, Jr. "Murphy," a heavily

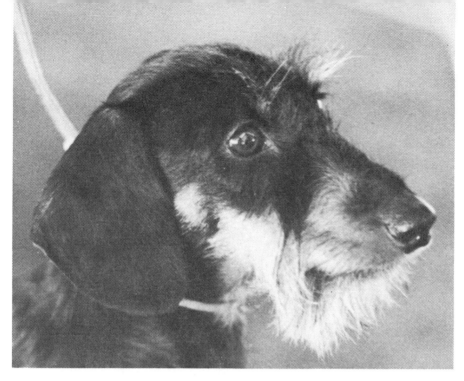

Am. and Can. Ch. Dorachar Jibe Ho MW, bred and owned by Mrs. Dorothy Poole, Carlisle, Massachusetts. Sired by Ch. Yaletown's Midnite Cowboy MW ex Ch. Wilheen's Schon of Dorachar MW.

sabled red standard Longhaired Dachshund, became the top winning Longhair of 1968 and 1969 and could trace his ancestry back to Ruby de Sangpur, the dam of William and Penny. "Murphy" won the variety at the DCA Parent Specialty in 1969 and was the last Dachshund that Grace campaigned widely.

The Dachshund fancy lost one of its most enthusiastic supporters and breeders when Grace B. Hill died on February 29, 1980.

DORACHAR

Dorachar Miniature Dachshunds are owned by Mrs. Dorothy C. Poole, Carlisle, Massachusetts, whose first Miniature Wire bitch came from California in 1971, purchased from the breeder-owner of the famous Wilheen's Mighty Mike, MW. Mike led the lists of outstanding Miniature Wire sires between 1960 and 1977, having sired sixteen champions. Quite an achievement for those times in the world of Mini-Wires! Dorothy Poole's Mike granddaughter, Champion Wilheen's Schon of Dorachar, is still alive and well as this book is being written.

Next came the purchase of a Mini-Wire bitch from Pat Wynne in Ohio (Wyndel Dachshunds), and from these two bitches the Mini-Wires of Dorachar were evolved.

Dorothy Poole also owns some lovely Mini Longhairs, which came to her kennel from Pat Beresford's noted Patchwork strain. It is interesting to study the pictures of Champion Patchwork Peter Piper and Champion Patchwork Marigold as they so handsomely illustrate the beautiful type of the Patchwork dogs. These two are full brother and sister from two different breedings of the same parents. Their sire, Champion Patchwork Love Bug, in his day was a top Group winning Mini Long. When Pat Beresford went to work as editor of the *American Kennel Gazette/Pure Bred Dogs*, Bug came to live with her good friend Mrs. Poole, and died during the winter of 1984-85 at the ripe old age of 16.

Although the Longhairs are all in the geriatric set now, Dorothy Poole continues the breeding and showing of the Mini-Wires. It always is fun for her, seeing a nice Mini at a show and, in checking the catalogue, finding that it is descended from her stock. A pleasure she enjoys quite frequently!

DOUBLE (SS)

Double (SS) Dachshunds are owned by Shirley Silagi at El Paso, Texas. It was many years ago that the Silagis obtained their first Dachshund, back when they were married in 1956. This was a standard red male who was a favorite family member for 12 years. After his death, it was not until 1976 that the Silagis again became Dachshund owners, at the urging of their son who so greatly missed the one he had loved as a youngster. Shirley finally agreed to let him purchase one, *provided* it was a miniature and a female. He tried to comply with her wishes, but this first "miniature" tipped the scales at 18 pounds so really was not what Shirley had had in mind. She was neutered as Shirley did not intend to breed her.

Then one day when the Silagis were out jogging in the park, they came upon a group of Dachshund fanciers who were having a practice session of preparing their dogs for an upcoming show. A *true* black and tan miniature caught Shirley's eye, and they stopped to inquire of the owner about her dog. This was how Shirley met Cynthia Bach and Ruckengrats Row Boat. Through Cynthia Bach, Shirley learned about the National Miniature Di-

Ch. Double (SS) My Kind of Town MS with his adoring breeder-owner-handler, Shirley Silagi. A judge has just awarded him Best of Breed at the Sooner Dachshund Club Specialty Show.

gest and began calling various breeders for a five-pound red miniature female. Dee Hutchinson at that time had what she considered to be a "very correct" black and tan bitch which she felt would be show quality but was too small for the show ring. Thus it was that "Mouth," Champion Rose Farms Talk Of The Town MS, came to live with the Silagis in March 1978, weighing in at just six pounds at age seven months. By May she tipped the scales at seven pounds, and Shirley thought her about the cutest Dachshund she had ever seen. Cynthia Bach convinced her to enter and show her new dog at the New Mexico Specialty where Ann Gordon was judging; brought her the entries, and helped her to fill them out. Shirley at that point never had even attended a dog show, and knew nothing about it all. She just had wanted a tiny Dachshund to love. Prior to the Specialty, in their front yard, Cynthia Bach had given Shirley lessons in moving the dog in different patterns as requested by judges, and in how to pose her dog, leaving Shirley with a book on junior handling for reference and study. Needless to say, the entire family attended this first show. You can well understand the excitement when Shirely won Best Puppy with "Mouth" in the Sweepstakes; then in the regular classes took Winners Bitch! Next day she again was awarded Winners Bitch, adding another two points—and Shirley forevermore was "hooked."

So exciting did she find it all that she decided she wanted a second Dachshund, this time a red Miniature Longhair. Again Dee Hutchinson was contacted, and this time Champion Rose Farms Dusty Romance ML was the result, coming to his new home at four months. From him Shirley learned about grooming, which took more time than she really wanted to spend. At about this time she decided that the sensible procedure would be to concentrate on one size and one variety of Dachshund, and for her, this would be the Miniature Smooth.

It took Shirley two years to find a stud she liked for her Talk Of The Town; and finally she settled on Champion Rose Farms Timothy MS, a lovely little dog but a red. He was being specialed at that time with Hannelore Heller, to whom Shirley delivered her bitch to be bred.

In July 1980 the puppies duly arrived, her first homebred litter-three puppies, which included a black male whom Shirley had the feeling immediately was very special. He was, and has grown up to become Champion Double (SS) My Kind of Town MS. Now four years old, he finished before reaching ten months in five shows with three majors including a five-pointer awarded by Howard Atlee at the Miniature Dachshund Round Up when just barely over six months. His wins include Best of Variety at the Santa Ana Specialty in California where he won his first Dachshund Club of America Bronze Plaque for defeating more than 50 smooth Dachshunds. He went on to win Best of Breed at the National Miniature Expo (a weigh-in competition) in Houston in 1982; Best of Opposite Sex to Best of Breed at the New Mexico Dachshund Specialty in May 1983 under Ed. Dixon; Best of Breed at the Houston Dachshund Specialty in October 1983; Best of Breed at the Columbine Dachshund Specialty in Denver in September 1984; and Best of Breed at the Sooner Dachshund Specialty in Oklahoma City during November 1984 judged by Mrs. Muriel Newhauser.

"My-T" as My Kind of Town is called by friends, has at time of writing, 65 Best of Variety awards; some 22 Group placements, including five times Best Hound (twice in Mexico, three times in the States) and four Specialty Bests of Breed. He has been entirely owner-handled as having bred and finished him herself, Shirley wanted it that way.

Shirley's first all-champion litter was sired by My-T from Champion Rose Farms Sara. The two puppies it produced are

Champion Double (SS) Your Kind Of Town MS, who finished quickly with three major wins, and Champion Double (SS) My Favorite Town MS who also went on to the title in short order. This litter is known as Bonnie and Clyde.

Shirley Silagi has now been showing for seven years and her breeding is very selective and limited. She has to date had only six litters, three of which have been just one puppy each. She already has five champions and is working on the sixth presently with Double (SS) Dolly Duz the Town MS who was Winners Bitch at her first four shows.

DUNKELDORF

Dunkeldorf Kennels were started in 1957 by Mr. and Mrs. T.R.Dunk, Jr., with the acquisition of their first Dachshund. Prompted by curiosity, they had attended a Fun Match, and after winning their class that urge "to get involved" came over them, making them feel it would be fun. Soon afterwards a man walking

Ch. Dunkeldorf Falson's Favorite, by Ch. Falcon of Heying-Teckel ex Ch. Fleming's Cherry Carmela, one of the breed's most prolific sires with 94 champions to his credit. He was on the Top Producers list for seven years, is a second generation Top Producer, and the sire of Top Producers. The total number of champions sired by Falcon's Favorite, his sire Falcon of Heying-Teckel, and the latter's sire, Ch. Favorite v Marienlust adds up to an awe-inspiring total of more than 275 champions! Falcon's Favorite was bred and owned by T. R. Dunk, Jr., Lake Helen, Florida.

a beautiful black and tan Dachshund passed their house, and they approached this gentleman with the idea of arranging to breed their bitch to this lovely dog. The dog turned out to be Champion Dachsland's Dynamo. The breeding was arranged, and the litter produced one male and one female. When both became champions, the Dunks quite naturally were "hooked."

In 1959 Champion Damaris of Anchorage was purchased, a Raven of Heying-Teckel daughter who went on to complete her championship. Next came Champion Triste of Anchorage (Champion Raven of Heying-Teckel ex Champion Alice of Heying-Teckel) who also gained her title in short order. With the addition of Champion Fleming's Cherry Carmela, a lovely clear red bitch, and Champion Timbar's Bubbling Over, who was a joy to show and who achieved an outstanding record in the ring, the Dunks had a strong foundation on which to base their breeding program.

They always aimed for quality rather than quantity, thus seldom had more than one litter each year. Also Tommy Dunk has a knowledge of genetics which they feel aided inestimably in their success as breeders.

Undoubtedly the best known Dunkeldorf litter was that by Champion Falcon v Heying-Teckel ex Champion Fleming's Cherry Carmela. This breeding produced Champion Dunkeldorf Falcon's Favorite, Champion Dunkeldorf's Falcon Forester, Champion Dunkeldorf's Falcon Fantasy, Champion Dunkeldorf's Falcon Fantasia, Champion Dunkeldorf's Falcon Frappe, and Dunkeldorf's Falcon Faveta. Favorite was a Top Producer for seven years with 94 American Champions. Fantasy was Best of Breed at the 1965 Dachshund Club of America Specialty. Forester will be remembered in the ring with Frank Hardy; he was Best of Breed at the 1964 Dachshund Club of America Specialty. When Forester won the Dachshund Club of America Specialty in 1964 and Fantasy did so in 1965, it was a first, and the record still stands, for littermates to win Best of Breed at the DCA National. Also, littermates have never won Best of Breed and Best of Opposite Sex at the same Dachshund Club of America Specialty as Fantasy (Best of Breed) and Forester (Best of Opposite Sex) did at the Dachshund Club of America in 1965.

In 1967, the Dunks' beautiful Champion Dunkeldorf's Rittmeister, by Champion Dunkeldorf Falcon's Favorite ex Dunkeldorf's Gimlet, was whelped along with five other champions. Rittmeister had an outstanding ring career, winning Bests in Show, Hound Groups, and Bests of Breed including the Dachshund Club of America in 1970. Dunkeldorf's Gimlet, Rittmeister's dam, was from Champion Timbar's Bubbling Over bred to her grandsire, Champion Fleet of Gera. Gimlet produced ten champions in two litters, bred to Favorite and to Forester. Rittmeister's early demise was a loss to his owners and to the breed.

They bred their last litter in 1971, but a large number of outstanding Dachshunds of today still carry Dunkeldorf bloodlines in their pedigrees.

The Dunks moved to Central Florida in 1974, where they built a house and small kennel on a lake in a rural area. At that time they had seven Dachshunds, all champions. In February 1985 they lost the last of these, thirteen-year-old Champion Dunkeldorf's Dratsab.

Words cannot even begin to describe the quality and excellence which these breeders attained in their 28 years "in" Dachshunds!

FIDDLERS HILL

Fiddlers Hill was registered as her kennel name by Catherine (Katay) Burg with the American Kennel Club on March 15, 1948. Her first Dachshund, however, had been purchased in January of 1940, a little black and tan bitch. Many generations have stemmed, like stairsteps, from that original bitch. Mrs. Burg attended her first dog show in 1941 or '42. The blue ribbon and trophy she won that day started it all!

Many famous Dachshunds have borne the kennel prefix "Fiddlers Hill." For example, Champion Fiddlers Hill Schottische and Champion Fiddlers Hill Polka who separately and together as a brace made their presence strongly felt in the show rings of the early 1950's. Schottische, born in 1948, was by Champion White Gables Basil from Hexe v Verrueckten Haus. Polka, a full sister, did considerable Best of Variety and Group winning and was the dam of Champion Fiddlers Hill Tiffany (by Champion Bergmanor Gay Guy) who in turn produced American and Canadian Champion Fiddlers Hill Tuppence (by Champion Showboy of Smith) the dam of Champion Fiddlers Hill Dubonnet (by Champion Falcon of Heying Teckel), who was born in October 1957. To show how the line traces down, Dubonnet was bred back to her sire, Falcon, producing Fiddler Hills Lark, who, bred to Champion

Am. and Can. Ch. Fiddlers Hill Tuppence taking Best of Opposite Sex to Best in Show at the Dachshund Club of Oregon Specialty, November 1954. Bred, owned, and handled by Mrs. Catherine (Katay) Burg, Portland, Oregon.

Herman VI, produced American and Canadian Champion Fiddlers Hill Cricket who, bred, to Champion Dunkeldorf Falcon's Favorite produced, in August 1968, American and Canadian Champion Fiddlers Hill Hickory Dick.

The previous year, 1967, Cricket had produced American and Canadian Champion Fiddlers Hill Cinnamon Bun when bred to American and Canadian Champion Jolly Dachs George. Then in 1969, bred to Champion Jay Bee's Toreador, Cricket produced Fiddlers Hill Mistletoe, Jingle Bell, and Drummer Boy.

Champion Fiddlers Hill Tuppence gained titles in both the United States and Canada during the early 1950's making some excellent wins in both countries.

Champion Fiddlers Hill Dubonnet completed championship at just past one year old going Best of Winners at the Dachshund Club of Portland Specialty. She was highly successful in the show ring making some excellent Best of Variety and Hound Group wins.

American and Canadian Champion Fiddlers Hill Cinnamon Bun was the Top Winning Dachshund for 1968, and a Best in Show winner when only 13 months of age.

Although no longer breeding dogs, Mrs. Burg continues her involvement with the Fancy as a judge. In 1969 she turned in an all-breed handler's license and was approved to judge Dachshunds that same year. By November 1977 she had been approved for all hounds, and currently is also approved for all sporting breeds except Spaniels. She has many exciting memories of the days when Fiddlers Hill Dachshunds were gaining titles, winning Groups and taking Best in Show honors, not only in the United States but in Canada as well.

FLEMING'S

Fleming's Dachshunds were founded by Polly Fleming, a Smooth breeder since 1947. This is a small West Coast kennel, located at Los Angeles, California, which seldom houses more than three or four adults.

The foundation stock for this highly successful kennel came from the Parker Kennels in St. Helena, California. The first champion was the noted Champion Flair of Gera, by Champion Badger Hill Nobby ex Champion Annette of Gera bred by Ray and Gene Shultis,

Among the homebreds in which Mrs. Fleming takes justifiable pride have been Champion Fleming's Cherry Carmela, by Red Locket Racketeer ex Fleming's Cherry Genevieve. Carmela was shown to her title by Jean and Tommy Dunk, then bred to Champion Falcon of Heying-Teckel from which she produced Champion Dunkeldorf Falcon's Favorite and Champion Dunkeldorf Falcon Forester, who between them sired a total of 117 champions.

Then there is Champion Fleming's Jolly Julie, by Champion Jolly Dachs George ex Jolly Dachs Victoria. Co-bred with Joy Levy (Jolly Dachs), Julie was shown to her title by the late Dr. Fred Lawrence. She was Top Winning Smooth in the United States for three years during the late 1960's. When bred to Champion Dunkeldorf Fashion's Favorite, Julie produced several champions, most notably Bob Cook's Champion Felsheim's Friendly Jester who was the sire of all 19 of Champion Moffett's Rosanne's champion kids. Rosanne was owned by the Moffetts.

Note the beautiful head and neck of Ch. Fleming's Tiny Timmy, by Ch. Barbadox Happy Derk ex Ch. Fleming's Falconer Teka. Sire of Top Ten winner Ch. Lyell's Master Thomas. Owned by Kimberley Lyell.

Champion Fleming's Jolly Dachs Torger, by Champion Dunkeldorf's Zahlmeister ex Jolly Dachs Victoria, was co-bred by Polly Fleming and Joy Levy. Torger was #2 winning Smooth in 1975, and sired 16 champions although seldom used at stud. In the East, Torger's little brother, Champion Teddy von Mardachs, sired several triple-titled winners ex Holmdachs (Betty Holmberg) bitches.

Yet another of the Fleming homebreds, Champion Fleming's Polly von Valona (Champion Fleming's Jolly Dachs Torger ex Fleming's Liebe von Ruhf Knabe), was shown to titles in both the United States and Canada by owner Ed MacDonald of Victoria, B.C. Polly, when bred to Champion Von Arbee's Razzle Dazzle, produced current Top Ten winner Champion Valona's Keeper of the Keys.

Mrs. Fleming's ambitions as a breeder include the eradication of short upper arms, short keels and steep stifles; the elimination of shyness with strangers, and the eradication, through genetic selection, of rear paralysis caused by disc degeneration. Some progress has been made in all of these areas, she is happy to say.

Since 1975 Polly Fleming has been judging, an activity which she enjoys. Currently she is co-breeding Dachshunds with Bette Anderson, Von Arbee Kennels.

GRENMAR

Grenmar Dachshunds, at Carencro, Louisiana, are owned by Leonce J. Romero whose time is divided between the care of his 25 Dachshunds, holding a full time job as a teacher of retarded children, and being Vice-President and Show Chairman for the Arcadian Kennel Club—a combination of activities which makes his a very full schedule with little free time to spare.

Among Mr. Romero's noted Dachshunds are Champion Sangsavant Grenadine, a lovely bitch with Best of Variety and Group placements to her credit. Champion Wagatome Marching Baron L is her sire; her dam Sangsavant Najma Al Jamila. She was bred by Patricia M. Crary. Following a short career in specials, she was retired to the whelping box where she has produced four champions. She is the foundation bitch at Grenmar; her background basically Wagatome, Mary Dean's color dogs, and an English import bitch of Patricia Crary's, Rockfall's Maid Marion.

Grenadine was Best of Opposite Sex to Best of Breed at the Silver Anniversary Specialty of the Houston Dachshund Club.

Champion Sangsavant Mardi Gras was bred by Patricia Crary by Sangsavant D'Appalussia ex Sangsavant Besamemucho. His championship was completed in 11 shows from the open class, and in finishing he became the first blue and tan dapple Dachshund of any size and any coat to earn the title. His dark blue color and excellent movement attracted much attention in the rings, and he is, as well, the sire and grandsire of champions. This is the foundation sire at Grenmar.

Champion Grenmaw Mosaic, C.D. was co-bred by Patricia Crary and Mr. Romero. A black and tan dapple, he earned his championship in ten shows from Bred-by Exhibitor and Open. He finished his C.D. obedience degree in three shows with excellent scores, one of them a 195, and he was in a tie for Novice B at Alexandria Kennel Club. A super happy working Dachshund!

Champion Grenmar Bourbon Cowboy, by Champion Sangsavant Mardi Gras from Champion Sangsavant Grenadine, was co-bred by Mrs. Crary and Mr. Romero, the latter now co-owner with Lee Ann Stagg. This dog marched swiftly to his championship, three times taking Best of Variety from the classes over specials, and a Group second as well, while on the way. He has been specialed only lightly, Mr. Romero preferring to concentrate his efforts on the classes.

Champion Grenmar Fashion Plate is by Champion Gerolf Das Zwergleinl ex Sangsavant Trilby. He is handled by Mr. Romero who bred him and co-owns him with Lee Ann Stagg. This handsome sabled red needed only eight shows in which to become a champion, winning majors at four of them plus first in a big class at the Dachshund Club of America's Specialty in Tennessee. He has been used three times at stud so far, and his first daughter has points from the puppy class. It is expected that he will become a champion producer.

Champion Grenmar High Fashion, full sister to Fashion Plate, finished quickly also with three majors.

Grenmar Satin, by Fashion Plate from Champion Grenmar Silhouette, is another successful homebred-owner-handled dog who promises an exciting future.

HAN-JO

Han-Jo Dachshunds are owned by Joseph and Hannelore Heller at Lake Villa, Illinois, and this name has become synonymous with excellence in Dachshunds, perhaps being the most widely known and admired by fanciers of Longhairs, although Hannelore has done notable winning with the other varieties as well.

Champion Han-Jo's Flaming Flare L, who was owned and campaigned by Hannelore Heller prior to her becoming a professional handler, has to his credit the imposing total of 72 champions of record. He was sired by Champion Robert de Bayard ex Champion Bayard Rosemonde, and he is to be found in a tremendous number of the best modern Longhaired pedigrees.

Among Flare's offspring was another immortal in the Dachshund world, Champion Von Dyck's Mr. Bojangles, owned by Dr. Helen G. Tiahrt. Handled by Hannelore, he was #1 Hound in 1974, Quaker Oats System, owned at that time by the late Mr. and Mrs. George Hendrickson, but is now back with Dr. Tiahrt.

Champion Han-Jo's Ulysses L was campaigned during his show career by Hannelore for Ingeborg Kremer, M.D. This remarkable dog attained such honors as #3 Longhaired Dachshund, in 1974 and 1975; #1 Longhaired Dachshund 1976 and 1977, these under "Dachshund Variety" System; #1 Canadian Longhaired Dachshund 1976; #3 Top Producer, 1981- 984; Silver Certificate Top Producer, Irene Phillips Khatoonian System; the sire of 42 champions from 21 dams.

Ulysses is a five times all-breed Best in Show dog; has over 20 Bests of Breeds at Specialties; more than 40 Group Firsts and numerous additional Group placements. He was Best of Variety at Westminster 1976 and 1977 with a Hound Group Third in 1976. He was Best of Variety at Knickerbocker Specialty in 1976 and 1977, going also Best of Breed there in 1976. Best of Variety, Metropolitan Washington Dachshund Club, 1976 and 1977. Best of Breed, Dachshund Club of St. Louis, 1975, 1977 and 1978. And Best of Breed at Lincolnland Dachshund Club 1976, 1977 and 1978.

The sire of Ulysses was Champion B's Javelin de Bayard, by Champion Bayard le Franchot ex Champion Robdachs Tambourine, who was owned by the late Mr. and Mrs. Hendrickson. Java was a multiple Best in Show, Hound Group and Specialty Best in Show winner. He is now, since the death of his owners, back with Hannelore who handled him so successfully, and he travels everywhere with the Hellers in their motor home, thoroughly enjoying life at close to 15 years of age.

The current campaigner out with Hannelore as we are writing is Champion Gerolf das Zwerglein, who is a grandson of both Ulysses and Mr. Bojangles. Carrying on in the family tradition, he was #1 Dachshund and #10 Hound in 1982; had three all-breed Bests in Show and three Specialty Bests of Breed that same year; was #1 Longhair sire in 1984; Best of Variety at Westminster 1980, 1981 and 1982; and sire of the Best of Variety at the Centennial American Kennel Club Show in 1984 and Westminster Variety winner in 1985.

Another splendid dog who is credited by his owner to Hannelore Heller's breeding program is Kenneth Andrews' Champion Han-Jo's 'Xtra Copy L. During the first year of his career this dog was tallied #2 with only 40 ring appearances, and his second year he will again be #2, just missing the #1 position by a few points. Even more than his success in the show ring, those associated with 'Xtra Copy are thrilled over the quality he is producing. Bred to bitches representing several different bloodlines, he is siring youngsters who are winning points on Specialty weekends from both puppy and open classes. He himself is a son of Champion Von Dyck's Mr. Bojangles (# 1 Hound in 1974) who is by the top producing Champion Han-Jo's Flaming Flare L. One of his recent successes as we write was that of Best of Breed at the prestigious

Ch. Han-Jo's Flaming Flare L, the sire of the famous Ch. Von Dyck's Mr. Bojangles, the sire of 72 champions, was owned and campaigned by Hannelore Heller prior to her becoming a professional handler.

Knickerbocker Dachshund Club Specialty Show at Westminster time in New York City 1985.

Hannelore's breeding program in Longhairs is based largely on the background developed by the late Mary Howell, so famous for the magnificent Bayard winners. We understand that it was Mrs. Howell's initial suggestions combined with Hannelore's own ideas, "dog sense," and capability as a breeder that provided the very solid and successful breeding program at Han-Jo which has produced such exciting results.

HARDWAY

Hardway Kennels are owned by Jeanette W. Cross, who now divides her time between her homes in Bennington, Vermont, and Delray Beach, Florida, whose first Dachshund was acquired in St. Louis, Missouri, in 1937. He was bred by Homer Steinhoff, was named Rudi, and was an intelligent and affectionate charmer, who by the time he had reached two or three years age had a repertoire of tricks that would be worthy of a circus performing dog. Jeanette Cross has had Dachshunds ever since.

Her first show dog of importance was Champion Gunther von Marienlust, purchased as a puppy from the Josef Mehrers of Marienlust fame. Brilliant is the only word with which to describe this dog's show career. He won his first points at Bar Harbor, Maine, in 1940 under Alva Rosenberg, by whom he was placed Best of Breed over specials from the classes. In 1941 he was Best of Breed at Westminster and Best American-bred Hound. He won the Dachshund Club of America Specialty in 1942 under Dr. Herbert Sanborn, in 1943 under William Held, and in 1945 the Golden Anniversary Specialty under Laurence A. Horswell. He was handled always by Mrs. Cross.

Gunther's grandson, Champion Hardway Welcome Stranger, had an imposing record, too. Bred, owned, and handled by Mrs. Cross, he established a breed record in the early 1950's when he completed his championship by winning Best in Show from the classes at the Old Dominion Kennel Club, then within the next month won Best in Show on three other occasions in strong Eastern competition. He won the 1953 Dachshund Club of America Specialty, and was Best of Breed at the Morris and Essex Kennel Club at one of its final shows.

In between these two outstanding males there were some lovely bitches. Champion Cornhill Linda, bred by Isobel Young of Massachusetts, who was the dam of Champion Hardway Welcome Stranger. Champion Hainheim's Olinda, bred by George Spradling of Wichita, Kansas was acquired following her win under Mrs. Cross at Westminster in 1955, who was so impressed with her quality that she then wheedled George Spradling into selling her; then went on to win multiple Groups with her, which was quite an accomplishment as she was completely untrained and unsure of herself. Olinda was later owned by Marcia Wheeler, for whom she became the dam of nine champions. The last bitch

Ch. Hainheim's Olinda winning Best of Variety in a huge entry at Westbury K.A. in 1955. *Left to right:* Ramona Van Court Jones presenting trophy; Jeanette Cross, owner-handler of Olinda; Mrs. Virgilio Cheda, the judge. Olinda was bred by George Spradling, Hainheim Kennels, Wichita, Kansas, very famous in those days.

shown by Jeanette was Champion Dixie Dachs Krushina, bred by Peggy and Wallace Alford of Raleigh, North Carolina. She made her title easily and was shown only once as a special, on which occasion she won over nearly all the top Eastern winners.

It was on the way home from the latter show, in the blistering heat and terrific traffic, that Jeanette, as she puts it, "came to my senses" and decided that she had had enough, and that she would prefer being out in boat or in a swimming pool, and that she was sure the little dog did not enjoy being dragged around the ring in such heat any more than she herself enjoyed being there.

Even though she no longer exhibits, Jeanette Cross remains a very active member of the Fancy as a highly respected judge.

HERTHWOOD

Herthwood Kennels, owned by Dr. and Mrs. George Pickett at Huntington, Connecticut now of Jekyll Island, Georgia, bred and showed many outstanding Dachshunds. Their Smooths were heavy in Marienlust bloodlines, like Champion Herthwood's Saffron, who exemplifies the soundness and elegance of the Marienlust dogs.

The Picketts also owned some outstanding Wires, including Champion Westphal's Wandering Wind and Champion Vantebe's Draht Kahlua.

Dorothy (Mrs. George) Pickett with her noted smooth dog, Ch. Herthwood's Saffron winning at Longshore-Southport in June 1962 under judge, the famous Dachshund expert L. A. Horswell.

JANDELO

It was back in 1946, while living in Grand Rapids, Michigan, that Elizabeth Van Valen purchased a Dachshund from the Schwarzwald Hof Kennels who breed such famous St. Bernards. After a few weeks people began saying "Oh! You have a Long-haired Dachshund," in a tone which implied "how foolish." By then the Van Valens had grown to love the pup so much that they were past being influenced by any such thinking. In fact they were so carried away that they went back to the kennel and purchased a second one, this time a bitch.

So it was that Jandelo Kennels came into being. The dog grew up to be Champion Midas de Sangpur, and was a son of that notable producer Champion William de Sangpur owned by Gracie Hill. Midas is described by his owner as "one of the most charismatic dogs I have ever seen." Certainly he did well by her and by his breed, for shown about 100 times, he was Best of Variety on 95 occasions and placed in the Hound Group on an average of about 25 percent of the time. In fact he was still winning groups at ten years of age!

The bitch was Champion Mitzi von Schwarzwald Hof, by Champion Steven of Gypsy Barn ex Priscilla Prim of Gypsy Barn. She was bred to Champion William de Sangpur, Champion Carlo v d Nidda, Champion Victor of Gypsy Barn, Champion Kelle of Gypsy Barn, and Champion Agne of Gypsy Barn, producing at least one champion in each litter. One son, Champion Jandelo's Don Juan, finished in four shows, including wins at the Florida East Coast Dachshund Club and Morris and Essex.

Shortly after purchasing the first of the Dachshunds, the Van Valens moved to Fort Lauderdale and established their kennel, choosing the identification "Jandelo" coined from parts of their names. Elizabeth, (or Jane as she is known to her friends) Van Valen was first President and Chairman of the Fort Lauderdale Dog Club and was active in that for a long time. She since has been elected a permanent member. Along with Charles and Mary Jane Davis of the Palm Beach County Dog Fanciers Association, and Charles and Madeline Fernsell of Palm Beach, the Van Valens started the Florida East Coast Dachshund Club.

In 1947, Jane was licensed by the American Kennel Club as an all-breed handler. Today she is a member of the Professional Handlers Association.

Ch. Mar-I-Lea's Wotan in 1965. Albert E. Van Court judging, Elizabeth (Jane) Derteen Van Valem handling.

In the early 1960's the Van Valens sold all of their dogs and re-tired—but that did not last for long. Champion Zachary de Bayard soon was purchased, as was a young dog named Mar-I-Lea's Wo-tan, who finished his championship on the Florida Circuit by beating five excellent specials under Kippy Van Court and Peter Knoop. Next a couple of bitches were acquired, eventually wind-ing up with a bitch named Jandelo's Patrician Knepper, strong in Champion Pegramos Paragon breeding, who became the founda-tion of the Jandelo dogs of to-day.

"Trish" had two litters, one by Champion Han-Jo's Flaming Flare L and one by Champion Delldachs Rolls Royce L. Nine puppies finished. *Kennel Review* listed her as the Top Producing Hound Bitch in 1977, tied with a Saluki. Her descendants have been producing well and winning in the show ring. She is dead now, but the Van Valens always will have a special place in their hearts for her.

Looking to the past as well as the future, there is a lovely young black and tan Standard, Champion Jandelo's Keedox Gypsy Baron, in the kennel, a return to the original Gypsy Baron strain Jane has loved right from the beginning, this time brought in by Emma Nance's Champion Dorndorf's Admiral L., in a youngster whom she hopes will be a "bright star" in Jandelo's future.

A couple of years ago, Jane Van Valen started thinking about the problems of constantly picking up Standard Dachsies thus decided that perhaps the time had come for her to try her hand with some Miniatures. Norma Love, a friend in Fort Lauderdale, was seriously ill at the time so let her Lovdox Josh's Dream Girl ML go to Jandelo. Now a champion, this lovely bitch has produced Champion Jandelo's Lucky Strike ML and Champion Jandelo's Philip Morris ML who was Best in Specialty Show at the Sunshine Dachshund Club of Jacksonville and has several Group placements. Yes, the breeding was repeated, and the puppies are coming on nicely. The sire is Champion Carawan's Jericho ML.

In 1974 the Van Valens moved their kennel to Fairview, North Carolina, just outside of Asheville. It is more convenient a location for getting to many shows, and the Van Valens love the North Carolina climate, so Jane and George are planning to remain there in the future along with their daughter Patricia Derteen.

KNOLLAND FARM

Knolland Farm is a very famous kennel in our American dog show world, known for outstanding excellence in a number of breeds. One of the most active here has been the Dachshund, of whom owner Edward Jenner, has long been an admirer. Now the breed is doubly fortunate to have the interest of Mr. Jenner's son, Daniel, who is usually to be found with several Dachshunds at his heels whenever one runs into him at Knolland Farm in Richmond, Illinois. Daniel prefers the Dachshunds to all the breeds who live there, and is determined to do his part to keep the breed active and in the limelight at this kennel.

Ed Jenner has been in Dachshunds since the early 1970's when he acquired Kleetal's Jolly Cookie, bred by Bob Welty and John Cook, a daughter of Tywell's Chaunesey from Jiridox Jingo, whom he had handled by Howard Atlee.

Since that time many famous Dachshunds in all three varieties have followed, the majority of them handled by Lorraine Heichel

Ch. Ram-Ral of Mar Lar, daughter of Ch. Risa's Heavy Chevy, is an excellent producing bitch owned by Daniel Jenner at Knolland Farm, Richmond, Illinois.

before her retirement from handling and eventual marriage to John Masley. One of the best-known of these was the red Smooth dog, Champion Moffett's Harvest, a Best in Show winner and a multiple Group winner. There was also the notable Longhaired Champion Kemper Dachs Marcel during the mid 1970's, widely admired for elegance and type.

Also, around this same period, another Dachshund carrying high the Best in Show banner for Knolland Farm was Champion Brandylan's Lanson of Lucene.

More recently has come the very famous and successful Champion Risa's Heavy Chevy, co-owned by Edward Jenner and Nancy Weber, who not only enjoyed an exciting ring career but who is siring some outstanding youngsters as well, among them Champion Knolland Karl and Champion Knolland Kranberry. Handled by Luc Boileau, Heavy Chevy is a son of Champion Moffett's Inca ex Champion Risa's Red Chevy, bred by Nancy and Carol Weber, born October 1978.

You can be expecting to see Daniel Jenner breeding Dachshunds for quite some time to come, and with the solid background of such bitches as his Specialty winning Champion Ram-Ral of Mar-Lee, who has proven herself a splendid brood matron as well as show bitch, we expect to see many more quality puppies coming from the Dachshund department at Knolland Farm owing to the interest of both Ed and Daniel.

KORDACHS

Kordachs Miniature Smooth Dachshunds are owned by Mrs. Raymond L. McCord at Winchester, Indiana, who has been raising Miniature Smooths since the early 1950's and exhibiting since 1963. At the time Mrs. McCord became an exhibitor, there were only four Smooth Miniature champions in the entire United States, the greatest number ever up to that time. Now Mrs. McCord has finished that number herself in the year of 1985! Smooth Miniatures have come a long way, but Mrs. McCord comments that she will never be satisfied until the Miniatures are separate from the Standards, a feeling shared by many who love and admire the Miniatures as she does!

Mrs. McCord has bred 15 Miniature Smooth champions, which is very likely the second or third highest number for an all-Smooth Miniature kennel in the United States.

Mrs. McCord has served the National Miniature Dachshund Club, Inc., in some capacity from Board of Directors to President, for more than 20 years. Currently she is Treasurer. She has taught Obedience classes, 4-H classes, conformation classes, judged matches and puppy sweepstakes. But her greatest challenge still is to try to breed the best Miniature Smooths and always to improve on the breed. She enjoys showing her own dogs personally, but lately, to quote her words "as I get older and busier" she is depending on Hannelore Heller to show them for her with increasing regularity.

Champion Kordachs' Wee Kamouflage has the distinction of being one of only three living dapple Smooth Miniature champion males in the United States. His sire, Champion Kordachs' Wee Konfetti, is also a black/silver dapple. A Kamouflage son, Champion Kordachs' Wee Kuartz, is the *only red dapple* Smooth Miniature champion ever to have finished to date—three generations of dapple champions bred and owned by Mrs. McCord. Four of Ka-

Miniature Dachshunds do quite well in obedience. *Left to right:* Kordachs' Wee Angel, C.D.; Kordachs' Wee Black Silk, C.D.; and Kordachs' Wee Caramel, C.D.X. with trophies won while they were earning their degrees in the 1960's.

mouflage's offspring completed their championships in 1984.

Champion Kordachs' Wee Pinocchio was the top winning Smooth Miniature Dachshund in the U.S. for 1972, as was his dam, Champion Kordachs' Wee Copper Candi, in 1968. He was shown to Best of Variety several times and an occasional Group placement by Mrs. McCord. His name is found back in the pedigrees of many present day Smooth Miniatures.

Kordachs Miniature Smooths have distinguished themselves in obedience competition as well as the conformation ring. Kordachs' Wee Angel, C.D., Kordachs' Wee Black Silk, C.D., and Kordachs Wee Caramel, C.D.X. each have won many honors, with Caramel taking Best Brace in Obedience Show nine times, with different partners.

These notable Smooth Miniatures were also shown in Brace conformation classes, and often placed first in Hound Brace Groups. Three times Kordachs has won Best in Show Team honors, with different teams.

LUCENE

Lucene Dachshunds are owned by Jeanine Sudinski at El Cajon, California, who purchased her first Dachshund in 1953, a black and tan female from an English breeder summering in Monterey, California. The bitch was from the Ascherhof-Jaegerhaus lines.

In 1956, Mrs. Sudinski bred her bitch to a young black and tan son of Champion Favorite v Marienlust, by name Champion Anchor of Heying-Teckel. For the next several years she continued breeding from this foundation stock, unfortunately still not quite certain about quality and type in the breed; thus, some beautiful puppies went to pet homes. Her enthusiasm mounted at a rapid rate, however, and she learned a great deal by attending every A.K.C. dog show and puppy match she possibly could manage. She also did some judging at the matches; but she took it slowly about showing her own dogs.

In 1961, Mrs. Sudinski leased a red daughter of Champion Aristo v Marienlust whom she bred to Champion Falcon of Heying-Teckel. Falcon was a son of Champion Favorite v Marienlust, who was a half-brother to Aristo. The litter consisted of nine black and tan puppies, of which only two were bitches, both of whom were kept by Mrs. Sudinski for her future breeding program.

One of the above two, Lucene's Fascination, was bred to Champion Hainhaim's Lance, son of Champion Lance of Heying-Teckel. This breeding produced American and Japanese Champion Lucene's Lantana to whom the other bitch, Champion Lucene's Flirtation (litter-mate to Fascination) was bred. From this came a smashing black and tan male, Champion Lucene's Lanson, who sired five champions.

Along about that time Mrs. Sudinski felt that she would like to introduce an outcross in her breeding program, for which she especially wanted a bitch of Blauruckenburg and Caseway lines. But for one reason or another nothing was available then from either of these kennels. Then a piece of good fortune occurred. A young couple who had been looking for a dog to whom to breed their bitch and especially admired the soundness of those from Lucene wanted to arrange to use Lanson. Their bitch was from the Blauruckenburg-Caseway lines Mrs. Sudinski was so anxious to try! The bitch was named Ballenger's Ballerina. In their first breeding she and Lanson produced Champion Lucene's Tanner who in his turn sired 11 champions. They were bred twice more, and the third time the litter consisted of two red bitches, who became Champion Lucene's Tanya and Champion Lucene's Lana v Brandylan. In her only breeding, Tanya produced Champion Kochana's Tanya of Lucene, who eventually became the dam of Champion Kochana's Sandman, a leading winner in 1979; Champion Gretl v BeaHal Rovna, also a consistent winner, and the one who stayed at home, Champion Lucene's Delight C.D.

Champion Lucene's Lana v Brandylan produced Champion Brandylan's Lanson of Lucene, a 13-time Best in Show winner in about six months of showing during the first half of 1976.

Mrs. Sudinski is a very talented artist as well as breeder of outstanding Dachshunds. She attended classes at the Chicago Art Institute in 1938, her special talents for drawing animals becoming immediately clear to her teachers, who had her transferred to the Chicago Field Museum where she attended school for ten years. Her biggest achievement, she modestly tells us, in her art work was the creation of the First Prize winning painting for the "Easter Seal," the original and the stamp both hanging in the Fine Arts Gallery in the Carnegie Institute.

Mrs. Sudinski has also painted gorgeous portraits of a goodly number of famous Dachshunds.

To speak a bit about the individual dogs at Lucene, let us start with Champion Brandylan's Lanson of Lucene, by Champion Birchwood High Command ex Champion Lucene's Lana v Brandylan, who was whelped in January 1974 and was the last dog before her retirement, handled by the well known Lorraine Heichel. Emily Bush was his breeder, who co-owned him with Edward Jenner, breeder-judge, for six months, during which time he won half dozen Bests in Show. He is the sire of champions for Mr. Jenner at Knolland Farm.

Champion Lucene's Delight of Kochana, CD. by Farmeadow Country Music ex Champion Kochana's Tanya of Lucene, is the only champion Smooth black and tan Dachshund ever to acquire a Companion Dog degree in San Diego County, which she did in three consecutive shows without benefit of a practice match! She is the dam of multiple Group winning Champion Lucene's Daily Double, whom her owner describes as "the ultimate of my 30 years of concentrated breeding." She was born in 1980.

Champion Lucene's Tanner and Champion Lucene's Tanya are

littermates. Tanner has made a glowing show record, winning his first Best in Show at seven months over 600 dogs at the Silver Bay Kennel Club Sanctioned Match, then a week later won the Dachshund Club of Southern California Specialty Sweepstakes. Two months later he finished his title in the mid-West handled by Lawrence Krebs.

It was more than seven years later when Tanner and his son, Champion Tar Tan were exhibited at the Dachshund Club of America Specialty where he was chosen first Best of Variety and then Best in Show. He is the sire of 12 champions, of which two are Canadian.

Tanya, meanwhile, was sent out with Hannelore Heller and completed title in ten shows. Returning to California, her first time out she was Best of Opposite Sex to Best of Breed at the Sierra Dachshund Breeders Specialty under the late Herman Cox. She is the dam of two champions.

MIDACHS

Midachs Miniature Smooth Dachshunds are owned by Sharon L. Michael of Johnstown, New York, who combined the first two letters of her own last name with the first five of her breed to create this kennel identification.

To date as we write, ten Miniature Smooth Dachshund champions have been bred at Midachs, including Champion MDPH Demonstration M, top producing Mini-Smooth dog in the breed; and Champion Midachs Penthouse Joker MS, the first Mini-Smooth ever to finish in the United States.

In addition to the Mini-Smooth conformation winners, Sharon Michael is very much "in to" field work with Dachshunds. Her partner, Roy R. Colverd, judges field trials (she, herself, is an A.K.C. approved Dachshund judge), and it was Sharon who started the annual field trials for the Albany Capital District Dachshund Club. Also for five years she has run the Dachshund Club of America's annual field trial.

Champion MDPH Demonstration M, Mini-Smooth male, was born in 1970, sired by Penthouse Daddy Goodness MW ex Midachs Auntie Em v Maybit M. Demo's importance as a sire becomes obvious when one realizes that he is behind almost all winning Smooths and Wires in the Miniature ring to-day. To date he has sired 12 champions, which has earned for him distinction as

Ch. MDPH Demonstration M, born in 1970, is the all-time top producing mini-smooth sire with 12 champions to date. Bred and owned by Sharon M. Michael, Johnstown, New York.

the leading producer in Mini-Smooths, plus some Longhairs also trace back to him. His descendants are to be found in Canada, England, Japan, and South America as well as here at home. He was bred by Sharon Michael.

Canadian and American Champion Midachs Christopher MSL is by Midachs Chancellor MS ex Midachs Ursala MSL. This red Smooth Miniature finished with four majors from breeder-judges, and has descendants all over the United States and Canada. Another of Sharon Michael's homebreds, she expects him one day to beat out Demo in the number of champions sired.

Champion Midachs The Heiress MS is by the same parents as Christopher from a later litter. She, too, finished easily and currently is producing some lovely puppies. Bred by Sharon Michael, she is co-owned with Roy Colverd.

Then, for the future, there is Midachs Zephyr MS, by Champion Midachs The Advocate MS from Midachs Francine MS. Her ring career started off in grand style when, at her first show, the prestigious Knickerbocker Dachshund Club Specialty, she took reserve winners in an entry of 35 bitches. Then at her second show she went Best of Variety at Elm City for a four-point major. Bred by Roy R. Colverd and Joan M. DuBuc, she is owned by Mr. Colverd and Sharon Michael.

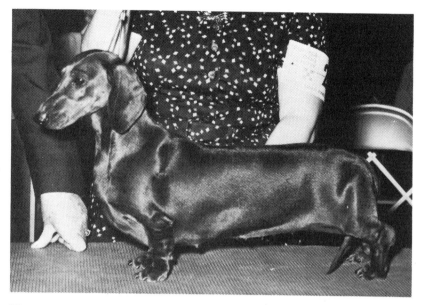

The great producing bitch.Ch. Moffett's Roxanne, by Ch. Crosswynd's Cracker Jack ex Moffett's Sandra, is the dam of 17 champions, including sons Harvester and Georgi who are also Top Producers as are some of Georgi's offspring. Thelma Moffett, owner, and Lorraine Heichel Masley, handler.

MOFFETT'S

Moffett's Standard Smooth Dachshunds are owned by Thelma Moffett of Flint, Michigan, whose husband, Russ, wholeheartedly shares her interest and enthusiasm. These folks have no kennel, just house dogs to be enjoyed for the "pleasure of their company" as well as for their beauty and accomplishments. And they have surely achieved some exciting success.

After beginning mistakes, Thelma Moffett acquired Janice of Gera from the noted Gera Kennels. Janice became a champion in eight shows, then was bred to Fleet of Gera. All of the Dachshunds produced by the Moffetts since are decended from her.

The approach was rudimentary. The best bitch puppy from each litter was retained, finished, and then bred to a carefully selected suitable stud. No more than one litter in any given year was ever produced by the Moffett bitches, and more frequently two, three or four years elapsed between litters.

These procedures seemed to work out well. Each litter produced at least one champion and usually more, somewhat depending upon who bought the puppies. Having no kennel, the Moffetts found it impossible to hold on to more than one puppy each time.

Within such restrictions, Thelma feels that they must have had some good luck, for when their Sandra came along she produced three champions from three litters, including Champion Rosanne. By Champion Crosswynd's Cracker Jack ex Moffett's Sandra, Rosanne accomplished the notable achievement of producing 17 champions in four litters!

Both Sandra and Rosanne are listed as Top Producers. Among Rosanne's 17 champions were Champion Moffett's Georgi and Champion Moffett's Harvest, both listed as fifth generation Top Producers on the dam's side and fourth generation on the sire's. Also Harvest garnered several Best in Show victories during his show career. Another brother, Jacket, quickly finished American and Canadian Championships, then acquired a championship title in India with two Best in Show Challenge Certificates.

Today Rosanne's descendants are widely evident among important dogs in the pedigrees of current winners. As Thelma Moffett comments, "it would seem that the road to winning is through the union of top *compatible* producers."

MURIEL'S

Muriel's Dachshunds, now at Lomita, California, were started by Muriel and Herman Newhauser back in the 1950's in an effort to breed and raise quality Miniature Dachshunds. Very dissatisfied with the Smooth Miniatures they had become accustomed to seeing during that decade, they decided that if they were going to have any to please themselves, they would have to breed their own. With this object in mind, three bitches were purchased, all from different bloodlines. None of these filled the bill as producers of the type of miniatures the Newhausers wanted, so they continued to look still further. It was the acquisition of Lo-Dachs Miss Fabulous M from Jim and Billie Ruffell that really did the trick. After seven years of showing the aforementioned first three, along with their offspring doing absolutely no winning (but making many friends as they made points for other exhibitors) the Newhausers felt that they had learned a good deal from the other breeders-exhibitors with whom they had become acquainted, and

Ch. Muriel's Miss Bam M finished with three 5-point majors for owner Muriel Newhauser, Muriel's Dachshunds, Lomita, California.

they set to work to make this knowledge work for them. As Muriel says regarding their kennel, "the Lo-Dachs bloodline changed our lives."

Two dogs stand out among those raised by the Newhausers. They are Champion Muriel's Semper Fidelis and Champion Muriel's Esprit de Corps. Muriel Newhauser has often remarked that the training she and her husband received when both were members of the Marine Corps had prepared them well for their years with miniature Dachshunds, all of whom they tagged with names chosen from their marine experiences. Champion Muriel's Esprit de Corps M was a daughter of Champion Muriel's Semper Fidelis ex Lo-Dachs Miss Fabulous M. Her points were won entirely from breeder-judges, and two of her three majors were at Specialties. Herman Newhauser considered her to be the finest Dachshund he and Muriel had ever bred. Sad to say, she died at only 14 months of age, long before she had enjoyed the opportunity of being widely seen and admired. She was #5 in 1970 in the Top 30 Miniatures, all coats. Her kennel-mate, and chief competitor, Champion Muriel's Miss Bam M, was #11. Their sire, Semper Fidelis, was #26.

Semper Fidelis, bred to Champion Hubertus Teddina (by Geam's Wee Reddy Teddy ex Geam's Wee Copper Gleam), was sire of Champion Verdon's Vici M who in 1968 was the top winning Smooth male Miniature Dachshund, Thomas System of the Top 100 Dachshunds. Starting his career on the Florida Circuit in 1968, he was finished by nine months later, but still going strong in 1970 when he made #76 under that same system.

Muriel Newhauser started judging Dachshunds in 1970, only a few months following the death of her husband who had greatly encouraged her to apply for American Kennel Club approval. She now does the entire Hound Group and, since retiring from teaching, is enjoying travel to many distant assignments (Australia, England, Canada, etc.) as well as being very steadily in demand for prestigious Specialty and all-breed shows here in the United States—a lady of knowledge and integrity who has contributed well to the Dog Fancy.

MUSELAND

Museland Kennels, Dorothy A. Muse and her late husband James G. Muse, are located at Mountain City, Tennessee. Their first Dachshund was purchased in 1951, after Jim Muse's retirement from the U.S. Air Force, and their move to Mountain City, where they could have dogs. This luxury had not been possible while the Muses were apartment dwellers in New York City, Washington, D.C. and other such locations. In the many years of attending dog shows prior to 1951, the Muses had been greatly attracted to the Smooth Standard Dachshund, especially so since they were shown natural. Stubbornly the Muses plugged away for years. Things really got to rolling, however, when they were able to purchase Timbar's Honeymoon Limited, who completed her title in both the United States and Canada. She was bred to Champion Nixon's Double Concerto owned by Jane Thomas, from

Mrs. Dorothy Muse owner-handling her great winning bitch Ch. Muse-land's Alysia. By Ch. Nixon's Double Concerto ex Ch. Timbar's Honeymoon Limited. Alysia's show record is an imposing one, and she is the dam of important winning progeny as well.

which she produced American and Canadian Champion Muse-land's Alysia, Museland's Atlantean, American Champions Muse-land's Athena and Bartholomew, and Canadian Champion Muse-land's Allegra.

Alysia earned a magnificent show record, which included 64 times Best of Variety, 37 Bests of Opposite Sex, and 14 Group placements. She was Best of Breed at four Specialties and Best Smooth at 12 Specialties. Bred to Champion Nixon's Fleeting Encounter, owned by Colette Kinch, she produced Champions Museland's Cybele, Cygnet, Cymric and Cyril (who has produced many champions for his owner, Barbara Haisch).

Dorothy Muse acquired Champion Dunkeldorf's Drachen as a youngster, later breeding her to American and Canadian Champion Museland's Atlantean. From this came four more champions, Museland's Daemon, Darius, Danae, and Dagmar.

Champion Sandwood Musette came to Dorothy Muse as a gift

while still a puppy from her co-breeder Jane Thomas. Musette had an exciting show career, including many Specialty wins (including the Dachshund Club of America) and Westminster.

To date the greatest show record has been with Champion Museland's Cybele. She was #1 Smooth Dachshund, all systems, in 1977 and 1978. She won four all-breed Bests in Show, three Specialty Shows, 24 Group Firsts, 59 additional Group placements, and 195 times Best of Variety!

Several years ago (the early 1980's), Mrs. Muse acquired her first Standard Longhair, Champion Poltergeist Brandy L, who completed her title in four shows and was Top Winning Bitch over a two-year period. She now has her first litter. Museland's Iona, Smooth Standard, also has her first litter sired by Champion Museland's Hickok.

Museland is a small one-woman operation, so breeding is limited. Dorothy Muse can well take pride in what her dogs have accomplished in the capable hands of Bobby Barlow, Michael Hagen, David Bolus, and Hannelore Heller, who have taken them to such outstanding success in the show rings.

PATCHWORK

Patchwork Dachshunds were established during the 1960's in Connecticut by Pat Beresford who is now editor of the *Pure-Bred Dog/American Kennel Gazette*, official publication of the American Kennel Club.

The first of Pat's litters was sired by the lovely and widely admired Miniature Longhair Champion Mighty Fine von Walder, Nancy Onthank's noted Group winner; and De Sangpur's Wee Rouge. Champion Westphal's Merry Mite, from Wee Rouge's first litter by Mighty Fine gave Pat her first homebred champion; and the second litter, a year later, added five champions to the Patchwork roster.

Since then Pat has bred many outstanding Miniature Longs, including at least one Best in Show winner. Five generations of Patchwork bloodlines were developed through a most careful and well studied breeding program.

Champion Patchwork Johnny Come Lately (by Mighty Fine ex Rouge) was making his presence felt in the late 1960's. Champion Patchwork Hill Calliope is another from the '60's, this one sold to Peggy Westphal.

PEGDEN

Pegden Dachshunds, belonging to Denny Mounce and Peggy Lloyd, located in Sugar Land, Texas, officially began breeding and exhibiting the breed in April 1974 with the purchase of Cal-Neva's Hap-Pea Tymes, MW, from Winston and Neva Calhoun, Stockton, California. Happy completed his championship in January 1975 by winning the Hound Group under judge Melbourne Downing. He retired from the show ring in February 1977 by winning the Hound Group under judge Mrs. Joan Urban. During the years between, he won numerous Bests of Varieties and Group placements, and was Best Wire at the Houston Dachshund Club in 1976. To date he has sired 11 champions, and is still producing top quality litters. The most famous of Happy's progeny is the top winning Dachshund bitch of all time, Champion Daiquiri's Fannie Farkle, MW.

In December of 1977, the bitch Champion Cal-Neva's Hy Tymes, MW, was purchased from the Calhouns, and subsequently her mother and grandfather, Champion Cal-Neva's Bight Bandit, MW. This was the start of what has become six generations of Miniature Wirehaired champion Dachshunds at Pegden.

Some of the dogs involved in the chain of Pegden champions include: the all-champion litter of Champion Pegden's Shotgun Willie, MW, Champion Pegden's Tizza Wire, M, and Champion Pegden's Sass Cee Wire M C.D. Sass Cee has since produced an all champion litter consisting of Champion Pegden's Goldrush MW, Champion Pegden's Texas Ranger MW (multiple Group winner) and Champion Pegden's Saddle Tramp MW. All in all, to date Pegden Kennels has owned or bred over 30 Miniature Wire champions, including three all-breed Best in Show winners as well as Specialty winners.

Since 1974, when Denny and Peggy started breeding Dachshunds, they have improved not only their dogs but the pedigrees of these dogs as well. With only one or two champions in each of the early pedigrees, they have successfully linebred and outcrossed until their pedigrees of today consist almost entirely of champions.

These girls believe that linebreeding can only be as successful as the dogs involved, which certainly makes sense. Although they have since the beginning bred for sound, typey Mini-Wires, they have from time to time introduced an outcross to improve on a particular trait. They believe that although pedigrees are impor-

Am., Mex., and Int'l. Ch. Batzenhof's Number Dri Sun, ML, No. 1 Miniature Long for 1978. Pictured here after completing his Mexican and International Championships with a Group 1st. He had several American Bests in Show as well. Pegden Kennels, Sugar Land, Texas.

tant, it is more important to breed dogs which complement one another rather than to base a breeding program on pedigree alone.

The newest Best in Show winner at Pegden is Champion Fannie Get Your Gun MW, co-bred with S.R. Whittaker, Jr. She is the result of the breeding of Champion Chris Harbor's Urban Cowboy MW with the bitch Fannie Farkle. Fannie Get Your Gun is the first black and tan Wire Dachshund ever to win an all-breed Best in Show. At this writing she has just begun her career and has already amassed 35 Bests of Variety, six Group firsts, and 22 Group placements. "Tush," as she is known by those who love her, is owned by Barbara Cosgrove, Barmere Kennels, Scottsdale, Arizona.

As an addition to this kennel story, we wish to pay tribute to the amazing achievements of American, Mexican, and International Champion Daiquiri's Fannie Farkle MW, the Top Winning Dachshund Bitch (any size or coat) in history!

Fannie's memorable career began when she was purchased by Samuel R. Whitaker, Jr., of Houston, Texas, and Mildred Bryant of Bridgeport, Texas, in 1979. She was a natural showdog, and from the very moment that her handler, Denny Mounce, set eyes on her, she knew that Fannie was destined to be a winner.

Ch. Pegden's Fanny Get Your Gun MW, black and tan daughter of Ch. Chris Harbor's Urban Cowboy MW ex Ch. Daiquiri's Fanny Farkle MW, owned by Barbara Cosgrove, Barmere Kennels. Handled by Denny Mounce, here winning a strong Hound Group under co-author judge Marcia Foy in 1985. Cowboy, Fanny, and his daughter all are Best in Show winners.

It was only a matter of weeks before Fannie became the first Miniature ever to win a Specialty Best of Breed from the Open Miniature class. The occasion was the Houston Dachshund Specialty, and the judge was Miss Dorothy Nickles. This was not to be the only time Fannie would win this show. She did so again the following year under breeder-judge Dorothy Hutchinson. Her other Specialty wins included the New Mexico Dachshund Club under judge John Seader, the Bayou Dachshund Club of New Orleans under judge Lyle Rethmeier, and the following year under Mrs. Aileen P.C. DeBrun, then the Dallas-Fort Worth Specialty under judge Mrs. Leota Seader.

Fannie was the #1 Wire Dachshund in 1980, 1981, and 1982. She was shown from coast to coast by Denny Mounce, and some of her most memorable and prestigious wins included her 100th Best of Variety won at Santa Barbara; Best of Variety three consecutive years at the Astroworld Series of dog shows; and she was High Dog in Trial at the International Field Trial in Mexico City while earning her championship there, undefeated, with four Group firsts.

Fannie retired to live at Pegden Kennels with Denny in November 1982. Her final ring appearance was an all-breed Best in Show under judge MSG/Ret. H.B. Cox, completing her record as the Top Winning Dachshund bitch of all time.

To Fannie's credit one finds the following:

> 10 all-breed Bests in Show.
> Six Specialty Bests in Show.
> Forty Hound Group Firsts.
> Two hundred Bests of Variety.
> Defeating a total of 34,268 dogs during her career.

In 1983, Fannie was bred to the #1 Dachshund for that year, Champion Chris Harbor's Urban Cowboy MW. The result was a smashing all-champion litter which included the Specialty winning Champion Pegden's Fred Farkle MW, owned by S.R. Whittaker, Jr., and the Best in Show winning bitch, Champion Pegden's Fannie Get Your Gun MW, owned by Barbara Cosgrove. This is the first black and tan Wire to win an all-breed Best in Show.

In 1984, Fannie was bred again to Urban Cowboy, and as the American Kennel Club celebrated its centennial, Fannie delivered another promising litter.

Fannie's accomplishments are many, but none more important than her ability to make people smile. She showed her heart out every time she entered the ring. A true champion in every sense of the word, she will remain in the hearts of her admirers for many years to come.

PENTHOUSE

Howard and Barbara Atlee, now of Teaneck, New Jersey, is a long time Dachshund enthusiast who has bred, owned, handled, and now judges the breed with knowledge and integrity.

Howard's "roots" in Dachshunds go back into at least the early 1960's. Although he loves good Dachshunds of either size, his particular breeding forte has been in miniatures, and his contribution to the improvement of miniature type and quality has been tremendous.

With the help of a Poodle breeder, Arthur P. Donahue, who has now become a famous sculptor, Howard set about trying to put more type and substance into the Miniatures. At first there was a weight limit of nine pounds which was raised later to ten. That helped. Howard recalls that Frank and Dorothy Hardy had a Miniature Smooth dog champion, a rare item back in the '60's, by the name of Champion Johannis Strauss. To him was bred the Standard Wire bitch, Champion Wilhemina W of Sharondachs, co-owned by Howard with Lloyd M. Case of Celloyd Kennels; and also a Miniature Wire champion bitch, Champion Val-Jeans Cinderella MW. Two of the offspring from each of these litters were crossed, or mated, which led to Penthouse Daddy Goodness, still alive and well at age 17 years as we write. This turned out truly to be "the key to the mint." Daddy was used on Standard and Miniature bitches. He was elegant, and reproduced this elegance into the miniature lines where it was so needed at that period. One of his sons, Champion Penthouse Demonstration, is among the outstanding studs in Miniature Smooths.

As with so many others, what had started out as a pet project developed into decades of showing and breeding dogs. Howard was introduced to the world of purebred dogs when he bought a bitch as a pet while traveling in Maine, which, quite naturally, he named Marlene Maine of Rudotin. Because he was doing a lot of traveling around to summer theatres at that time, he found it necessary to board her during some of his trips. Through the recommendation of writer Kurt Unklebach, whom Howard knew through the publicity business, she was put in the care of Betty Dunn Cummings, a professional handler. Betty started showing the bitch, and Howard stopped in at one of the shows, only to promptly become "hooked" immediately. Through Betty Cummings, Howard met Lloyd Case, and when it came time for Marlene to be bred, it was to Lloyd's wonderful Smooth dog, Champion Celloyd Daniel. This was the start of a long and valued friendship.

It was Lloyd and Celia Case who presented Howard with a birthday gift, the puppy who was to become Champion Celloyd Virginia Woolf. Howard was so deep in his Miniature project at

Ch. Zebediah W of Sharondachs, Wirehaired Dachshund owned by Howard Atlee of New York and the late Lloyd Case, Torrington, Connecticut. Bred by Sharon King. Handled by Howard Atlee. Shown winning Best of Variety at Philadelphia in the 1960's.

the time she was born that he hadn't really thought of the possibility of owning her, greatly as he admired her. But, when Lloyd called and said they wanted to present her to him for his birthday, Howard soon was devoting the principal part of his Dachshund interest to her and to her exciting show career.

Champion Celloyd's Virginia Woolf was born November 3, 1962, daughter of Willo-Mar's Hero ex Pixdown Cleo. She was handled by Howard Nygood. Through 1965 Virginia's record stood at five times Best Hound, 18 additional Group placements, 47 times Best of Variety, twice Best of Opposite Sex to Best of Breed, and 48 times Best of Opposite Sex to Best of Variety.

Howard took up the challenge of breeding Dapple Miniatures at one period, doing so successfully. The first Smooth Miniature dapple champion was Champion Midach Penthouse Joker MS, which Howard followed with the first miniature bitch of that color to finish, Champion Penthouse Splash MS and also with Champion Penthouse Speck Teckel MS.

One of Howard's first top winning Miniature Smooths was Champion Penthouse MS, who had the elegance and type for

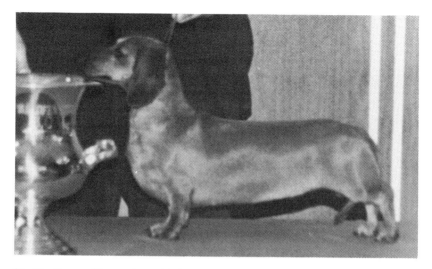

Ch. Penthouse Emmy Award MS, the first Miniature Smooth bitch to win Best of Breed at a Dachshund Specialty. Bred, owned, and handled by Howard Atlee, Penthouse Kennels, Teaneck, New Jersey.

which he was striving. MS became a consistent winner, even making her presence felt in Hound Group competition.

Also, Howard Atlee was handler of the lovely Champion Tywell's Pegeen, who had been bred by the late Robert Welty, to some splendid wins for Robert A. Houslohner including an all-breed Best in Show at Watertown.

The sisters, Champion Penthouse Class Act and Champion Penthouse Emmy Award are two of Howard Atlee's finest Miniature Smooths, and certainly attest to the success of his breeding program. Together they are a fantastic brace whose honors have included Best Brace in Show, all breeds, at the big Western Reserve Kennel Club event in 1980. While on her own, Emmy Award is the first Miniature Smooth bitch to have won Best of Breed at a Specialty show and one of the first to win a Hound Group.

RAVENRIDGE

Ravenridge Kennels were located in Fox Chapel, a suburb of Pittsburgh, Pennsylvania. Owned by Ann and Michael Gordon, Ravenridge was active in breeding and showing for about 20 years, from 1958 to 1978.

The goal of the breeding kennel at Ravenridge was to produce a Dachshund with substance, yet one that possessed elegance. To achieve this goal, the von Marienlust and Gera lines (which stemmed from Badger Hill) were selected to be the foundation bloodlines. Thus Willo Mar's Ruby of Ravenridge, a Champion Saba of Gera daughter, and Champion Dresel's Allegro, a Champion Falcon of Heying-Teckel son (thus a Champion Favorite v Marienlust grandson) were purchased. These two individuals produced Champion Ravenridge's Big Red and Champion Ravenridge's Ravenette.

Later, Champion Jolly Dachs George, also a son of Champion Falcon of Heying-Teckel, was acquired. He had an illustrious show career as well as being one of the top producing stud dogs in his era. Many of his approximately 30 champion progeny became leading show winners in their time.

Champion Ravenridge's November Morn, along with all the Dachshunds who bore the Ravenridge identification, did fulfill their breeder's ambition for the kennel, exemplifying the Dachshund of substance combined with elegance which those at Ravenridge had worked for from the beginning.

Ch. Ravenridge's November Morn, by Ch. Jolly Dachs George ex Ch. Ravenridge's Ravenette. Bred and owned by Michael and Ann Gordon, Pittsburgh, Pennsylvania.

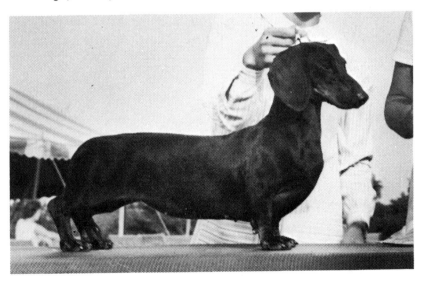

Ch. Mighty Fine von Walder at the Greater Miami Dachshund Club in 1962. Dorothy Hardy handled for owner, Nancy F. Onthank, Greenwich, Connecticut.

ROSE FARM

Rose Farm Dachshunds were originally started in the 1940's by Nancy F. Onthank in Greenwich, Connecticut. The kennel was founded on standard smooths, and over the years she bred many top winning dogs. Among the most famous of these were Champion Venture of Hardway; winner of many Bests in Show, handled by Frank Hardy. Champion Herthwood's Mark of Rose Farm was a Venture son who won a great many Groups and Specialty Shows for Mrs. Onthank.

On trips to England, Mrs. Onthank selected and imported a number of leading winners. The most famous of these was Champion Pondwick's Hobgoblin, undefeated in more than 100 shows. Hobgoblin went on to become the Top Producing wire stud in the breed with a total of 89 champions.

Mrs. Onthank also imported a Miniature Longhair male, Champion Mighty Fine von Walder. This handsome little dog can be found in most of the Miniature Longhair pedigrees today. He was also a highly successful show dog under the handling of Frank Hardy. Nancy Onthank herself bred more than 50 champions over the years.

Rose Farm Kennels have been carried on over the past 20 years, or since the mid-'60's, by Dee Hutchinson who is Mrs. Onthank's daughter, at Pound Ridge, New York. Dee has bred Dachshunds in all coats and both sizes, the total number of champions bred or co-bred by her exceeding 60 as we write. Her accomplishments as a breeder, the quality of the dogs being produced generation after generation at Rose Farm, and the part her dogs have played in the foundation of other newer successful kennels speaks eloquently for what she has accomplished.

While still a youngster, Dee's interest in the dogs started with her mother's kennels. She was always available when needed, and she showed some of them upon occasion. Following her marriage to Bruce Hutchinson, and the rearing of their youngsters in the early days, Dee's activities with the Dachshunds were somewhat limited. But now for awhile she has been putting a good deal of time into her Dachshunds, most of which she always owner-handles in the ring; and to raising puppies which seem to become even more outstanding with every generation, a true mark of success as a breeder!

Dee's winners during the early 1970's included a gorgeous Wire, Champion Rose Farm's Moon Rockette W, who among numerous exciting wins, was Best of Variety at the Dachshund Association of Long Island (DALI) Specialty in 1971. Bred by Nancy Onthank, owned and handled by Dee, Rockette was a daughter of Champion Westphal's Timber W ex Champion Pondwicks Queen of Night.

One of Dee's most outstanding dogs has been the great black Standard Smooth Champion Karstad's Lionel, bred by Barbara Murphy. Lionel was a multi-Group winner during his show career, won the Dachshund Club of America Specialty among other prestigious honors, and sired 35 or more champions.

Then there has been the Longhair, Champion Rose Farms Merrakesh Express, by Champion Kemper Dachs Bad Habits ex Champion Rose Farms Ginger Girl, who has won well in that variety during the early 1980's.

The Standard Wire Champion Rose Farms Moonbow has been a great asset to this kennel as Top Dam in 1980 and 1981.

ROYALDACHS

Royaldachs Dachshunds are the result of the Royal S. Copelands, who upon returning to the United States in 1956 following a military tour in Japan owned two pet type Dachshunds. They were then stationed at Fort Monmouth, New Jersey and took the suggestion that they call on Betty Holmberg who lived in that area. She was the breeder of the famed Holmsdachs Dachshunds. They did so, and that was the beginning! Betty Copeland immediately fell in love with Betty Holmberg's marvelous Standard Longhaired Champion Holmdach's Wonderous Star L. Betty Holmberg took Betty Copeland under her wing so to speak, taking her to match shows and, as she says, "shoving me into the ring" with some of the Holmdachs puppies. Later they started attending the point shows together, with Betty Copeland's enthusiasm for the whole thing growing by the minute.

As soon as possible, which was in 1959, the Copelands purchased a Wonderous Star daughter, who became their first show dog and first champion, Holmdachs Wonder's Gay Star. Betty Copeland will never forget the thrill when Bill Kendrick gave this youngster her first two points—from the puppy class—owner-handled! Gay finished at age 11 months, her points gained under the handling of her owner with either Betty Holmberg or Frank Hardy taking over for the majors. Then the following spring and summer she garnered some Best of Variety wins over some of the top males in the Northeast, including her illustrious sire.

Royal Copeland retired from the army, and in late 1961 they moved to southwest Florida, where at last there was a bit more space in which to keep dogs. Gay's most notable offspring was Champion Royaldachs Ebony Echo, of whom Bobby Barlow was very fond, and handled her a bit. Echo went on the January circuit, coming home with a good Best of Variety win over the top winning male "special" of that time. Another Gay Star son completed his championship. Unfortunately her loveliest daughter had to be spayed just one point short of her title.

At the first opportunity, Betty Copeland purchased another Wonderous Star daughter, and bred her to Champion Lucifer of Knocknegree. From this came Champion Royaldachs Angel's Beezlebub. Betty had fun showing him, but finally turned him over to Bobby Barlow to be finished because she could not compete successfully with Bennie Dennard; then he was later cam-

Ch. Royaldachs Ebony Echo, by Ch. No Ka Oi's Irisher ex Ch. Holmdachs Wonder's Gay Star, was the first homebred champion owned by Betty E. Copeland, Venice, Florida. Handled by Bobby Barlow.

paigned by that same Bennie Dennard, and for three consecutive years "Beezie" was among the Top Fifteen Longhairs. At this same time, Betty was showing his daughter, Champion Royaldachs Sea Magic, the two making a handsome pair of winners. After a nice career, "Beezie" was retired except for appearing in the Veterans Parade at the annual Florida Gulf Coast Dachshund Club Specialty Show.

Beezlebub produced Champion Royaldachs Whispering Echo, who is an Ebony Echo granddaughter as well. Bred to Champion Tallavast Odyssey, a son of Champion Han-Jo's Ulyssis, Whispering Echo produced Champion Royaldachs Christmas Cherub, who started his career winning Best Puppy in Sweepstakes at the Alabama Dachshund Club Specialty, and had a Best of Variety on the way to his championship. Shown by his co-owner Donna Collins, this dog for two years was in the Top Fifteen Longhairs, garnering a Group 1st and a Group 2nd along the way. He also holds a Certificate of Gameness from the AWTA, and as of this date is the sire of ten champions and one C.D.X with points. Mrs. Copeland comments, "To me this seems rather remarkable considering the fact that he has been bred only seven times, and the ten champions are from five of those bitches, four of them from one litter."

Now at last Betty Copeland has a kennel large enough and surrounded by five acres! She also has a treasured niece and her daughter close by to help with the care and showing of her dogs, and notes that they are learning fast, in December having shown two six month-old puppies to Reserve Dog and Reserve Bitch! Also they are now involved in obedience training a couple of the puppies.

SLEEPYTIME

Sleepytime Miniature Longhairs are owned by Susan and Johnny Jones at Durham, North Carolina.

Behind the Mini-Longs at this kennel are three excellent bitches who have served as its foundation. They are Champion Wildwood Solitary Splendor ML, a daughter of Champion Foxfire von Bayern Hutte ML ex Ellis' Midnight Mist ML; Champion Lehigh's Wee Kooka Boo ML, by Champion Foxfire von Bayern Hutte ML ex Veeshund's Wildwood Minx ML; and Champion Wildwood Seasons In The Sun ML C.D., also by Champion Foxfire von Bayern Hutte but in this case from Champion Liebchen Palantyr ML. Thus all three are Foxfire daughters but each from a different dam.

These three bitches all have produced champions. Champion Wildwood Solitary Splendor is the first Miniature Dachshund to have earned the Dachshund Club of America's Versatility Certificate. She is the dam of Champion It's Sleepytime at Wildwood ML C.D. Champion Lehigh's Wee Kooka Boo is the dam of two champions, as is Champion Wildwood Seasons In The Sun.

Susan Jones speaks with pride of Champion Flachshund's Exquisite, by Champion Wildwood's Deep Darkness ex Flachshund's Oriane who finished with four majors in only eight outings in the classes, gaining the majors at Lincolnland, Alabama and Louisville Specialties and at the Westminster Kennel Club in New York's Madison Square Garden. This lovely bitch was bred by Lowell and Alberta Flachs.

Champion Lehigh's Sarah of Brayton ML was Winners Bitch at the Dachshund Club of America National Specialty in 1983. She was bred by Druid and Cynthia Sartin. Sarah made an exciting finish to her championship when she completed title at the big National Miniature Dachshund Club 1983 Round Up.

Champion Wildwood's Initial Action, by Champion Lehigh's First Encounter ML ex Wildwood Misty Blue ML, was Best of Breed at the Dachshund Club of St. Louis Specialty in 1983 under breeder-judge Mrs. Muriel Newhauser. This multiple Best of Variety winner also has gained multiple Hound Group placements.

Champion It's Sleepytime At Wildwood ML C.D., C.G., is the first, and to date, only, Miniature Dachshund to have earned the coveted Versatility Certificate, as we have already mentioned. Added to this is a conformation title; a Companion Dog certificate; and a trailing certificate; plus now starting out in field trials.

The three foundation girls at Sleepytime, *Left to right:* Ch. Wildwood Solitary Splendor ML, Ch. Lehigh's Wee Kooka Boo ML and Champion Wildwood Seasons In The Sun ML. Owned by Susan and Johnny Jones, Durham, North Carolina.

Ch. Threesteps Liza W, a top show winner in the 1970's and a top producer being the dam of five champions. By Ch. Pondwicks Hobgoblin ex Ch. Holmdachs Tam O'Shanter, bred and owned by Harvey and Laura Mueller, Preston, Washington.

SUNTURA

Suntura Dachshunds, featuring Miniature Longhaired Dachshunds and Standard Smooths, are owned by Edith M. Nelson at Mason, Wisconsin, who has been active in the breed since 1974. During this period of time, Suntura has made over 18 champions. Also some outstanding imports have come there from both England and Germany.

Edith Nelson's very special pride and joy, however, is her exciting homebred Champion Suntura's Blue Max ML, who was the 1982 winner of the Best of Breed award at the Dachshund Club of America National Specialty, thus becoming the *only* miniature in history to have won this Specialty—certainly a marvelous achievement. Max also completed his championship in style, doing so with back-to-back majors on two weekends.

Another lovely dog at Suntura is a son of the English import from Champion Suntura's Scheherazade ML, Blue Max's litter sister. He is Suntura's Royal Salute ML, who will undoubtedly be a champion before you are reading this.

Then there is a very special Smooth Standard sired by Champion Fleming's Jolly Dachs Torger ex Champion Suntura's Debutante that has finished and now been retired as the Suntura Dachshunds are specialed only on a very limited basis.

THREESTEPS

Threesteps Wirehaired Dachshunds are owned by Harvey and Laura Mueller, Preston, Washington, Champion Holmdachs Tam O Shanter having been their foundation bitch back in the early 1960's.

"Tammy" was purchased by the Muellers from Betty Holmberg's daughter, Jane Paul. Betty and Jane traveled across the country by car from New Jersey and delivered Tammy in person to her new owners in Oregon at the Eugene Kennel Club Dog Show. She was exhibited during their trip across the country, finishing her championship in California. She is the dam of five champions: Champion Holmdachs Bewitching Wire, a top show winner nationally; Champion Threesteps Rita W, a top show winner nationally; Champion Threesteps Wistful W; Champion Threesteps Tam O'Shanter W, a top show winner nationally and a top producer; and Champion Threesteps Liza W, a top show winner nationally and a top producer; plus an obedience degree dog, Threesteps Lucas W, C.D.X.

During her lifetime, Tammy was bred three times, on each of these occasions to Champion Pondwicks Hobgoblin. Bewitching Wire, Rita, Wistful and Lucas were from the first breeding. Tam O'Shanter was from the second, Liza from the third and last breeding.

Champion Holmdachs Bewitching Wire finished her title at less than one year old, then became one of the top winning Wires of the 1960's. She is a granddam of Champion Midernochs Wild Card W, a top producer who is a granddam of Champion Midernochs Wild Card, a foundation bitch at Barhar Kennels.

Champion Threesteps Rita W was also a top winner of the 1960's, and dam of Champion Threesteps Pepper, a top show winner nationally in the 1970's and top winning Standard Wirehair in Canada in 1975; and Champion Threesteps Pixie W, a top producer. Pixie is the dam of six champions. Rita won many varieties from the classes on the way to her championship.

Champion Threesteps Wistful W, owned by Pat Strnot, was the dam of three champions from her only litter, the sire of which was Champion Charlamar's Noah W.

Champion Threesteps Tam O'Shanter W was a top show winner nationally and a top producer of the 1960's and 1970's; Dam of six champions including the multiple all-breed Best in Show and Specialty Show winner and top producer, Champion Midernoch's Sextus Wire.

Champion Threesteps Liza W was a top show winner of the 1970's and a top producer. She finished from the classes at the Cascade Dachshund Club Specialty in June 1974 winning Best of Variety and Best of Opposite Sex to Best of Breed. She was again Best of Variety at this Specialty the following year; and in 1980 she was Best Brood Bitch in Show there. She is the dam of five champions, they being Champion Threesteps Caroline W, Champion Threesteps Tammy W, Champion Threesteps Columbine W, Champion Threesteps Thunder W, and Threesteps Peanut W.

Champion Threesteps Pepper W, by Champion Whiskie's Hi-Ho Henneree from Champion Threesteps Rita W, bred and owned by Harvey and Laura Mueller, was another top winner nationally in the United States during the 1970's and top Standard Wirehair in Canada in 1975. He is the sire of six champions, and has other pointed offspring and puppies who will be shown. His litter sister is Champion Threesteps Pixie W, dam of Champion Threesteps Cricket W.

Cricket, by Champion Barhar Minnie's Boy W ex Champion Threesteps Pixie W, was bred and is owned by the Muellers. She was Top Winning Wire Bitch in the United States under the *National Dog* System for 1977 and *Dachshund Variety* System for 1978. During her show career she won 65 Bests of Variety and 20 Bests of Opposite Sex, 15 Group placements, two Specialty Bests in Show and three Specialty Bests of Opposite Sex to Best in Show. She is the dam of Champion Threesteps Trooper who finished in 16 calendar days at age 13½ months and won the Group at 14½ months. Also Champion Threesteps Essie W and some others nearing the title are among her offspring.

Other noted Dachshunds from Threesteps Kennels include Champion Threesteps Caroline W (by Pepper ex Liza W), who first time out as a special was Best of Variety and Best of Opposite Sex to Best of Breed at the Golden Gate Specialty in 1979. She is the litter sister to Tammy W. Then there is Champion Threesteps Columbine, (Pepper-Liza W), Champion Threesteps Thunder W, and Champion Threesteps Peanut W, littermates from the repeat breeding of their parents. All three of these have Group placements. And Champion Threesteps Trooper W (Thunder W-Cricket W), who was a top show winner nationally during 1983 and 1984. Currently Champion Threesteps Audacious W is doing well as a special, having completed title from the Bred-by Exhibitor Class in just seven shows. She is by Pepper W ex Audacious W.

This family of Wires has distinguished itself well both in the show ring and as producers.

TORI JARICE

Hilda, Tom and Jeanne Rice began the love affair with Miniature Dachshunds which was to result in Tori Jarice kennels at Valley Stream, New York, back in the spring of 1966 with the purchase of a black and tan Smooth male whose parents were of England's Wagon Wheel Kennels. The personality and antics of this little dog so captivated the Rices that they wanted a companion for him. Thus Marguerite Green, owner of Kinkora Kennels in Syosset, New York, invited them to come to see a four-week-old litter of red Smooths. Tom Rice picked one from the litter of three, and at seven and a half weeks' age, Tori Russet Princess joined the Rice household where she remained for the next 17 years. Through Princess, the family learned about, and became involved with, dog shows and with breeding. At age four months, Tori was awarded a Hound Group 1st at a match show, and at ten months she gained a Best in Match over 372 dogs. At maturity, Tori tipped the scale at eight and a quarter pounds. Her show career took this tiny mite to American and Canadian championships and gained her the honor of being one of the top 30 Miniature Dachshunds in the United States in 1968. Her Canadian title was earned in three shows with three Bests of Breed and a Group placing. Shown only six times in Canada during 1968, Tori was the second highest scoring Smooth Miniature in Canada that year.

Tori was first bred to Champion Hubertus Petrus MS and produced three males who grew to weights between nine and a quarter-nine and a half pounds---just over the nine pound weight limit for Miniatures at that time. Though none of these males were shown, two produced Miniatures who have completed their championships, and these in turn are producing show quality dogs.

In 1970, Tori was bred to Champion Verdon's Vici M owned by Tom and Kathryn Curtis, the Top Winning Miniature Smooth Male in 1968. This breeding was highly successful for it produced Canadian Champion Tori Jarice's Wee Angus MS who shares the title "Top Producing Miniature, All Time" with Sharon Michaels' Champion M.D.P.H. Demonstration M. Angus produced record-setting Miniature Dachshunds, and his record will probably stand well into the future.

Angus was the sire of Champion Tori Jarice's Wee Nicodemus MS who in 1975 became the 28th Smooth Miniature male to achieve championship in the United States. The first Smooth Miniature male to do so had earned status some 19 years earlier, which gives our readers some insight into the difficulty of finishing a Smooth Miniature! Nicodemus then made his own page in history by becoming the first Miniature Smooth Dachshund to earn a Specialty Best in Show award, which he did at the Reserve Dachshund Club in Cleveland, Ohio, under breeder-judge Mary Garner over an entry of 253 Dachshunds from all parts of the country. Nicodemus was the Top Winning Smooth Miniature Dachshund of 1975. The Rices believe that Nicodemus is still the only Smooth Miniature male to have won a Specialty Best in Show in the United States. Along with being an outstanding winner himself, Nicodemus has also sired champion Miniatures.

Champion Spartan's Sloe Gin Fizz was the result of A. Bernie Caluwaert's breeding her Spartan's Mynni Wyre MW to Angus. This Smooth-Wire cross produced Fizz, the top winning Dachshund in the history of the breed.

Another Angus son, Champion Tori Jarice's Wee Pettijon MW, was the #7 Wirehair Dachshund in 1975, with multiple Bests of Variety and Hound Group placements. He, too, is the sire of Miniature winners.

Angus inherited a recessive gene for Longhair, apparently from Konrad of Allendale who is 14 generations back in his pedigree. The Rices' first encounter with this gene was through a Smooth-to-Smooth breeding which produced a litter of one puppy, a black and tan Longhair who later produced a champion. The Rices have made a point of informing everyone that Angus did carry this Longhair gene, and have made every effort to keep their Wire and Smooth lines free of this recessive. Angus may very well be the only Miniature who has sired Miniatures in all three coats.

The Tori Jarice miniatures are family members of the Rice household. Tom and daughter Jeanne train the Miniatures, Hilda specializes in the nutritional department, and all three of them share in keeping everyone socialized.

Am. and Can. Ch. Tori Russet Princess, June 10, 1966-September 10, 1983, by Ardencaple's Wee Tomboy ex Kinkora's Pooka Chili Bean M, was the foundation smooth bitch at Tori Jarice Kennels. Bred by Marguerite Green. Owned by Thomas J. Rice, Valley Stream, New York.

In all three coats, foundation behind the Tori Jarice bitches came from the Kinkora bloodlines. Each has produced a minimum of one champion. Both English and American bloodlines have been incorporated into the breeding program to assure production of excellent quality. American and Canadian Champion Favorite v Marienlust is nine or ten generations behind the Smooths and Wirehairs who have made Tori Jarice so famous and respected.

During the past few years, Tori Jarice has made somewhat fewer trips to the dog shows than in the past. Yet 16 of their Miniatures have completed title, the most recent Champion Tori Jarice's Jon Eric MW in January 1985. Nearly all have been owner-handled, and of the 16 referred to, the Rices are the breeders of 12. There are also four more headed for the title as we write, having one or more majors already to the credit of each. In addition to these champions at Tori Jarice, the Rices have bred three other champions finished by new owners. Tori Jarice is noted for type, bone, substance, balance, and lowness to ground in its Miniatures.

v. GEIL

Helen S. Hyre is the owner of two very handsome winning dogs who, despite the fact that they seldom travel more than 250 miles from home to be shown, have made some very proud and exciting records in the show ring.

American and Canadian Champion Wadeldorf Baron Teckel v Geil was born in 1974, bred by John P. Wade. Sired by Champion Moffett's Harvest ex Sea Mist Tempest Dream, Teckel, despite limited showing, was ranked in the Top Ten for five years in at least one system. He was #2 in the old Dachshund Variety Breed System in 1979. Teckel has the look of the old Gera dogs.

Teckel's retirement announcement began "Teckel proves that house pets can be top winners." Additionally, he has proven that a novice can win with a worthy dog!

Another multiple Group winner belonging to Helen Hyre is Champion Moffett's Boondox Maxin v Geil, born in 1982, bred by Helen Moffett. A son of Champion Moffett's Boondox Crockett ex Champion Moffett's Miss Flint, "Maxie" finished his first year as an owner-handled special ranked #5 in the *Kennel Review* System for 1984 with limited showing. He is also ranked in *Canine Chronicle* and *Dachshund reporter* Systems, and in *Canine Chronicle* Top 100 Hounds.

VILLANOL

Villanol Dachshunds at East Greenbush, New York, have had a long and illustrious career in our dog show world. It was in 1956 that the owners, Gordon and Jean Carvill, went in search of an English Springer Spaniel puppy to replace a beloved dog who had died. At the kennel where they found what they wanted in a Springer, they also discovered that the breeder raised Dachshunds, too, a breed which Jean Carvill had always loved. So when they returned home, they were accompanied not only by the Springer but by a black and tan Smooth Standard Dachshund puppy as well, the Springer for Gordon, the Dachshund for Jean.

Thrilled over her new puppy, Jean started out to learn all about Dachshunds, which led her to first attending a match show as a spectator, then to joining the Albany Capital District Dachshund Club and then into an obedience class. Eventually Jean and the Dachshund showed at their first match in competition, and the Dachshund, Beaupeg's Borag, went Best in Match. Almost without their realizing it, the Carvills' life-style was changing. By 1959, two more Dachshunds had been added: Bel-Clar's Lady Vycksen, a red, and Beaupeg's Tarryson, another black and tan. At that point, Jean and Gordon moved to a rural area where they proceeded to build their second home, this house on a hill being appropriately named Villanol.

The Carvills have bred Miniature Smooth and Miniature Wire Dachshunds, Standard Longhaired Dachshunds, and Standard Smooth Dachshunds, but at the present time are concentrating mainly on the Standard Smooths. Their first litter was whelped in 1960, Standard Smooths of which we will speak further along.

The first Miniature owned by the Carvills was purchased from Mrs. William Burr Hill, De Sangpur Wee Honey, who was bred back to her grandsire, De Sangpur Wee Fancy Package, C.D. This produced a red bitch puppy who was kept by the Carvills and who became Villanol's Wee Widget. Bred to Champion Talla-

Ch. Villanol's Troubadour as a youngster. Breeder-owner, Gordon H. Carvill, East Greenbush, New York.

vast Eddie M, she produced Champion Villanol's Wee Mignon who was bred back to her paternal grandsire Champion Tallavast Frank-M. From this litter Jean and Gordon kept a black and tan male, Villanol's Jamie-M, who earned points but never completed title. Later on a Miniature Wire bitch, Scoshire Amelia MW, was bred to Jamie, which gave the Carvill's their Champion Villanol's Scampi MW. Much later the Carvills purchased a red Miniature Smooth male who became Champion Tallavast Amos-M.

The Carvills purchased their first Longhaired Standard from Harriet Crocker. He was Crocker's Rob Roy L, by Champion Man of War of Marin ex Steele's Empress. Bob and Ann Wlodkowski bred their Lee Lo's Beatrice to this dog, and the Carvills took two bitches from that litter. One, Champion Villanol Lovely L, was bred to Champion Rickjon's Man About Town producing Champion Villanol's Gentle Ben, a black and tan male. "Lovely's" litter sister was co-owned by Gordon with Barbara Jill Carter and they selected Champion Bayard Le Pernod as the stud to whom she (Villanol's Lucy Fussbudget) should be bred. From that litter, Gordon selected a red bitch puppy who became the well-known winner Champion Villanol's Maxine.

Two litters were born to Maxine, the first by Champion Bayard L'Aquilon; the second by Champion Von Dyck's Mr. Bojangles L. From the first litter, Champion Villanol's Heritage still resides with the Carvills. From the second, Champion Villanol's Radiance was kept.

Now to the Smooth Standards! The first of the Carvills' Dachshunds, Beaupeg's Borag, known as "Tarry," had many fine dogs in his lineage, including some of the leading ones from Marienlust. The first bitch purchased by the Carvills, Bel-Clar's Lady Vycksen, a daughter of Champion Venture of Hardway, was bred to the first male, producing a dog and a bitch puppy which the Carvills kept. These puppies were whelped in January 1960. The bitch, Villanol's Lady Belle, was eventually bred to Dark Deacon of Wingalore, owned by Harriet Crocker, producing two black and tan puppy dogs whom Gordon and Jean kept, one of which became the first champion bred by them, Champion Villanol's Troubadour. He and his brother, Villanol's Deacon, were very similar, and Gordon trained them to work as a brace, leading to many exciting wins.

Jean decided to breed Bel-Clar's Lady Vycksen to her grandson,

Villanol's Deacon, thereby producing a puppy who was sold and later earned his title, Champion Villanol's Valiant Jonathan. He returned to Villanol and went on to win some excellent honors, such as Best of Breed at the Metropolitan Dachshund Club and a Hound Group first at K.C. of Buffalo along with several other Group placements.

In 1961, Crocker's Bambi v d Krista was purchased from Charles and Harriet Crocker. She was an elegant black and tan bitch with sparkling personality, a daughter of Champion White Gables Ristocrat ex Champion Nicoli's Krista. After earning a few points, including a major, she retired to motherhood, bred to Champion Nicoli of the Walls, her grandsire. Villanol's Krista, a black and tan daughter, was kept and bred to Champion Sealybourne Sirius v Velvet who had been purchased by the Carvills along with a bitch, Champion Sealybourne Royal Miss, from Sealybourne Kennels to add to their bloodlines. Bambi was bred twice to Champion Kleetal's Raven Wing owned by Peggy Westphal. From the first of these litters the Carvills kept Champion Villanol's Wendy v Bambi; from the second, Champion Villanol's Mandolin.

Here is where the lines began to blend! Champion Villanol's Wendy v Bambi was bred to Champion Villanol's Valiant Jonathan from which came Champion Villanol's Sampson. Then going back to Villanol's Krista, half-sister to Wendy and bred to Champion Sealybourne Sirius v Velvet, her second litter produced five puppies. Three became champions; American and Canadian Champion Villanol's Camille, Champion Villanol's Jason and Champion Villanol's Rachel, the latter co-owned by Jean Carvill with Faith N. Hoffman.

Other champions produced by Krista include Champion Villanol's Richie v Krista, by Champion Kleetal's Rich Return, and Champion Villanol's Lorelei from a second litter by Champion Sealybourne Sirius v Velvet.

To speak a bit about Rachel, the bitch co-owned by Jean with Faith Hoffman: twice she was bred to Champion Crosswynd's Firecracker, and from a total of nine puppies in the two litters, eight finished. They are Champions Villanol's Vanguard, April Love, Marigold and Black Jade from the first litter; Christopher, Companero, Zucker, and Canadian Champion Villanol's Sonata from the second litter.

Ch. Villanol's Rachel, by Ch. Sealybourne Sirius v Velvet ex Villanol's Krista, was bred by Jean Carvill and co-owned with Faith N. Hoffman. She is the dam of 8 champions. Gordon Carvill handling.

From Rachel's first litter, April Love was bred to Champion Villanol's Sampson and from the resulting puppies the lovely future American and Canadian Champion Villanol's Red Rose was chosen to be kept. Champion Villanol's Red Rose was bred to Champion Villanol's Redson von Piercen, who came to live at Villanol and is co-owned by Gordon and Jean. Both he and Red Rose have made notable show records, he having been #10 Smooth in the *Dachshund Variety* system for 1978. Red Rose was #3 Smooth bitch for 1974 and tied in 1975 for #3, same system.

Red Rose's litter of four produced one male among the four puppies. He is Champion Villanol's Gladiator, noted winner, #5 Smooth in the Variety System and #8 Smooth in the Group System of the *Dachshund Reporter* for 1980.

Gladiator is the sire of the elegant red male, Champion Wavecrest's Adam of Fabeland, bred by Raymond L. Phillips and Donald A. Ingamells from their bitch Champion Wavecrest's Lyric of Fabeland. He was #2 Smooth Dachshund *Canine Chronicle* Points System and #2 Smooth under the *Dachshund Reporter* Group System, both for 1983.

Jean and Gordon Carvill have owned or bred 43 champions of record. Sometimes they speculate as to what their lives might have been like had they not gone in search of that first puppy! What is for certain is that the World of Dogs has been a large part of their lives for nearly 30 years.

Champion Villanol's Heritage, Longhaired, was 14 years "young" in January 1985. Champion Villanol's Zucker will celebrate her 14th birthday this same year. These are the oldest two in residence, and very dearly loved.

Gordon and Jean have been active in many aspects of the Fancy. Jean has been President of the Albany Capital District Dachshund Club and is presently its Vice-President. Gordon has been Show Chairman for Albany Kennel Club and President of that Club; and A.K.C. Delegate for Troy Kennel Club and their Secretary; is a former President of the Dachshund Club of America, Inc., and is now a member of their Board of Directors. He is President of Associated Dog Clubs of N.Y. State, and President of the American Dog Owners Association Inc. He is also a very popular and busy judge of all Hounds and now some of the Sporting breeds.

VON RELGIB

Von Relgib Dachshunds came about through Mrs. Ethel Bigler's husband wishing to own a Dachshund, which led to the purchase of Tina Nedimo Tenroc. That is how it began. Both Biglers had always been involved with dogs as they grew up—Boston Terriers in Ethel's family; Collies on the farm where Jim was raised. It proved difficult to locate a puppy who looked like the type of Dachshund Jim Bigler had in mind (a bitch named Greta who was from Marienlust Kennels, they later learned) in the Washington, D.C. area where they were stationed at that period. But after several months of answering advertisements, they learned, from the veterinarian who had cared for their 15½ year old English Cocker Spaniel, of a litter he thought the Biglers would like.

They did, indeed, and Ethel brought home Tina Nedimo Tenroc to her husband on April Fool's Day 1949. Tina's dam was of Bencelia breeding (Ben Klimkowitz) and sired by Champion Hermon von Tenroc from the Louis Cornets' line.

With Dr. Cornet's advice, the Biglers bred Tina to Champion

Ch. Von Relgib's Style, noted winner and dam of ten champions owned by Ethel Bigler, Von Relgib Kennels, Studio City, California.

Harborvale Constellation, owned by Mr. Hendricks of Philadelphia and the Biglers kept the one female puppy in the litter. Again following Dr. Cornet's advice, the Biglers decided on Relgib for their kennel name---Bigler spelled backwards, which is what the Cornets themselves had done in the naming of their own kennel, Tenroc. This first homebred puppy then was named Madchen Hannah Von Relgib.

In 1952 the Biglers moved to California, by which time Ethel had studied all available Dachshund books and learned a little about who was who in the Dachshund world. She took Madchen Hannah to the Heyings for breeding. Of the five Favorite sons Rose Heying offered for her, Ethel chose the one red, not so much for his color as for his beautiful elegance and aristocratic carriage. Champion San Souci's San Pedro thus became the sire of the Bigler's first champion, Madchen Salome Von Relgib. To her Ethel Bigler pays tribute as she states, "I feel she has passed on her sire's elegance and lovely head carriage thru all my future breeding."

When the time came that Ethel Bigler felt she was ready to embark on a serious breeding program, it was again to the Heyings she went, this time falling in love with a handsome eight-month-old Favorite son, Anchor of Heying-Teckel. He and Madchen Salome produced beautifully together, three champions in their first litter and many more later on.

At the present time, Ethel Bigler has produced eight generations of bitches who have produced champion bitches. From Madchen Hannah Von Relgib came Champion Madchen Salome Von Relgib; she produced Champion Von Relgib's Charm; Charm produced Champion Von Relgib's Amulet; Amulet was the dam of Champion Von Relgib's Vision; Vision produced Champion Von Relgib's Image; Image was the mother of Champion Von Relgib's Emblem; Emblem's daughter Champion Von Relgib's Dream is the dam of the newest champion, Von Relgib's Dream Come True. These, and many others of Von Relgib breeding, have produced numerous champions in addition to the ones listed here who have been splendid producers.

For example, Champion Von Relgib's Zenith (Champion Dunkeldorf Falcon's Favorite ex Champion Von Relgib's Style), a multiple Group and Specialty winner bred and owned by Ethel Bigler sired six champions from the two litters he sired for her.

Champion Von Relgib's Commandant, by Champion Von Relgib's General ex Champion Von Relgib's Classic, a multiple Group and Specialty winner, sired six champions from one litter out of Champion Von Relgib's Silhouette (Champion Von Relgib's Zenith ex Champion Von Relgib's Image).

Champion Von Relgib's Image, multiple variety and breed winner, produced five champions from her two litters.

Champion Von Relgib's Vision, by Champion Wayt A While Parade ex Champion Von Relgib's Amulet, was the dam of eight champions.

Champion Von Relgib's Style, by Champion Herman VI ex Champion Von Relgib's Charm, was the dam of ten champions.

Currently, Ethel Bigler is pleased with three young littermates by Champion Choo Choo's Billi v Barbadox ex Champion Von Relgib's Dream who have been winning well. They include Champion Von Relgib's Challenge who finished at 11½ months of age; Champion Von Relgib's Dream Come True, who won the Best of Variety at Sierra Dachshund Club Specialty in January 1985, first time out as a special, and Von Relgib's Omen, needing just a point to finish, who was Best of Winners at the Golden Gate Specialty in 1985.

Ch. Saba of Gera, a son of Ch. Badger Hill Nobby ex Lisa of Gera, bred by Gera Kennels. An outstanding Best in Show winner of the 1950's, sire of many champions, owned by Marcia Wheeler, Willo-Mar Dachshunds, Fairfax, Virginia.

WILLO-MAR

Willo-Mar Kennels at Fairfax, Virginia, were started by Marcia Wheeler when she was just out of college and seriously interested in beginning to breed Smooth Dachshunds. This was in the mid-1950's. With the acquisition of several dogs who had already done considerable winning she was on her way. These dogs were Champion Saber of Gera, an all-breed Best in Show winner bred by Gera Kennels and handled by Woodie Dorward; Champion Hainheim's Olinda, bred by George Spradling, then owned and shown to many Group wins by Jeanette Cross; and Champion Zwei von Dorville, a Group winner bred by Dora Faville.

Saber continued his show career under Marcia's ownership, winning numerous Groups with Lloyd Case handling. Olinda was retired from the ring and bred to Saber, giving Marcia her first multiple champion litter. Champion Zwei von Dorville, also bred to Saber, produced Champion Willo-Mar's Firebrand who was sold to Dora Faville and campaigned on the West Coast by Woodie Dorward to #1 Smooth Dachshund in the country. Bred to Champion Willo-Mar's Ace of Spades, Zwei produced Champion Willo-Mar's Night and Day, Best of Variety at Westminster and Best of Breed at the Dachshund Club of America Specialty in 1962. Night and Day was the dam of two Group winners and her grandson, Champion Crosswynd's Crackerjack, bred by Mrs. Lovering, was one of the all-time top winners in the breed.

Returning to Marcia's first all champion litter, by Saber from Olinda, these included Champion Willo-Mar's Ace of Spades, kept by Marcia; Champion Willo-Mar's King of Clubs, a Group winner sold to Betty Wick; Champion Willo-Mar's King of Hearts, sold to and successfully campaigned by Betty Munden; Champion Willo-Mar's Queen of Spades, sold to Barbara Lovering; and Champion Willo-Mar's Queen of Hearts, also kept by Marcia Wheeler. A repeat breeding produced three more champions. Saber sired, among his many champions, three all-breed Best in Show winners.

Another great winner bred by Marcia Wheeler at Willo-Mar in the late 1950's was Champion Willo-Mar's Lucky Star (Champion Saber of Gera-Bayard's Elise), who was sold to Mrs. O.J.S. de Brun and handled by Jerry Rigden to #1 Dachshund in the country with three all-breed Bests in Show among his countless honors. Marcia Wheeler also acquired, from Woodie Dorward, Champion Red Locket Roberto, another who won three all-breed Bests in Show under Jerry Rigden's handling.

A great many other champions have been bred at Willo-Mar during this period, often co-owned with Barbara Lovering, prior to Marcia's taking a five-year break in her breeding and showing activities. In the late 1960's she returned to the ring with Champion Crosswynd's Firecracker (Kenneth of Crosswynd ex Crosswynd's Moonglow), bred by Mrs. Lovering. Firecracker did much winning, including nine Specialty Bests of Variety and Best of Variety at Westminster. Additionally he sired the impressive total of 18 champions.

During recent years Marcia has bred only occasional litters, still managing, however, to produce an admirable number of winners. Her Champion Willo-Mar's Gem of Countryside bred to Champion Mullen's Bold Venture produced, in two litters, six champions: Champion Willo-Mar's Gemini, Champion Willo-Mar's Gala, Champion Willo-Mar's Diamond Jim, Champion Willo-Mar's Diamond Jubilee, Champion Teckel Falcon of Willo-Mar, and Champion Willo-Mar's Houdini, the latter sire of a Best in Show winner for Bennie Dennard.

Champion Willo-Mar's Gemini bred to Champion Boondox Chuckie Bunyan, produced Champion Willo-Mar's Takoma Persephone, Champion Willo-Mar's Great Expectations, and Champion Danimere's Mr. Jigs v Willo-Mar, a Group winner.

Marcia Wheeler's daughter, Sharon Kachovee, is now carrying on the Willo-Mar kennel name and tradition, breeding Longhairs and Smooths.

The foundation bitch at Braaehaus Kennels, Celloyd Penthouse Sadie, by Ch. Crosswynds Cracker Jack ex Ch. Celloyd Virginia Woolf, at three and a half years old. Owned by Carol and Uffe Braae, Schomberg, Ontario.

Can. and Am. Ch. Braaehaus Big Buoy is the only Canadian Dachshund dog in breed history to win Best of Variety at the Dachshund Club of America Specialty. Pictured here at age of one year. Carol and Uffe Braae, owners, Schomberg, Ontario.

Chapter 5

Dachshunds in Canada

The Dachshund long has enjoyed popularity among Canadian dog fanciers, and on many of the occasions when I have judged them there, I have been highly impressed by the type and quality. Here, as in England, all six varieties compete in the Hound Group, all three coats and both sizes having classification. It is an imposing sight to watch the full half dozen of them make their way merrily around the ring!

Unfortunately some very important historical papers on the breed have been lost to their owners, disposed of inadvertently by people who "did not realize they were valuable." Thus we do not have for you the extensive Canadian history we would have enjoyed presenting. Just to look at the Dachshunds from Canada pictured in this book, however, and the two important Canadian kennel stories on the following pages will make it clear that Canadian breeders have the Dachshund situation well in hand, as they are producing dogs not only of consistent winning quality at home, but well able to visit the United States and attend our most prestigious shows, coming away with exciting honors from these trips.

For a very long time Jean Fletcher, in Western Canada, has bred notable Dachshunds. Other Canadian breeders whose names, and dogs, come to mind are Lily Turner, Patrice Fisher, and Helen Sinclair Langford.

BRAAEHAUS

Braaehaus Kennels were established in 1970 by Carol and Uffe Braae at Schomberg, Ontario, where some very famous winners since have been raised, making this Canada's top winning and top producing Dachshund kennel of all time. The Braaes are breeders-owners of nearly 100 champions to date in Canada and the United States, and theirs has been the home of Canada's top winning Dachshunds for over five years.

Foundation bitch on which this kennel began was Celloyd Penthouse Sadie, daughter of the top winning Dachshund dog and bitch in the United States for the year 1965 American Champion Crosswynd's Cracker Jack, her sire, who was three times Best of Variety at the Dachshund Club of America Specialty, 1966, 1967, and 1968; and American Champion Celloyd Virginia Woolf, granddaughter of Champion Celloyd Daniel, a top winning Dachshund in the States during the 1950's when he was a multiple Best in Show winner.

Sadie, in her only litter by Patchwork Penthaus Prospero (American Champion Sheen v Westphalen ex American Champion Tywell's Tempest) produced the first of the Braaes' top winning bitches, Canadian and American Champion Braaehaus Gretchen To Train, and their first top producing stud dog, Braaehaus Footnote.

Gretchen, in turn, in her only litter, by Nixon's Petey Penthouse (Canadian Champion Heidenhelm's Black Falcon ex American Champion Nixon's Penthouse Falforita) produced two bitches. These were Canadian Champion Braaehaus Gretchen Again and Canadian Champion Braaehaus Sister Train. These, in their turn, produced Canadian and American champion offspring, and are the granddams of the two recent top winners and producers, Canadian and American Champion Braaehaus Big Buoy and Canadian and American Champion Braaehaus Traveling Man.

Big Buoy is the only Canadian Dachshund in breed history ever to have won Best of Variety at the Dachshund Club of America Specialty, and is the sire of 12 Canadian and American champions to date. Traveling Man is Canada's top winning Dachshund of all time in Canada and the United States.

To elaborate a bit, Big Buoy, by Canadian Champion Joydachs Fleet of Nikobar ex Canadian Champion Braaehaus Margarethe, was Canada's #1 Standard Smooth Dachshund for 1981 and is a multiple Specialty winner. At Washington, D.C., in 1982, owner-handled by Uffe Braae, he became the only Canadian Dachshund in breed history to win Best of Variety at the prestigious Dachshund Club of America Specialty, which he did that day under judge Eleanor Bishop.

Traveling Man, by Canadian and American Champion Fabeland Blue Chip of Nikobar ex Canadian Champion Braaehaus Royal Ensignia, is a multiple Best in Show winner in Canada and the United States at all-breed and Specialty events. He was Canada's #3 Top Hound in 1984; #7 in 1983, making him Canada's Top Dachshund, all varieties, in those two years. In very limited showing here, he also was among the Top Dachshunds in United States competition in 1983 and 1984. To date he has sired 24 champions in Canada and the United States.

As a six-month-old puppy, Traveling Man began his show career and completed his American championship in three consecutive Specialty Shows at the Dachshund Club of America weekend in Washington, D.C. in 1982. His Canadian career began with a Hound Group first, and by a few months later he had become Canada's Top Standard Smooth Dachshund for 1982, while still a puppy! Many more Groups and group placements followed to his credit, including a Best in Specialty Show. He, too, has always been handled by his co-breeder-owner Uffe Braae for himself and Carol Braae.

The current winners and producers at Braaehaus are linebred many times on their foundation bitch and her progeny.

VONDIXONER

Vondixoner Kennels, owned by Ed Dixon, Toronto, Ontario, Canada, has made an outstanding record in this breed with some very memorable and exciting dogs, since Mr. Dixon showed his first Dachshund during the late 1950's. When asked what to him was the most thrilling victory of a Vondixoner Dachshund, Mr. Dixon replied without hesitation that it was on the occasion when Canadian and American Champion Vondixoner Stardachs Johann came out of retirement at ten and a half years' age, and went on to Best in Show, all breeds, that day, adding to his already impressive Best in Show record.

Johann, still alive and well at 15 years of age now, is the Top Winning Best in Show Dachshund *of all time* in Canada. A son of Champion Dunkeldorf Falcon's Favorite, this handsome dog has won the acclaim of noted authorities on numerous occasions.

Breeding all six varieties of Dachshund, the Vondixoner kennel prefix made further history with Miniature Wirehaired Canadian and American Champion Vondixoner Stardachs Julie who became

Can. and Am. Ch. Vondixoner Stardachs Johann came out of retirement at age 10½ years and won Best in Show under judge William Bowden. Katie Rodley, grandaughter of the famous all-breed judge Doris Wilson, is handling for owner Ed Dixon, Vondixoner Dachshunds, Toronto, Ontario.

the only female Miniature Wirehaired in Canada to date to have captured a Best in Show. This is a daughter of Canadian and American Champion Spartan's Knight Star and granddaughter of the all-time record holding American Champion Spartan's Sloe Gin Fizz.

Other of Mr. Dixon's most famous winners include Champion Vondixoner Stardachs Jet Star, a consistent winning Miniature Smooth who, interestingly, is a Smooth recessive grandson of the noted Mini-Wire Champion Spartan's Sloe Gin Fizz.

Then there is Champion Vondixoner Stardachs Jacob, a leading Best in Show Canadian winner during the 1970's, and two lovely Dachshunds who won well both separately and as a brace, they being Champion West Dox Jessica and Champion Vondixoner Stardachs Jhennie.

Ed Dixon ceased his breeding and showing activities in 1983 to pursue a busy, and highly successful, international judging career. He is one of the world's most respected authorities, and his services are constantly in demand one place or another.

1▲   2▼

←Overleaf:

1. Standard Smooth bitch, Hydax Encounter Of Sevorg, born in 1982, by Carracot Crackerjack of Hydax (grandson of the American import, Clarion Call von Westphalen) ex Hydax Comet (winner of one Challenge Certificate, three Reserve Challenge Certificates and four Bests in Show). Owned by Mr. and Mrs. Groves, Sevorg Dachshunds, Blackwood, Gwent, United Kingdom.

2. This is Ch. Karstad's Lionel, handsome black Standard Smooth Dachshund, a multi-Group winner with 35 champion offspring, winner at the Dachshund Club of America. Bred by Barbara Murphy, owned by Dee Hutchinson, Rose Farms Kennel, Pound Ridge, New York.

Overleaf:→

1. Ch. Von Relgib's Zenith, multiple Group and Specialty winner, sire of six champions. Breeder-owner, Mrs. Ethel Bigler, Studio City, California.

2. Ch. Holmdachs Tam O Shanter W, by Ch. Happy Go Lucky of Willow Creek ex Ch. Hot Wire of Hawthorne, was the foundation bitch at Threesteps Kennels, Harvey and Laura Mueller, Preston, Washington.

3. Ch. Birchwood High Command, by Fleming's Capricon is a Top Ten winner. Photo courtesy of Polly Fleming, Los Angeles, California.

4. Ch. Jandelo's Sweet William finishing with four majors. Here taking points at the Dachshund Club of Metropolitan Atlanta in 1982. Owned, handled by Jane Van Valen, Jandelos Kennels.

5. Ch. Barhar Take Me Along W owned by Lucy Moden, Murfreesboro, Tennessee.

6. The noted Longhair, Ch. Kemper Dachs Bad Habits, sire of 18 champions, handled by co-owner Charles Baris for himself, Patricia D. Kemper, and John Hart, co-owners.

← Overleaf:

1. Ch. Jandelo's Wizard in 1977. Elizabeth Van Valen owner-handling. Peter Monks was judge.

2. Ch. Jandelo's Jessica of Charlane with owner-handler Elaine Baum, Long Boat Key, Florida, who was the former owner of Charlane Afghans in California.

3. Ch. Moffett's Garnet, by Ch. Felshire's Friend of Jester ex Ch. Moffett's Rosanne, was the third in her litter to complete title. Pictured November 1972. Owned by the Russell Moffetts, Flint, Michigan.

4. Ch. Moffett's Gayla, winning the Hound Group at Licking River in 1973. A lovely daughter of Ch. Felsheim's Friendly Jester ex Ch. Moffett's Rosanne. Mr. and Mrs. Russell Moffett, owners, Flint, Michigan.

5. Ch. Knolland Kranberry is a lovely homebred daughter of Ch. Risa's Heavy Chevy. Edward Jenner owner, Knolland Farm, Richmond, Illinois.

6. Ch. Crosswynd's Firecracker, by Kenneth of Crosswynd ex Crosswynd's Moon Glow, bred by Barbara Lovering making an important win. The late Dachshund breeder-judge Mrs. Ramona Von Court Jones was the judge at this occasion.

1. Von Relgib's Omen should by now be a champion having needed just one more point. Best of Winners here at Golden Gate Dachshund Club. Breeder, owner and handler Ethel Bigler, Studio City, California.

2. Ch. Cozy v Westphalen, daughter of Ch. Call to Arms v Westphalen ex Ch. Pennies From Heaven III, one of many outstanding Dachshunds co-owned and shown by Peggy Westphal and Edward Jenner. Now owned by Daniel Jenner, Knolland Farm, Richmond, Illinois.

3. Ch. Rose Farms Choo Choo winning the Hound Group at Mississippi Valley in June 1978. This is Dan Harrison's first champion, bred by Dee Hutchinson and Judy Anderson, co-owned by Dan Harrison and Dee Hutchinson.

4. Ch. Sleepytimes Wildwood Omen ML, by May's Dream Along ML ex Ch. Wildwood Seasons In The Sun ML, C.D., was bred by owners, Susan and Johnny Jones, Sleepytime Dachshunds, Durham, North Carolina.

5. Ch. Bristleknoll Bedwarmer W, co-owned by Lynn Cope and Lucille Moden, Murfreesboro, Tennessee.

6. Ch. Canebrake Pandora Wire here has just defeated eight dog champions to take Best of Variety at Cheyenne Kennel Club in 1979. Bred and owned by Frank and Monica Canestrini, Wheat Ridge, Colorado.

7. Ch. Dunkeldorf's Dratsab, by Ch. Dunkeldorf Falcon's Favorite ex Schreurs' Kleines Majestat. Bred by Diana Schreurs, owned by T.R. Dunk, Jr.

8. Ch. Grenmar Bourbon Cowboy, by Ch. Sangsavant Mardi Gras ex Ch. Sangsavant Grenadine, co-owned by Leonce J. Romero and Patricia M. Crary, winning Best of Variety in a large entry at the Houston Dachshund Club Specialty under Dr. W. Nixon.

1

2

3

4

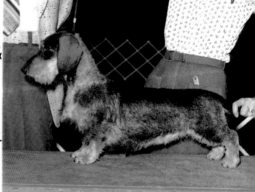

5

6

7

8

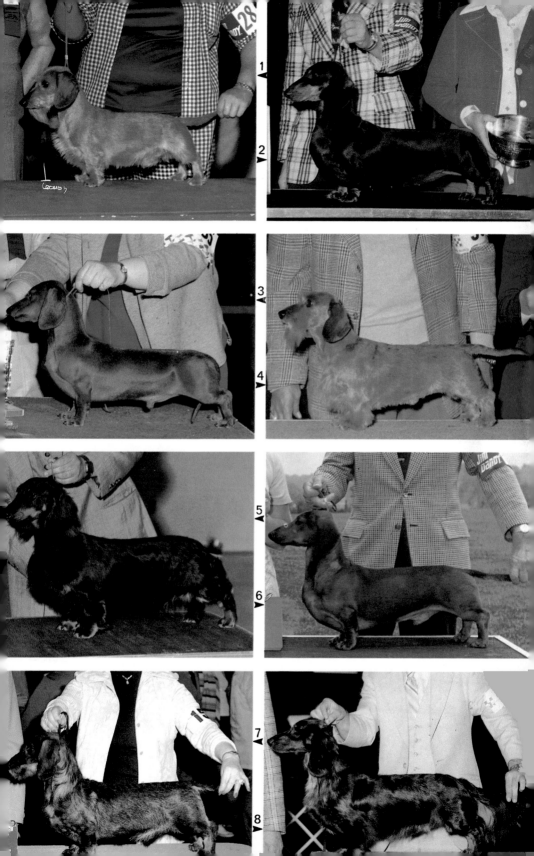

←**Overleaf:**

1. Ch. Cal-Neva's Hap-Pea Times MW, was bred by Neva and Winston Calhoun. This is the sire of the famed multiple Best in Show winner Fannie Farkle as well as ten other champions, and has two Best in Show winning grandchildren. His owners are Denny Mounce and Peggy Lloyd, Pegden Kennels, Sugarland, Texas.

2. Ch. Museland's Cybele, by Ch. Nixon's Fleeting Encounter ex Am. and Can. Ch. Museland's Alysia, winning the Metropolitan Dachshund Specialty Show in 1977. Bred and owned by Mrs. Dorothy Muse.

3. Am. and Can. Ch. Midachs Christopher MS, red Miniature Smooth male bred and owned by Sharon M. Michael, Midachs Kennel, Johnstown, New York. Lorraine Heichel Masley, noted Dachshund specialist, here making the Best of Breed award.

4. Ch. Spartan's Sloe Gin Fizz, famous record-breaking multiple Best in Show and Group winning Miniature Wire. Handled by Jerry Rigden. Owned by Mrs. Christy Ann Gordon Creed.

5. Ch. Rose Farms Zesabel v Boondox, Group winning black and tan Standard Longhaired Dachshund bitch, multiple Specialty winner. Bred by Dan Harrison and Dee Hutchinson. Owners, Mr. and Mrs. Walt Jones and Dan Harrison, Mecca, Indiana.

6. Ch. Villanol's Redson von Piercen, by Can. Ch. Redstart v Westphalen ex Am. and Can. Ch. Villanol's Sonata. Owned by Jean Carvill and Gordon Carvill.

7. Ch. Selkert's Randy, noted Wirehaired Dachshund en route to title. Handled by Lorraine Heichel Masley for Edward Jenner.

8. Ch. Grenmar Mosaic, C.D., owned by Leonce D. Romero, Granmar Dachshunds, Carencro, Louisiana.

Overleaf:→

1. Ch. Dachsborough Nedrum, C.D.X., by Ch. Bigdrum Close Call v Westphal ex Ch. Nedra of Dachsboro, Best Smooth Dachshund Brood Bitch at the 1980 National. Owned by Carl and Candace Holder, Lumberton, Texas. Winning High in Trial and leg No. 2 on C.D. Candy Holder handling.

2. Double (SS) Your Kind of Town MS, son of Ch. Double (SS) My Kind of Town MS ex Rose Farms Sara, taking points at the Silver Bay Kennel Club en route to his future title. Bred and owned by Shirley Silagi, El Paso, Texas.

3. Ch. Tori Jarice's Wee Maruss MS, by Tori's Russet Prince MS ex Ch. Tori Jarice's Wee Marietta MS. Breeder-owner-handler, Jeanne A. Rice.

4. Ch. Moffett's Boondox Crockett v Geil, by Ch. Moffett's Boondox Crockett ex Ch. Moffett's Miss Flint. Bred by Thelma Moffett. Owner-handled by Helen S. Hyre, Madeira, Ohio.

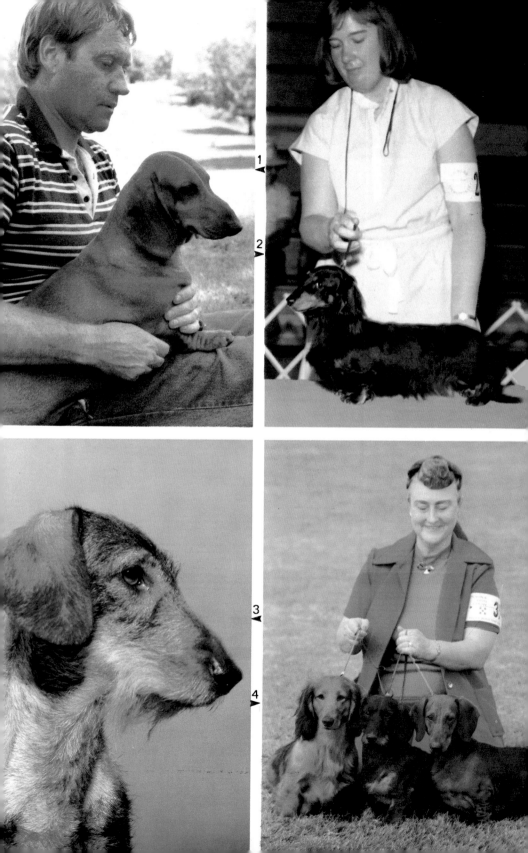

←Overleaf:

1. Uffe Braae and his dog! A handsome study of Can. and Am. Ch. Braaehaus Traveling Man with his co-owner. Owned by Carol and Uffe Braae, Schomberg, Ontario, Canada.

2. The very successful Ch. Flachshund's Exquisite ML, by Ch. Wildwood's Deep Darkness ML ex Flachshund's Orianel winning Best of Variety over four Standard specials. The judge was co-author Marcia Foy. Bred by Lowell and Alberta Flachs. Owned by Susan and Johnny Jones, Durham, North Carolina.

3. Ch. Threesteps Cricket W., one of the outstanding winning Wires owned by Threesteps Kennels, Harvey and Laura Mueller, Preston, Washington.

4. Lorraine Heichel Masley with three famous champions she handled some years back for Edward Jenner of Knolland Farm. *Left to right,* the Smooth, Ch. Moffett's Harvest, the Wirehair, Ch. Selkert's Randy, and the Longhair, Ch. Kemper Dachs Marcel. All important and outstanding campaigners who have brought many show honors to their owner.

Overleaf:→

1. Ch. Rose Farms Talk of the Town MS, bred by Dee Hutchinson, the foundation bitch behind Shirley Silagi's highly successful line of Miniature Smooth Dachshunds. A daughter of Champion Rukengrats Stanley Steamer MS from Rose Farms Rebecca MS.

2. Black and tan Longhair, English Ch. Africandawns Yank Go Home with three of his kennel-mates, all winning bitches. Photo by Sally Anne Thompson, submitted by owner of dogs, T.L. Johnson, Huntingdon, Cambs, England.

3. A Fleming puppy owned by Mrs. Polly Fleming, Los Angeles, California.

4. Can. and Am. Ch. Vondixoner Stardachs Johann, top winning Best in Show Dachshund *of all time* in Canada, won his last Best in Show at age 10½ years. Sired by Am. Ch. Dunkeldorf Falcon's Favorite. Bred and owned by Ed Dixon, Toronto, Canada.

5. Ch. Wyndel's Charisma MW winning Best of Breed at the Bay Colony Dachshund Club Specialty 1974. Owner-handler, Ray Patenaude. Judge, Muriel Newhauser.

6. This nicely balanced head is one of the assets of the Group winning bitch, Ch. Canebrake Pandora Wire. Bred and owned by Frank and Monica Canestrini, Wheat Ridge, Colorado.

1

2

3

4

5

6

1▲   2▼

←Overleaf:

1. Can. and Am. Ch. Vondixoner Stardachs Julie, a granddaughter of Am. Ch. Spartan's Sloe Gin Fizz. The first Canadian-bred Dachshund ever to win a Canadian Best in Show. Ed Dixon, owner, Vondixoner Kennels, Toronto, Ontario, Canada.

2. The great Ch. Han-Jo's Ulyssis L with his breeder-handler, Hannelore Heller. Ulyssis is the sire of 42 champions and an outstanding winner during the late 1970's. Owned by Ingeborg Kremer, M.D.

1. Ch. Dorachar Golden Lace-MW owned by Mrs. Dorothy Poole, Carlisle, Massachusetts.

2. Ch. Westphal's Sincerely Yours, black and tan Longhair owned by Peggy Westphal, von Westphalen Kennels, now at New Milford, Connecticut.

3. This Standard Smooth Dachshund puppy, three months of age here, grew up to become Can. and Am. Ch. Braaehaus Traveling Man. Owned by Carol and Uffe Braae, Schomberg, Ontario, Canada.

4. Am., Mex., and Int'l. Ch. Daiquiri's Fannie Farkle MW, with the Challenge Trophy she retired at the Houston Dachshund Club, having won it from the Open Miniature Class, the first time ever from that class for a Specialty Best of Breed. Fannie is owned by Samuel R. Whittaker, Jr. and handled by Denny Mounce.

5. Ch. Hollydach's Betsy Ross-W, by Ch. Tharp's Oliver W (by Ch. Pondwick's Hobgoblin ex Ch. Charlamar's Lori W) from Tharp's Bonnie Boom W (by Ch. Tharp's Boom-Boom W ex Ch. Tharp's Cee Zee W) was bred by Holly Diane Darnell and is owned by Lucille Moden, Murfreesboro, Tennessee.

6. Ch. Kleetal's Raven Wing, influential Smooth dog of the late 1950-1960 period, was bred by Peggy Westphal, von Westphalen Kennels.

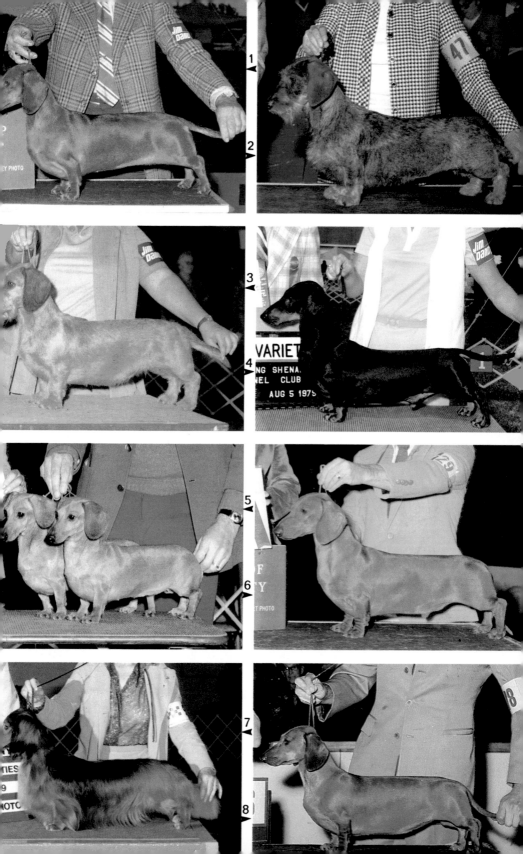

← **Overleaf:**

1. The noted winning bitch, Am. and Can. Ch. Villanol's Red Rose, by Ch. Villanol's Sampson ex Ch. Villanol's April Love. Breeder-owner, Jean M. Carville. Handler, Gordon Carvill. Here winning a Hound Group.

2. Ch. Rose Farm's Moonbeam taking Best of Winners and Best of Opposite Sex at Westminster 1977. Bred, owned, and handled by Dee Hutchinson, Pound Ridge, New York. A Top Dam in 1980 and 1981.

3. Ch. Hollydachs Betsy Ross W finishing her championship. The foundation bitch of Lucy Moden's famed Bristleknoll Kennels, "Holly" was No. 1 Hound Producing Dam and No. 1 Producing Dam of All Breeds in 1982. She is the Top Producing Dachshund Dam, all varieties, *for all time.*

4. Am. and Can. Ch. Wadeldorf Baron Teckel v Geil, noted winner, owner-handled by Helen Hyre, Madeira, Ohio.

5. Ch. Penthouse Class Act MS and Ch. Penthouse Emmy Award MS, sisters, are among the leading top winning Smooth Miniature braces. Here winning Best Hound Brace, and later Best Brace in Show, Western Reserve Kennel Club 1980. Howard Atlee, breeder-owner-handler, Penthouse Dachshunds, Teaneck, New Jersey.

6. Ch. Farmeadow Light Up The Sky, famous Smooth Standard, with 55 champions to his credit to date. A Best in Show, Best in Specialty Show and Group winner. Owned by Barhar Kennels, John Hart and Charles Baris, Montrose, New York.

7. Ch. Von Dyck's Johnny One Note L taking Best of Breed at the Minnesota Dachshund Club Specialty, June 1979, under judge Muriel Newhauser. Hannelore Heller handled for owners Ron and Nancy Lockhart.

8. Can. and Am. Ch. Braaehaus Gretchen Go Teain, Canada's Top Winning Dachshund Bitch for 1972, by Patchwork Penthouse Prospero ex Celloyd Penthouse Sadie, handled here by Howard Atlee for Carol and Uffe Braae, Schomberg, Ontario, Canada.

150

1. Royaldachs Christmas Cherub, by Ch. Tallavast Odyssey ex Ch. Royaldachs Whispering Echo, winning the Puppy Sweepstakes at Alabama Dachshund Club Specialty, handled by Donna Collins, co-breeder-owner with Betty E. Copeland.

2. Ch. Tori Jarice's Wee Robyn MS, by Tori's Russet Prince MS ex De Sangpur Jarice's Tamara MS, bred by Jeanne Rice. Handled by Hannelore Heller for owner, Maurice E. Klinke, Madison, Wisconsin.

3. Ch. Tori Jarice's Jon Eric MW, by Ch. Tori Jarice's Wee Pettijon-MW ex Ch. Valenhofen's Funny Girl MW, bred, owned, and handled by Jeanne A. Rice, Valley Stream, New York.

4. The outstanding Longhaired Dachshund, Ch. Han-Jo's Ulyssis L, bred by Hannelore Heller; owned by Ingeborg Kremer, M.D., pictured winning the Lincolnland Dachshund Club Specialty, May 1976. Judge was John Cook, handler, Hannelore Heller.

5. Ch. Tori Jarice's Michael Magee MW, by Ch. Wyndel's Michelob MW ex Ch. Verdon's Shady Lady MW, bred, owned, and handled by Jeanne A. Rice.

6. The noted Ch. Villanol's Gladiator, by Ch. Villanol's Redson von Piercen ex Am. and Can. Ch. Villanol's Red Rose, bred and owned by Jean M. Carvill, handled by Gordon Carvill, judge Dachshund breeder and all-breed judge James Walker Trullinger.

7. Homebred son of Ch. Risa's Heavy Chevy, this is Knolland Karl en route to the title; owned by Edward Jenner, Knolland Farm, Richmond, Illinois.

8. Ch. Bristleknoll Bonus O'Barhar W owned by Mrs. Alan Robson, Albelarm Kennels. Lucy Moden handling, Murfreesboro, Tennessee.

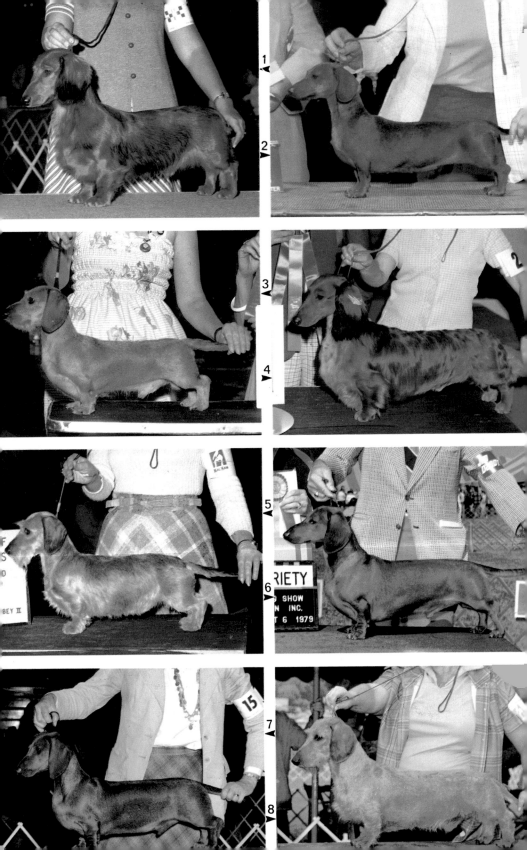

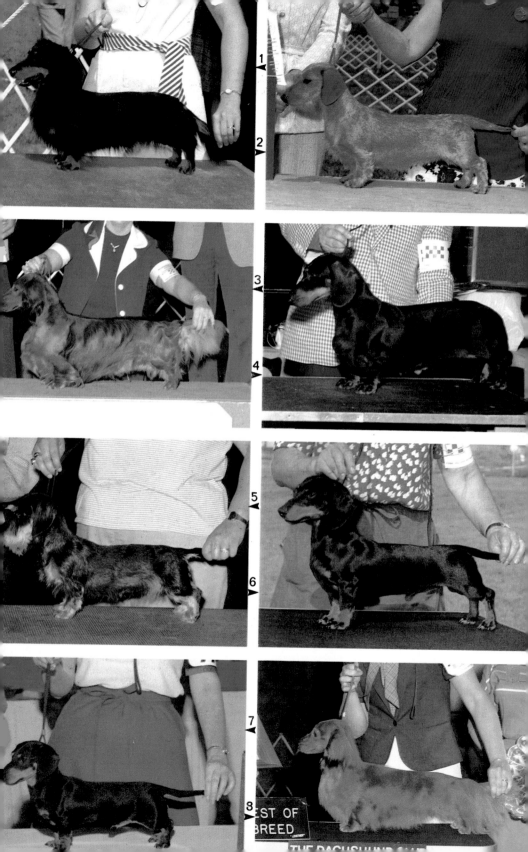

← **Overleaf:**

1. Ch. It's Sleepytime at Wildwood ML, C.D., C.G. was bred and is owned by Susan and Johnny Jones, Durham, North Carolina.

2. Ch. Wyndel's Nutmeg MW, by Ch. Wyndel's Knight On The Town MW, ex Ch. Wyndel's Butterscotch MW, was in 1976, No. 2 Wire Bitch, *Dachshund Variety* System. Bred by Pat Wynne. Owned by Dorothy C. Poole, Carlisle, Massachusetts.

3. The beautiful Longhaired Dachshund Ch. Kemper Dachs Marcel winning a Best in Show in 1974. Handled by Lorraine Heichel Masley for Edward Jenner, Knolland Farm, Richmond, Illinois.

4. Ch. Ram-Ral of Mar-Lar winning the Dachshund Club of Great Lakes Specialty Show in 1977. Owned by Daniel Jenner, Knolland Farm, Richmond, Illinois.

5. Ch. Cal-Neva's Hy Tymes MW, bred by Neva A. and Winston Calhoun. A strong contender for Top Producing Mini Wire bitch, "Weezie" has eight champions to date. She is the foundation bitch at Pegden, owned by Denny Mounce and Peggy Lloyd, handled by Denny Mounce.

6. Ch. Badgerlands Wee Bo Jangles MS taking Winners Dog in Smooths at the Midwest Dachshund Specialty Show in 1982. Hannelore Heller handled for owner Maurice E. Klinke, Madison, Wisconsin.

7. Ch. Tori Jarice's Toral Anson MS, last born son of Can. Ch. Tori Jarice's Wee Angus MS. Co-bred by Jeanne A. Rice and Mary Castoral out of Penthouse Tony Award. Anson pictured taking Winners Dog for a 4-point major at the famous D.A.L.I. Specialty under Doris Wilson at seven months old. Anson is the first Miniature to retire any of the D.A.L.I. Challenge Trophies in competition for 33 years. Owner-handled by Jeanne A. Rice, Valley Stream, New York.

8. Ch. Wildwood's Initial Action ML winning the Dachshund Club of St. Louis Specialty in May 1983. Owned by Susan and Johnny Jones, Durham, North Carolina.

1. Ch. Valona's Keeper of the Keys in 1982. Bred and owned by Polly Fleming, Los Angeles, California.

2. Aust. Ch. Te Puke Firefly earned her championship at just eight months of age. Owned by J.H. Genford, Drofneg Dachshunds, Mount Pritchard, New South Wales, Australia.

3. Aust. Ch. Drofneg Dagobert, by Millewa Storm King ex Drofneg Dagmar, at the time of his retirement from the show ring in 1983 had become the biggest winning Dachshund in New South Wales. He had a total of more than 1000 points and at least 30 Hound Group 1sts to his credit. Owned by J.H. Genford, Drofneg Kennels, Mount Pritchard, New South Wales, Australia.

4. Miniature Wirehaired bitch, Gaygait Lovable Lily of Sevorg, by Gaygait O'Grady ex Gaygait Miss Groucho, born August 1981. Owners, Sevorg Dachshunds, Mr. and Mrs. Groves, Blackwood, Gwent, United Kingdom.

5. Aust. Ch. Zwerg Rough Caste, Miniature Wire by Australian Ch. Gisbourne Bisto Kid (U.K. import) ex Aust. Ch. Zwerg Harrys Tweed, an exciting young dog just starting his career. Best of Breed and Best Wire in Show at Dachshund Club of New South Wales 1985. Owned by N.J. and G.D. Cowie, Rouse Hill, New South Wales, Australia.

6. Suntura's Royal Salute ML is a lovely Miniature Longhair Dachshund by an English import sire from Ch. Suntura's Scheherazade ML. Bred and owned by Edith M. Nelson, Suntura Dachshunds, Mason, Wisconsin.

7. Aust. Ch. Zwerg Little Walloper, by Aust. Ch. Komaha Komander ex Zwerg Interpol, owned by N.J. and G.D. Cowie, Zwerg Kennels, New South Wales, Australia.

8. A noted Best in Show winner of the mid-1970's. Ch. Brandylan's Lanson of Lucene owned by Edward Jenner, Knolland Farm, Richmond, Illinois.

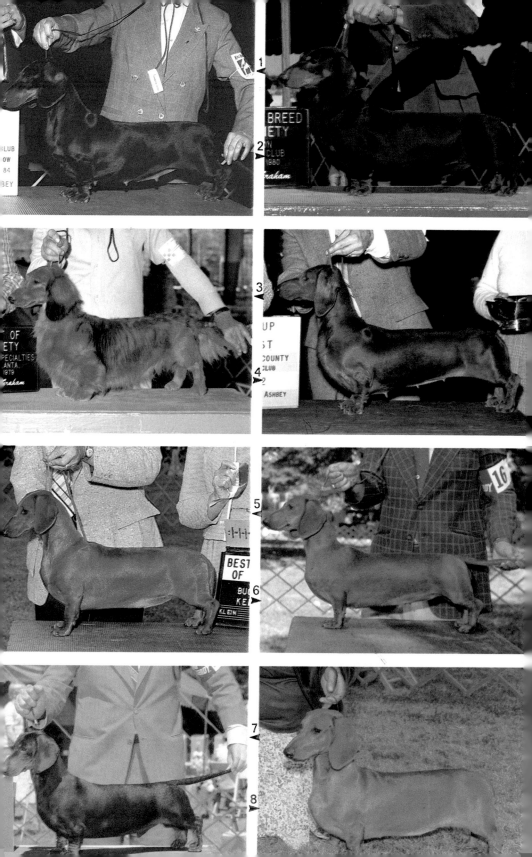

←Overleaf:

1. Apothecary Black Rosey Rose, by Ch. Boondox Chuckie Bunyan ex Ch. Tom-Mar's Lyra Nick, taking Best of Variety at the American Kennel Club Centennial Dog Show in November 1984. Hannelore Heller handles this handsome Smooth for Waldemar Rivera, breeder-owner, and Ivelisse Seda, co-owner, Guaynabo, Puerto Rico.

2. Ch. Museland's Darius, by Am. and Can. Ch. Museland's Atlantean ex Ch. Dunkeldorf's Drachen. Handled by David Bolus for owner Mrs. Dorothy Muse.

3. Ch. Jandelo's Trick or Treat earned several Group placements. Here taking Best Longhair at the Atlanta Specialty in 1979. Jandelo Kennels, owners, Mr. and Mrs. George Van Valen, Fairview, North Carolina.

4. Ch. Doxhaus Starmaker of Barhar, daughter of Ch. Farmeadows Light Up The Sky, making one of her exciting wins for Charles Baris and John Hart, Barhar Kennels.

5. Ch. Curtsey v Westphalen taking Best of Winners en route to title at Bucks County in 1983.

6. Ch. Dunkeldorf's Drachen, by Ch. Texdox Eric ex Ch. Yardley's Favorite Star, handled by Davis Bolus for Mrs. Dorothy Muse, Mountain City, Tennessee.

7. Ch. Museland's Daemon by Ch. Museland's Atlantean ex Ch. Dunkeldorf's Drachen. Owner-handled by Tony Rizzo to Best of Winners at Greenwich Kennel Club 1976. Daemon completed championship while still a puppy.

8. An outstanding Smooth bitch, Ch. Westphalen's Pennies From Heaven, owned by Peggy Westphal.

1. Ch. Von Roblos Portos, a most handsome silhouette study of an excellent Smooth Dachshund. Photo courtesy of Peggy Westphal, von Westphalen Kennels, New Milford, Connecticutt.

2. Ch. Lucene's Delight of Kochana, C.D., owned by Jeanine Sudinski, El Cajon, California.

1▲   2▼

BEST OF BREED

MANATEE
KENNNEL CLUB

JANUARY 1984

PHOTO BY MEYER

1▲   2▼

←Overleaf:

1. Ch. Apothecary The Say Hey Kid, by Ch. Boondox Chuckie Bunyan ex Ch. Tom-Mar's Lyra Nick, bred and owned by Waldemar Rivera, Guaynabo, Puerto Rico, winning Best Smooth Dachshund at Manatee Kennel Club in 1984. Hannelore Heller handling.

2. This important photo of famous winning Miniature Longhairs is of the noted Ch. Patchwork Peter Piper *(left),* and Ch. Patchwork Marigold. Both were bred in successive litters by Pat Beresford, Patchwork Kennels, and both eventually belonged to Dorothy C. Poole, Dorachar Dachshunds. They are by Ch. Patchwork Love Bug ex Nired v Frauenbrunnen.

1. The authors of this book love the older dogs and are happy to include this lovely informal snapshot of three famous "oldsters" at Canada's famous Braaehaus Kennels. *Left to right,* Can. Ch. Braaehaus Pretty Girl, age 10 years; Am. Ch. Penthouse Salome, age 14 years (Pretty Girl's aunt); and Celloyd Penthouse Sade, age 14 years (Pretty Girl's dam).

2. These Miniature Smooth dapples are Ch. Penthouse Speck Teckel MS and the first Smooth Miniature dapple champion bitch, Ch. Penthouse Splash MS, here winning Best Hound Brace. Owned and handled by Howard Atlee, Penthouse Dachshunds, Teaneck, New Jersey.

3. This stunning little Smooth Miniature is Ch. Rose Farm's Elsie, multi-Group winning bitch bred by Dee Hutchinson and owned by Robert Hauslohner.

4. Ch. Rose Farm's Satellite W on the way to title. Handled by Howard Nygood for Dee Hutchinson, Pound Ridge, New York.

5. Ch. Chris Harbor's Stardom MW, by Am. and Eng. Ch. Drakesleat Komma-MW ex Ch. Chris Harbor's Wire Strudel MW, is a homebred owned by Jim and Betty Christian, Panama City, Florida.

6. A current winner from Rose Farm, Ch. Harmo's Royal Ermine taking Winners Bitch at the Dachshund Club of America in 1984. Bred by Anna H. Boardman, owner-handled by Dee Hutchinson.

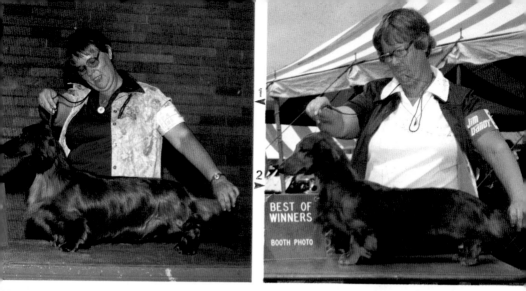

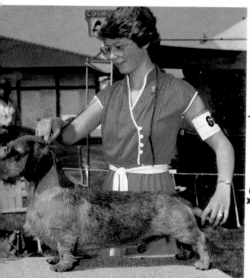

BEST OF
WINNERS

BOOTH PHOTO

OF
ERS

MINION
L CLUB
84

ENS PHOTO
BY GILBERT

NNERS
TRULIS

← **Overleaf:**

1. Ch. Solong Squire of Bristleknoll owned by Sidney Stafford, Stony Brook, New York.

2. Ch. Ballardach's Applause, by Ch. Han Jo's Flaming Flare was handled by Lucy Moden to a good win under co-author Marcia Foy.

3. Ch. Royaldachs Christmas Cherub, GC, by Ch. No Ka Oi's Irisher ex Ch. Royaldachs Whispering Echo, pictured making a good Hound Group win. Dam of ten champions and a C.D.X. to date. Handled by Donna Collins, co-owner with Betty E. Copeland.

4. Ch. Bristleknoll Beauty Spot W. Handled by Doug Holloway for owner James Grinder, New Canaan, Connecticut.

5. Ch. Bristleknoll Barbarian W, by Ch. Barhar Take Me Along ex Ch. Hollydach's Betsy Ross W, was bred by Lucy Moden. Owned by Barbara and Keri Lasila, junior-handled by Keri to this and many other good wins.

6. Ch. Bristleknoll Brawny Lad W, by Ch. Barhar Take Me Along ex Ch. Hollydachs Betsy Ross W, owner-handled by Lucy Moden, Bristleknoll Kennels, Murfreesboro, Tennessee.

1. Ch. Rose Farm's Xavier making the impressive win of Best of Winners, November 1984 at the A.K.C. Centennial Dog Show under specialist judge John Cook, himself a noted Dachshund breeder. Breeder-owned by Dee Hutchinson.

2. Ch. Danimere's Mr. Jigs v Willo-Mar, by Ch. Boondox Chuckie Bunyan ex Ch. Willo-Mar's Gemini. Robert S. Forsyth was judge. Co-owned by Ursula Merritt and Marcia Wheeler.

3. Ch. Gerolf das Zwerglein L, No. 1 Dachshund and No. 10 Hound in 1982, No. 1 Longhair sire in 1984. Gerolf is a grandson of those two famous Longhairs Ch. Han-Jo's Ulyssis and Ch. Von Dyck's Mr. Bo-jangles. Handled by Hannelore Heller, Lake Villa, Illinois. Pictured winning the Minnesota Specialty.

4. Am. and Mex. Ch. Dachsborough Dorion, by Ch. De Sangpur Eric von Copano out of Ch. Nedra of Dachsborough, is just one of many Dachshund champions handled by Denny Mounce. Also a Top Pro-ducer, he sired 11 champions. A gorgeous mahogany Dachshund with many Variety wins and Group placements to his credit. Owned by Vance and Helen Carlin, Houston, Texas.

5. Ch. Grace's Diane of Dachsborough, by Ch. Big Drum Close Call v Westphalen ex Ch. Her Grace of Dachsborough, was Best Puppy in Show, Dachshund Club of America Specialty at Houston, Texas and Best Puppy in Sweepstakes at Houston Dachshund Specialty the same weekend. Denny Mounce handled for Helen and Vance Carlin.

6. Ch. Big Drum Close Call v Westphal, by Ch. Call To Arms v Westphalen ex Burny Ember v Westphalen, winner of 57 Hound Groups, 19 Bests in Show and six Specialty Shows, was also Top Hound in the country for 1981.

7. Ch. Royaldachs Angel's Beelzebub, by Ch. Lucifer of Knocknegree ex Hallhaven Star of Wonder. This sire of four champions was in Top 15 Longhairs for three years. Handled by Bennie Dennard for breeder-owner Betty E. Copeland, Venice, Florida.

8. Ch. Big Drum Bonus v Westphalen, by Ch. Call To Arms v Westphalen ex Burnt Ember v Westphalen, during one year of showing is a Best in Show winner, a Specialty winner, and a multiple Group winner. Owned by Mr. and Mrs. Sidney G. Sims, Houston, Texas.

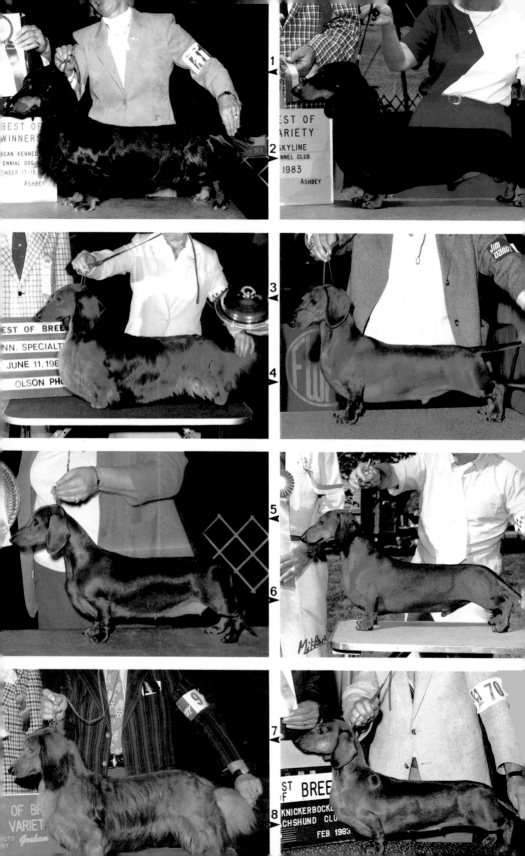

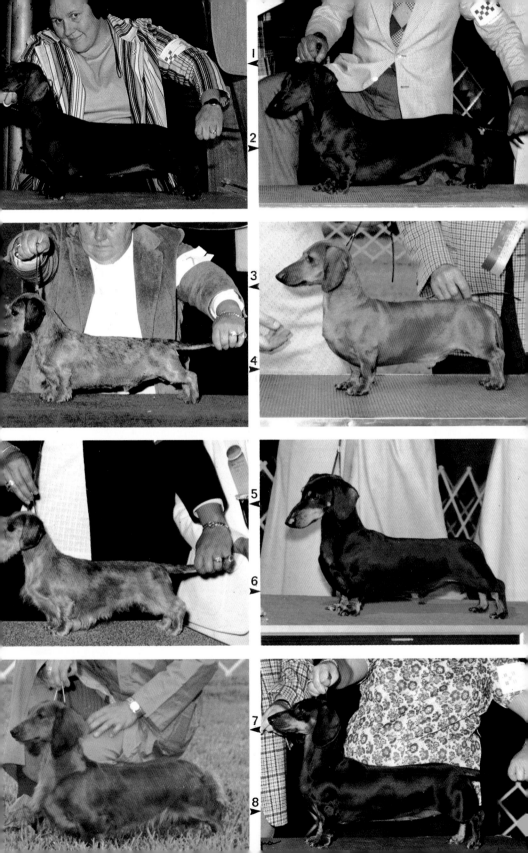

←Overleaf:

1. Am. and Mex. Ch. Her Grace of Dachsborough, the No. 1 Smooth Dachshund of 1979. Her sire was Ch. De Sangpur Eric von Copano, her dam Ch. Pruitt's Lady Diane. She had over 80 Bests of Variety with six Group 1sts and Specialty Best in Show. Handled to all of her wins by Denny Mounce. Owned by Helen and Vance Carlin.

2. Ch. Risa's Heavy Chevy, noted multiple Group winner owned by Edward Jenner and Nancy Weber, has an outstanding record in the ring.

3. Ch. Chris Harbor's Urban Cowboy MW, the No. 1 Dachshund, all coats, for 1983. Sire of the Best in Show winning Ch. Pegden's Fannie Get Your Gun MW. Pictured here winning one of more than 30 Group 1sts. Handled by Denny Mounce, Cowboy is owned by Samuel R. Whittaker, Jr., of Houston, Texas.

4. Ch. Kordachs' Wee Pinocchio was the top winning Smooth Miniature Dachshund in the U.S. during 1972, as had been his mother, Ch. Kordach's Wee Copper Candi, in 1968. Bred, owned, and handled by Mrs. Raymond L. McCord, Winchester, Indiana.

5. Am., Mex., and Int'l. Ch. Daiquiri's Fannie Farkle MW is pictured here winning one of her six Specialty Bests of Breed. Owned by Samuel R. Whittaker, Jr., and Mildred Bryant. Handled by Denny Mounce.

6. The noted black Miniature Smooth Dachshund, Ch. Double (SS) My Kind of Town, by Ch. Rose Farms Timothy MS ex Ch. Rose Farms Talk of the Town MS. Bred, owned, and handled by Shirley Silagi, El Paso, Texas.

7. Ch. Poltergeist Brandy L, by Ch. Gerolf das Zwerglein L ex Champion Delldachs Jasmine L. Owned by Dorothy A. Muse, Mountain City, Tennessee.

8. Ch. Nedra of Dachsborough was a third generation Top Producer. She was Top Producer in 1979. Best Smooth Brood bitch at the Dachshund Club of America and Columbine Dachshund Specialty Shows. This daughter of Ch. Dunkeldorf's Sundlich ex Ch. Pruitt's Lady Diane was owned by Helen and Vance Carlin. Handler, Denny Mounce.

Overleaf:→

1. Ch. Von Arbee's Cherry Suzanne, by Ch. Fleming's Jolly Dachs Torger ex Ch. Von Arbee's Dazzling Deabra, was bred by the Andersons and belongs to the Fred Johnsons.

2. Ch. Rose Farms Dolly v Boondox, Best of Opposite Sex to Best of Variety, Dachshund Club of America 1984. A multiple Specialty winner. Bred and owned by Dan Harrison and Dee Hutchinson.

3. Ch. Chris Harbor's Urban Cowboy at 15 months with his breeder Betty Christian, when just on the threshold of his great career in the show ring.

4. Ch. Muselands Hickok, by Ch. Nixon's Fleeting Encounter ex Ch. Museland's Dagmar, winning points towards the title handled by Michael Hagen under co-author and judge Marcia Foy.

←Overleaf:

1. Ch. Lehigh's Sarah of Brayton ML, by Ch. Sleepytime's Wildwood Omen ex Veshund's Scarlett Ribbon ML was Winners Bitch at the Dachshund Club of America National Specialty in 1983. Pictured finishing at the 1983 Miniature Dachshund Club round-up. Bred by David and Cynthia Sartin, owned by Susan and Johnny Jones.

2. Ch. Tori Jarice's Wee Nicodemus MS, No. 1 Smooth Miniature 1975. The first Smooth Miniature to earn a Specialty Best in Show and still the only male to do so. By Can. Ch. Tori-Jarice's Wee Angus-MS ex Jarice's Dach-Haven Aurora MS. Co-breeders and owners, Jeanne A. Rice and Kathryn M. Curtis. Handled by Jeanne Rice.

3. This lovely Wire Dachshund is Ch. Rufus One II, by Ch. Fleming's Randolph Karim (Smooth) ex a Perocima's bitch (Wirehair) winning the variety at Del Monte in August 1982. Handled by Clay Coady for owner Andrea Davidson.

4. Ch. West Dox Jessica and Ch. Vondixoner Stardachs Jhenny, a popular brace winning pair of the 1970's. Owned by Ed Dixon, Vondixoner Kennels, Toronto, Ontario, Canada.

1. Ch. Willo-Mar's Diamond Jim, by Ch. Mullen's Bold Venture ex Ch. Willo-Mar's Gem of Crosswynd, bred and owned by Marcia Wheeler winning Best of Variety.

2. Ch. Threesteps Trooper W, a top show winner of 1983 and 1984. Bred and owned by Harvey and Laura Mueller, Threesteps Kennels, Preston, Washington.

3. Ch. Dachsborough Nedrum, C.D.X. winning first in Novice A in entry of 89 dogs with a score of 198 for the third leg on his C.D.. Owned by Carl and Candace Holder, Lumberton, Texas.

4. Standard Smooth puppy at two months old on his first day in the United States. Bred at the Braaehaus Kennels, Carol and Uffe Braae, Schomberg, Ontario, Canada.

5. Ch. Lucene's Tanya, sister to Ch. Lucene's Tanner, taking Winners Bitch for a 3-point major. John Cook was judge. Hannelore Heller handled for owner Jeanine A. Sudinski.

6. Am. and Can. Ch. Von Dyck's Mr. Bojangles L, by Ch. Han-Jo's Flaming Flare L ex Ch. Dachs Ridge Midnight Blues L, was No. 1 Hound in 1974 to gain the *Kennel Review* Hound Group Award. Handled by Hannelore Heller for Dr. Helen G. Tiahrt, Salem, Iowa.

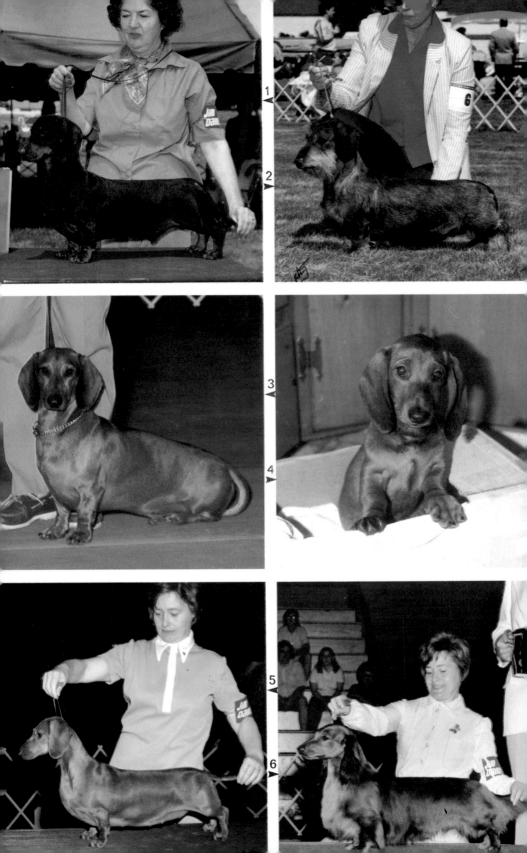

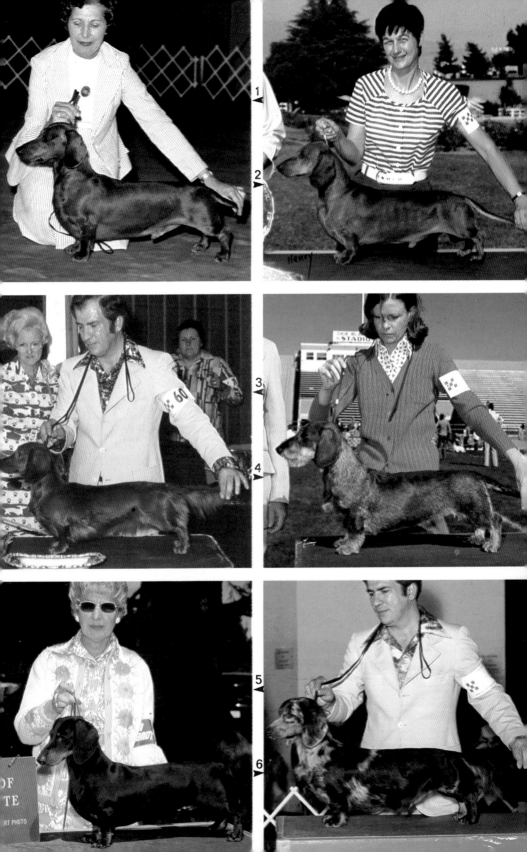

←Overleaf:

1. Ch. Von Relgib's Commandant, multiple Group and Specialty Show winner, sire of six champions from one litter. Bred and owned by Ethel Bigler.

2. Ch. Lucene's Tanner taking Best of Breed over 138 entries, Dachshund Club of California, September 1975. Judge, Mr. Lawrence Krebs. Breeder-owner-handler, Jeanine A. Sudinski, El Cajon, California.

3. Ch. Sangsavant Grenadine, a Group-placing Best of Variety winner by Ch. Wagatome Marching Baron ex Sangsavant Najma Al Jamila, bred by Patricia M. Crary. Owned and handled by Leonce J. Romero, Carencro, Louisiana.

4. Ch. Canebrake Diamond Lil Wire, by Ch. Sky-Hi Diamond Jim Wire ex Canebrake Zelda Wire, winning at Laramie Kennel Club in August 1975. Owned by Frank and Monica Canestrini, Wheat Ridge, Colorado.

5. Ch. Willo-Mar's Gemini, by Ch. Mullen's Bold Venture ex Ch. Willo-Mar's Gem of Countryside, co-owned by Marcia Wheeler and Barbara Lovering.

6. Ch. Sangsavant Mardi Gras is the first blue and tan dapple Dachshund to finish championship, any size and any coat. Owned by Leonce J. Romero, Carencro, Louisiana.

1. Ch. Rose Farms Sally of Trebor MS winning Best of Variety, Badger Kennel Club 1984. Hannelore Heller handled for owner Maurice E. Klinke, Madison, Wisconsin.

2. Ch. Von Relgib's Image, noted winner and dam of five champions, bred and owned by Ethel Bigler, Studio City, California.

3. Ch. Delfisk L'Enfant d'Amour ML, a top winning Miniature Longhair. Bred by Ken Fields, owned by Robert A. Hauslohner and handled by Howard Atlee.

4. Ch. Brundox Daiquiri's Kid MW, by Ch. Rose Farms Thorn In My Side MW ex Ch. Daiquiri's Pick-A-Daisy MW, winner of 26 Hound Groups, five times Best in Show, and six Specialties. Owned by Mr. and Mrs. Sidney G. Sims, Houston, Texas.

5. Ch. Midachs Penthouse Joker MS, the first Smooth Dapple Miniature Dachshund champion in 1973. Howard Atlee, owner, Penthouse Kennels, Teaneck, New Jersey.

6. Ch. Double (SS) My Kind of Town by Ch. Rose Farms Timothy-MS ex Ch. Rose Farms Talk of The Town-MS, is a very important Mini-Smooth who has made a notable record. Breeder-owner-handler, Shirley Silagi, Double (SS) Dachshunds, El Paso, Texas.

7. Ch. Valerna's Keeper of the Keys winning a Hound Group at Tucson in 1983. Bred by Ed MacDonald, by Ch. Von Arbee's Razzle Dazzle ex Ch. Fleming's Polly von Valerna (Polly Fleming, owner Los Angeles, California). Owned by John and Arvilla Mayhall.

8. Ch. Penthouse Critics Choice MS, although still a puppy, here is taking a Group placement at the Cheshire Kennel Club in 1984. The judge was Tom Stevenson. Now winning consistently as she matures, this outstanding Miniature Smooth bitch is adding many laurels for her owners Ann Carey and breeder-co-owner-handler Howard Atlee.

←Overleaf:

1. Ch. Boondox Chuckle Bunyan taking Reserve winners Dog from 6-9 months Puppy Class at Dachshund Club of America in 1980. This Group and multiple Specialty winner was also Top Smooth Sire for 1984. Bred by Dan Harrison and Dee Hutchinson. Owned by John Thompson and Terry Snyder.

2. Ch. B's Javelin de Bayard, famous standard Longhair Dachshund owned by Hannelore Heller, Han-Jo Kennels, Lake Villa, Illinois. This famous multiple Best in Show, Group and Specialty winner, sire of Ch. Han-Jo's Ulyssis-L, won under the late great Dachshund authority, Dr. Herman Cox. Mrs. Heller handled.

3. Ch. Trebor's Mr. Rose Farm MS, a recently finished champion at Rose Farm, bred by Robert A. Hauslohner. Owned and handled by Dee Hutchinson.

4. The distinguished winning Longhair Ch. Han Jo's Candyman. Owner-handled by Beverly Kelly Dodds of San Mateo, California.

5. Am. and Can. Ch. Museland's Atlantean, by Ch. Nixon's Double Concerto ex Ch. Timbar's Honeymoon Limited, in 1972 at the Canadian National Sportsmen's Show.

6. Ch. Dorachar Golden Lace MW, No. 1 Wire Bitch, Dachshund Variety System, for 1977, is by Ch. Poohdach's Boaregard MW ex Ch. Wilheen's Schon of Dorachar MW. Homebred owned by Mrs. Dorothy Poole, Carlisle, Massachusetts.

7. Ch. Dunkeldorf's Rittmeister, by Ch. Dunkeldorf Falcon's Favorite ex Dunkeldorf's Gimlet, was the winner of three all-breed Bests in Show and was a Best of Breed winner of the Dachshund Club of America Specialty. Bred and owned by T.R. Dunk, Jr., Lake Helen, Florida.

8. Top Winning Dachshund in Canada and the United States, Can. and Am. Ch. Braaehaus Traveling Man, age two-and-a-half years, winning the Dachshund Fanciers of Berks County Specialty Show over 300 Dachshunds on DCA weekend 1984. Bred, owned, and handled by Uffe Braae, Braaehaus Dachshunds, Schomberg, Ontario, Canada.

1. Ch. Chris Harbor's Jezebel MW, by Ch. Melody Run's Vagabond Lover MW ex Melody Run's Kiss of Fire MS, bred and owned by Betty and Jim Christian, Chris Harbor Dachshunds. Top Producing Dachshund Bitch, all coats, from April 1983 to March 1984 and currently the *all time* Top Producing Miniature Wirehaired Dachshund Bitch.

2. Ch. Murgam's Cassie Bunyan, by Ch. Moffett's Ingram ex Ch. Murgam's Polly Bunyan, bred and owned by William F. Magrum and Richard E. Bunyan, Naples, Florida.

3. Ch. Double (SS) My Favorite Town MS, by Ch. Double (SS) My Kind of Town MS ex Rose Farms Sara MS, bred and owned by Shirley Silagi, El Paso, Texas.

4. Ch. Vondixoner Stardachs Jet Star, a popular winning Miniature Smooth Dachshund, a smooth recessive grandson of Am. Ch. Spartan's Sloe Gin Fizz. Owned by Ed Dixon, Vondixoner Kennels, Toronto, Ontario, Canada.

5. Ch. Penthouse Ms owned by Robert Hauslohner and handled by Howard Atlee at Ladies Dog Club in 1974.

6. Ch. Pegden's Fred Farkle MW, is the Specialty winning litter-mate to Best in Show winning Ch. Pegden's Fannie Get Your Gun MW. He is owned by Samuel R. Whittaker, Jr., and resides at Pegden Kennels with his handler Denny Mounce.

7. Ch. Kordach's Wee Kamouflage is one of only three living Smooth Miniature black/silver dapple champion males in the U.S. He represents three generations of dapple champions breeder-owned by Mrs. Raymond L. McCord, Kordachs, Winchester, Indiana.

8. Ch. Penthouse Ms MS, one of Howard Atlee's first top winning Smooth Miniatures, a Group winner with the elegance of line he had been working to perfect.

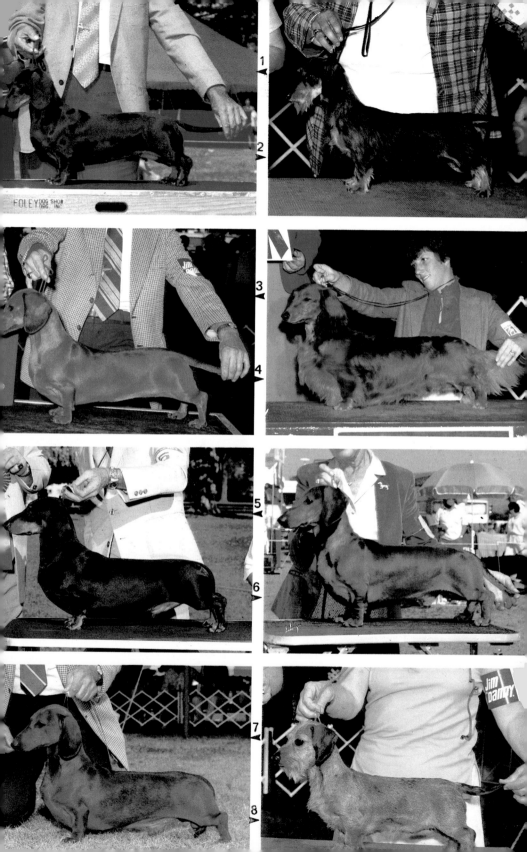

←Overleaf:

1. Ch. Villanol's Lorelei, by Ch. Sealybourne Sirius v Velvet ex Villanol's Krista, bred and owned by Jean M. Carvill. Lorelei is the dam of three champions.

2. Ch. Pegden's Sass Cee Wire M, C.D. is the producer of an all-champion litter. The fourth bitch in a chain of six generations of Pegden champions owned and bred by Pegden Kennels. Owned and bred by Denny Mounce and Peggy Lloyd, Sugarland, Texas. Handled by Denny Mounce.

3. Ch. Villanol's Victoria, by Ch. Villanol's Sampson ex Ch. Villanol's Zucker, bred and owned by Jean Carvill. Handled by Gordon Carvill.

4. Ch. Han-Jo's 'Xtra Copy L, a multi-Group winner and a multi-Specialty Best of Breed winner, including the 1985 Knickerbocker Dachshund Club Specialty Show. Owned by Kenneth M. Andrews, Denver, Colorado. Handled by Lorene Hogan.

5. Ch. Lyell's Master Thomas, by Ch. Fleming's Tiny Timmy ex Lopsee, winning the Hound Group. Photo courtesy of Polly Fleming.

6. Ch. Von Relgib's Challenge taking his third major. Bred, owned, and handled by Ethel Bigler, Von Relgib Kennels, Studio City, California.

7. Ch. Wavecrest's Adam of Fabeland, by Ch. Villanol's Gladiator ex Ch. Wavecrest's Lyric of Fabeland, owned by Jean M. Carvill, handled by Gordon Carvill, Villanol Kennels.

8. Ch. Dorachar Peanut Butter, by Ch. Ruckengrat's Joker MW, ex Ch. Dorachar Nut Buttercrunch MW. Bred, owned, and handled by Mrs. Dorothy C. Poole, Carlisle, Massachusetts.

Overleaf:→

1. Ch. Barhar Minnie's Boy W, famous Best in Show, Specialty Show and Group winning Wire who is as well the sire of 14 champions. This No. 1 Standard Wire in 1976 was bred and is owned by John Hart and Charles Baris, Barhar Dachshunds, Montrose, New York.

2. Ch. Von Relgib's Dream Come True winning Best of Variety at Sierra Dachshund Specialty in January 1985. Bred, owned, and handled by Ethel Bigler.

3. Ch. Moffett's Harvest, famous Best in Show winner, owned by Edward Jenner, Knolland Farm, Richmond, Illinois.

4. Ch. Bristleknoll Brass Buttons W winning Best of Variety and Best of Opposite Sex to Best of Breed at the 1982 Dachshund Club of America Specialty, Houston, Texas. Bobby Fowler handled for owner Kellie Williams.

5. Ch. Chris Harbor's Wendy Wire MW, by Ch. Hericher's Prime Candidate MW ex Ch. Chris Harbor's Jezebel MW, bred and owned by Jim and Betty Christian, Panama City, Florida. Lem Strauss, judge.

6. Fleming's Mariposa Poppy, by Ch. Barbadox Happy Dirk ex Fleming's Sweet Alice, here taking Winners Bitch from the puppy class, Dachshund Club of San Diego, 1973. Handled by Ray McGinnis for owner Polly Fleming.

7. Am. and Can. Ch. Jolly Dachs George, by Ch. Falcon of Heying-Teckel ex Georgette of Heying-Teckel, bred by Joy and Al Levy. Owned by Michael and Ann Gordon, Pittsburgh, Pennsylvania.

8. Ch. Lucene's Daily Double winning a Hound Group placement, Los Encinos Kennel Club, May 1982. Handled by Miss Mechelle A. Sudinski for breeder-owner Jeanine A. Sudinski, El Cajon, California.

← **Overleaf:**

1. Ch. Rose Farms Hannelore Boondox taking Best of Winners at the Dachshund Club of America Specialty in 1984, completing title on the day. Owned by Dan Harrison and Melanie Maurey.

2. Ch. Chris Harbor's Wire Strudel MW, by Ch. Hericher's Prime Candidate MW ex Ch. Chris Harbor's Jezebel MW, bred and owned by Jim and Betty Christian, Panama City, Florida.

3. Ch. Pegden's Fannie Get Your Gun MW, the No. 1 Dachshund Bitch for 1984, with more than 40 times Best of Variety, six Group firsts, and an all-breed Best in Show at the age of only a year and a half. She is writing the record for black and tan Wires with her unprecedented wins. Owned by Barbara Cosgrove. Bred by Denny Mounce and Samuel R. Whittaker, Jr., and handled by Denny Mounce.

4. Am. and Can. Ch. Metzler's Gypsy Mack v Lucene winning Best in Specialty over 134 entries at 1982 Golden Gate Dachshund Club Specialty. Owned by Maybelle B. Metzler, Fresno, California. Bred by Jeanine Sudinski. Handled by Miss Lori Turner.

1. John Hart *(left)* and Charles Baris with three of their Dachshund "greats": *left,* Ch. Kemper Hill Bad Habits (Longhair); *center,* Ch. Barhar Minnie's Boy (Wirehair); *right,* Ch. Farmeadow Light Up The Sky (Smooth).

2. Family portrait! Waiting to enter the ring for Brood Bitch competition are Ch. Hollydachs Betsy Ross W, Top Producing Dachshund Bitch of all varieties, with some of her offspring. *Left to right:* Betsy Ross, Ch. Bristleknoll Brass Bell W, Ch. Bristleknoll Bedwarmer W, and Ch. Bristleknoll Bonus O'Barhal W. Betsy Ross owned by Lucy Moden, Bristleknoll Dachshunds, Murfreesboro, Tennessee.

1▲ 2▼

Chapter 6

Dachshunds in Australia

Considerable rapport exists between the Australian Fancy and ours here in the United States, with an increasing awareness of each other's dogs fostered by the frequency with which judges from Australia travel to the United States to fulfill assignments in the show rings here, and vice-versa. This exchange of opinions can only be beneficial to both countries, enlarging the true scope of what is taking place worldwide within the breeds of interest to us.

In Australia, as in England and in Canada, Dachshunds compete as six separate breeds, with the best of each competing in the Variety Group. Thus the classification is for Longhair, Smooth and Wirehaired Miniature Dachshunds and the same in Standard Dachshunds.

Popularity seems especially high in the Longhairs, with quality dogs in both sizes. Among those of whom I have heard good reports are the standard dogs Champion Marandoo Ezechial owned by Miss S.L. Bennett and Champion Tischamingo Dazzler owned by Miss S.A. Bower who seem to wind up with high awards at the Royal shows. Ezechial was born in October 1979, by Australian Champion Millewa Royal Gem ex Australian Champion Marandoo Bonnie. Dazzler was born in 1982 by Australian Champion Nicholyev Highland Lad ex Nicholyev Moon Shadow. Dazzler also has a littermate, Champion Tischamingo Nite Lite doing well in the ring. Nite Lite is owned by R.J. Walker. These two were champions before leaving the Junior Dog classes.

Miss Bennett also has a splendid bitch in her kennel, Champion Charlemagne Odette, by an importation from the United Kingdom, Australian Champion Imber Irish Coffee ex Australian Champion Charlemagne Red Rebecca.

Aust. Ch. Sonderbar My Way, by Aust. Ch. Bowbank Red Remus (U.K. import) ex Eng. Ch. Bowbank Colombine. Owned by W. Hardie, Hornsby, New South Wales.

E. Berge Phillips is another with a truly lovely bitch, Champion Lohengrin Tapestry, born in 1980, by Australian Champion Jamanean Maxie, imported from the United Kingdom, ex Bredena Amandas Girl.

In Mini-Longs, the bitch Champion Saintbarbara Flipside, daughter of Australian Champion Saintbarbara Playboy ex Australian Champion Saintbarbara Spindle, has many enthusiastic admirers, as does the dog, Champion Artemus Mini Kinsman by Champion Minard Miss Magnum (imported U.K.) from Beanochen Lavender Lady (also from U.K.).

In Standard Smooths, Champion Drofneg Dagobert is a consistent winner for J. H. Genford. Born in 1977, he is a son of Millewa Storm King ex Drofneg Dagmar. This dog also has a noted daughter in Australian Champion Valdachs Charisma owned by Mrs. V. Palangas.

We also take note, in Smooth Standard dogs, of New Zealand Champion Marictur Black Major who was imported from the United Kingdom and is owned by K.A. and D.W. Hardwick. Born in 1980, he is a son of English Champion Matzell Midas and English Champion Marictur Black Modiste.

A leading Smooth Standard bitch is Edwald Appassionata, a winner at the Royals sired by Australian Champion Edwald Nytflyt, owned by K.H. McCarthy. And Heinton Kennels has Champion Heinton Michelle by Australian Champion Heinton Nicholas ex Millewa Mirama.

Mini-smooths of note include Champion Paper Tiger of Hundsburg, born in 1982, by New Zealand and English Champion Willowfield Woodcock ex New Zealand Champion Sonderbar Carrie, a young dog belonging to W. Hardie. Two bitches among Mini-Smooths of whom we've heard enthusiastic comment are Champion Kilsherry Duel Choice, by Australian Champion Sonderbar Substitute ex Kilsherry Marsha Hines, Mrs. R.A. Crastin, owner; and Champion Sonderbar Money Honey, by Australian Champion Sonderbar That's All ex Ardmore Pale Pale Ale, W. Hardie owner. One cannot help but note the frequency with which the Sonderbar prefix appears in and behind the names of successful Mini-Smooths in Australia. Among them Australian Champions Sonderbar Starlight, That's All, Lady Madonnah, Lady Bird, Love Game, Substitute, Maggie May, Oh Brandy, Carrie, Security, Cathy's Clown, and Desiree to list a few we have noted. Truly a highly successful and dominant kennel.

In Standard Wires Miss L.A. MacDonald has Champion Ardmore Hopsack winning Challenge Certificates in dogs, while Mrs. M.E. Fitzgerald is taking the Certificates in bitches with Champion Talshund Sophia Jane.

Mini-Wires have two strong kennels in those belonging to N.J. and Mrs. G.D. Cowie and J.C. and Mrs. D. Brown. the Cowies have Zwerg Gravy Boat, Zwerg Tabby Cat, and Zwerg Magnolia in the winners circle, all sired by their well-known Champion Gisbourne Bisto Kid (Gisbourne Little Bisto ex Redworth Fern). The Browns have Woodfall's Crispy Critter and Champion Woodfall's High Society among their winning contenders, both sired by New Zealand Champion Ludworth Enterprise, an importation from the United Kingdom.

DROFNEG

Drofneg Dachshunds, located at Mount Pritchard in New South Wales, Australia, is owned by J.H. Genford, who has been breeding Standard Smooth Dachshunds since the late 1950's, doing so with considerable success.

D'Arisca Disco Dancer was bred in England and imported to Australia in 1984 by J. H. Genford, Mt. Pritchard, New South Wales.

Some of England's finest bloodlines have been incorporated into this kennel, one of whose most prominent winners is Australian Champion Drofneg Dagobert. He is out of Drofneg Dagmar, by Millewa Storm King, both sire and dam being black and tan. He was born on December 29, 1978, and his forebears go back into the famous Silvea and Womack lines.

Dagobert enjoyed a spectacular career in the Australian show ring where, at the time of his retirement in 1983 he had amassed 30 Group First awards, and was Reserve Hound on about forty occasions. In all he had earned a total of 1000 points, thus the biggest winning Dachshund of any variety in New South Wales.

A very prolific sire, Dagobert has winning progeny throughout most of the Australian states.

Dartlowe Lady Emma came to Drofneg from Victoria, where she was bred by Mrs. Jean Smith. This elegant daughter of Dartlowe Prince Kim ex Dartlowe Gretal also carries back to the Silvae strain, and she was purchased by Drofneg for the express purpose of being bred to Dagobert. Although shown only sparingly thus far, she is, as we write, well started towards Australian championship.

Another outstanding black and tan bitch is one born in 1982, the result of mating a daughter of still another Silvea import to Dagobert. She is Australian Champion Te Puke Firefly, an excellent show dog who gained championship when only eight months of age. Her dam was Te Puke Frances owned by Mr. and Mrs. R.R. Gore, Castle Hill, NSW.

During 1984 Drofneg brought out an English import in whelp to English Champion Benjamin of Raylines. Mrs. Lovaine Coxon of the D'Arisca Kennels bred her, and she is by English Champion D'Arisca Commodore ex English Champion D'Arisca Caprice. While in quarantine she produced a litter of three puppies, two dogs and a bitch, all black and tan. In the short time that she has been shown as we write, D'Arisca Disco Dancer is close to her championship, but principally she was imported for the purpose of introducing new blood to the Drofneg line. When mated to Australian Champion Drofneg Dagobert, she produced five puppies, four black and tan dogs and one chocolate colored bitch, all looking very promising at three months. We wish them a successful future!

LINDENLEA

Dachshunds were introduced into her Lindenlea Kennels in 1958 by Mrs. P.F. MacDonald of Charlestown, New South Wales, when she purchased a Standard Smooth from Windswept Kennels. As owner of a highly successful Irish Setter kennel, she thought it would be fun having a smaller dog which required less in show preparation than the Setters; as it has turned out, it did not take long at all for the Dachshunds to become #1 with her.

Over the years, Lindenlea has owned and/or bred all six types of Dachshunds, but now concentrate only on the Miniature Smooth variety. Over 60 champions have been campaigned to their titles by this kennel.

The breeding program at Lindenlea has been influenced by English bloodlines, going back to Wendlitt, Bowbank, Stargang and Hobbit Hill. As the Miniature Smooth variety is now the strongest both in numbers and depth of quality in her area, Mrs. MacDonald notes that most of the breeders have six or more generations of locally bred dogs in their pedigrees.

Among Mrs. MacDonald's winners are two whose photos we show you in this book. They are Australian Champion Lindenlea

Aust. Ch. Lindenlea Lorikeet, red Miniature, owned by Mrs. F. Mac Donald, Charlestown, New South Wales.

Let's Cheer, by Champion Hobbit Hill Lenwe (imported from United Kingdom) ex Champion Sonderbar Cathy's Clown. Born in November 1983, this dog attained his championship at 11 months' age. Still only a youngster, he already has a Best in Show, all breeds, to his credit, plus multiple Best Exhibit in Hound Group awards, several times Best Puppy in Show, (Baby Puppy twice, at Dachshund Club of New South Wales under the American judge Mrs. C. Burg and at Novocastrian Dachshund Club under the breed specialist, Dr. I.I. Hamilton; Minor Puppy once, North of the Harbour K.C. Winter Classic 3,000 entries, judge Mr. Roy Ayres from the United States), and Challenge Dog at the Spring Fair under Canadian judge and Dachshund breeder, Ed Dixon. Other wins include the Junior Dog Class at Sydney Royal 1985, Australia's largest all breeds show, where the judge was Mr. H. Jordon, Dachshund specialist from the United Kingdom.

Then there is Australian Champion Lindenlea Lorikeet, by Champion Sondebar That's All from Champion Sondebar Ladybird, born in 1980.

Lorikeet attained her championship title at eight and a half months of age, and is now a multi-Best in Show All Breeds winner; was Best Exhibit in Show at the Dachshund Club of New South Wales Specialty judged by Mr. S. Kershaw, a Miniature Smooth Dachshund breeder, owner of Hobbit Hill Kennels, in the United Kingdom; and Best Exhibit in Show at the Novocastrian Dachshund Club under the New Zealand Hound specialist, P. Kersey, plus numerous Group and "in Show" awards in keenest specialty and all-breed competition.

NICHOLYEV

Nicholyev Kennels, owned by John R. Bower, Edgeworth, New Castle, New South Wales, Australia, was started more than twenty years ago (during the mid-1960's) with the purchase of a black and tan Standard Smooth male. He was shown three times, then kept as a much loved pet for 17 years. Prior to this time, the Bower family had been breeders and exhibitors of rough coated Collies, so they were "into" dogs from the start.

Aust. Ch. Nicholyev Highland Lad, one of the outstanding Standard Longhaired Dachshunds owned by John R. Bower, New Castle, New South Wales. This dog is an all-breed Best in Show winner and a Specialty Best in Show winner, and an important sire in both Australia and New Zealand.

The Bowers next purchased a male and a female Standard Longcoat, both of leading bloodlines, and through the years they have maintained a very careful breeding program through which they have produced Best in Show winners at both all-breed and Specialty events, Royal Challenge winners, and consistent in show-winning stock both in Australia and New Zealand.

More than 40 championships have been completed by Nicholyev Dachshunds, quite a few of them with New Zealand and Australian Dual titles. Many dogs have been sold by this kennel to New Zealand and other Australian states in addition to their own.

At present the kennel consists of between 30 and 35 Dachshunds of the Standard Long variety. But over the years the Bowers have also raised Standard Smooths, Miniature Smooths, and Miniature Longs, despite the fact that their first love is for the Standard Longs.

Mr. Bower is a Dachshund judge who enjoys officiating at Specialty Shows and does so frequently in both Australia and New Zealand.

Australian Champion Nicholyev Dynasty, born in March 1980, is a black and tan Longhaired son of Australian and New Zealand Champion Nicholyev Irish Coffee ex Australian Champion Lohengrin Sugar Candy. This is a combination of Imber, Albany and Mountchlown bloodlines, which is predominant, along with a bit of older Australian stock, behind most of the Nicholyevs.

Dynasty is shown only at Specialty events, and has won Best in Show at the Dachshund Club of New South Wales under the British specialist judge, J. Crawford; has a Specialty Best in Show under American breeder-judge P. Bishop; and a Specialty Best in Show under New Zealand breeder-judge G. Johnson. He was point score winner of the Dachshund Club of New South Wales, 1982-83 and 1983-84 in males, and Dachshund of the Year at the Novocastrian Dachshund Club in 1983-84. Not only is Dynasty a consistent winner, he is also a sire of quality.

The red dog, Australian and New Zealand Champion Nicholyev Highland Lad, is a son of Australian and New Zealand Champion Lohengrin Black Bean ex Australian Champion Garthela Highland Fling (New Zealand). He is an elegant and stylish dog, Inber and Albany bred on one side, Inber and New Zealand breeding on the other.

Lad is an all-breed Best in Show winner in Australia and in

New Zealand; in addition he has been Best Hound exhibit on numerous occasions. As a stud dog, his worth has been proven repeatedly with Best in Show winning stock to his credit.

The lovely bitch, Australian Champion Nicholyev Tabariz, born in 1981, is a black and tan daughter of Irish Coffee and combines Imber, Albany and Mountchlown breeding. Her show career has been very successful, starting with the winning of her first Challenge Certificate at seven months of age. She was Challenge Bitch at the Sydney Royal Show in 1983, 1984, and 1985; has been Challenge Bitch and Best of Breed at the Dachshund Club of New South Wales, and has a long list of additional honors in the New South Wales area.

SAINT BARBARA

Saint Barbara Kennels raise Longhaired Miniature and Longhaired Standard Dachshunds and Miniature Smooths under the ownership of Mrs. B. Hill at Ridgewood Heights in Queensland, Australia.

Established in 1956, Saint Barbara had the pleasure of introducing Miniature Smooths and Longhairs to Queensland, and over the years they have bred and made up more than 68 champions.

Aust. Ch. Saint Barbara Flipside, homebred owned by Mrs. B. Hill, Saint Barbara Dachshunds, Ridgewood Heights, Queensbury, Australia.

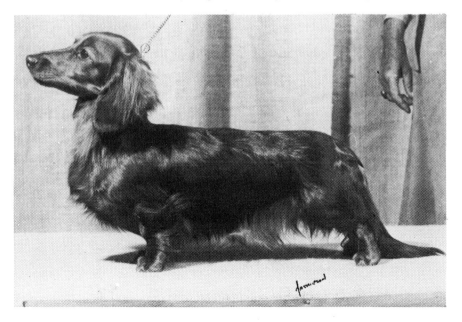

Many overseas judges have liked Mrs. Hill's dogs, and they have brought home numerous exciting honors, wins made under judges from the United States and other countries as well as from the Australian authorities.

Recently Mrs. Hill has been showing two sisters, Mini-Longs who have been top bitches in all the eastern states of Australia. For instance in 1983 between them they won Challenges at all four of the eastern state Royal shows. One of these, Australian Champion Saint Barbara Flipside, has won numerous Bests in Show, including all breeds. She has been "Champion of Show" at four consecutive Dachshund Club of Queensland events, a record which will be hard to beat. Flipside was born in 1981, and is a daughter of Australian Champion Saint Barbara Playboy ex Champion Saint Barbara Spindle.

Over the years Mrs. Hill has bred and owned a number of Australia's leading stud dogs. However, recently it has been necessary for her to reduce her kennel quite drastically, and she has transferred all but a few bitches to other kennels.

SONDERBAR

Sonderbar Miniature Smooth Dachshunds are owned by Mr. W. Hardie, at Hornsby in New South Wales, Australia. The first of Mr. Hardie's Dachshunds was purchased by him in 1961. By the time she had completed her title, she had him thoroughly sold on her breed and on the fun of showing dogs. Thus the following year what was to become Sonderbar's foundation bitch joined the family, Australian Champion Windswept Hold Me Close. She produced Australian Champion Sonderbar Say It Again, the granddam of Australian Champion Sonderbar Mrs. Robinson.

In 1971, Bill Hardie felt that some new blood would be useful in the progress of his line; thus he took a trip to England specifically to look at Dachshunds and to select something he liked for his breeding program. Bowman Red Remus was purchased at that time from Mrs. Dorothy Solomon, a grandson of the famed English Champion Bowbank Red Riordan from English Champion Bowbank Colombine. Coming out of quarantine at seven months' age, Remus attained his championship in no time flat, then was retired to stud.

Remus proved to have been an excellent selection, for not only was he himself a handsome dog but he proved as well to be a most

The well-known Miniature Smooth Dachshund, Australian Ch. Sonderbar Money Honey, by Ch. Sonderbar That's All ex Ardmore Pale Ale, is owned by W. Hardie, Hornsby, New South Wales.

prepotent sire, even when mated to less than outstanding bitches. His offspring include 37 champions, surely an impressive number!

The second importation from England to Sonderbar Kennels was Australian Champion Hobbithill Yorke of Limberin in 1974, who became the sire of eight champions. Then in 1977, English Champion Stargang Wurlitzer, bred by Mrs. Ellen Blackburn, was selected by Dorothy Solomon on Bill Hardie's behalf, as a sire to complement the "Remus" line. With his arrival in Australia, Wurlitzer attained his championship there and has sired 34 champions.

In 1982 an additional complementary bloodline was introduced with the acquisition of Australian Champion Paper Tiger of Hundsburg, this one imported from New Zealand. Tiger was by English and New Zealand Champion Willowfield Woodcock, imported from the United Kingdom, out of New Zealand Champion Sonderbar Carrie (imported from Australia) a full sister to Australian Champion Sonderbar Oh Brandy. He is the sire of Australian Champion Sonderbar Fascination.

ZWERG

Zwerg Dachshunds were started in 1979 by N.J. and G.D. Cowie of Rouse Hill, New South Wales, Australia. Miniature Smooths were the first Dachshunds there, the foundation bitch being principally from Lady Dick Lauder's Willowfield bloodlines from Scotland. Miniature Wires, now the principal interest, followed closely, the foundation for those being the Peredur lines from Mrs. Ruth Spong in Wales. In 1982 Australian Champion Gisbourne Bisto Kid was imported from Mrs. Eve Quick in the United Kingdom.

Over these few years, the Cowies have "made up" 20 Australian champions, 17 of which they bred themselves. There are also two Zwerg bitches in New Zealand who have gained championship there.

The Cowie's latest champion as we write is Australian Champion Zwerg Rough Caste, who at only eight months old has already won Baby Puppy in Group on three occasions; Baby Puppy in Show once; Minor Puppy in Group four times; Minor Puppy in Show once; and Best Wire in Show at a Dachshund Specialty Show. She is a daughter of Australian Champion Gisbourne Bisto Kid and has indeed made a most promising start in her show career.

Aust. Ch. Zwerg Tabby Kat, Best of Breed Miniature Wire and Best Wire in Show at the Dachshund Club of New South Wales Speciality. Multiple class, in-Group and in-Show winner owned by N. J. and G. D. Cowie, Rouse Hill, New South Wales.

Aust. Ch. Gisbourne Bisto Kid, U.K. import, by Gisbourne Little Bisto ex Redworth Fern. The sire of eight Australian Champions to date. Owned by Zwerg Dachshunds, N. J. and G. D. Cowie, Rouse Hill, North South Wales.

Bisto Kid, the U.K. importation mentioned above, has proven a valuable asset to the kennel. He is a multiple Group and class and in-Show winner, including Best in Show under Dr. Harry Spira.

The Miniature Wire sisters, Australian Champions Zwerg Alley Kat (now in New Zealand where she is owned by Mrs. Dawn Smith) and Australian Champion Zwerg Tabby Kat are two lovely bitches representing their breeder very well. They are by Australian Champion Gisbourne Bisto Kid from Australian Champion Zwerg Arpeggio. Tabby Kat was Best of Breed Miniature Wire and Best Wire in Show at Dachshund Club of New South Wales Specialty judged by the British authority Mrs. Ruth Spong, and has multiple class, in-Group and in-Show awards.

Among the other winning Miniature Wires are Australian Champion Zwerg Witch Tartan, by Crofton Downs Wee Wizard, N.Z. ex Australian Champion Zwerg's Harry's Tweed. Also Australian Champion Zwerg Allegretto, by Australian Champion Crofton Downs Rag-a-mufin.

A promising Mini-Wire "star of the future" is Zwerg Irish Tweed, by Australian Champion Andyc Ima Driver ex Australian Champion Crofton Downs Red Tweed, both parents imported from U.K.

Miniature Smooths include the handsome Australian Champion Zwerg Little Walloper and his litter sister Zwerg Black Maria. These are by Australian Champion Komahi Komander ex Zwerg Interpol.

Breeder-owner Grace B. Hill is pictured showing De Sangpur Wee Allene, the first American-bred Miniature Longhair Champion and granddaughter of Champion William de Sangpur. Sire, Tinyteckel Black Silk. Dam, Shantee Linda de Sangpur.

Chapter 7

The Miniature Dachshund

The Miniature Dachshund is growing steadily in interest for many fanciers, and is at the same time establishing himself as an important member of the Dachshund breed. People are looking with respect upon these tiny dogs, as indeed should be the case when one considers the winning numerous specimens have done, and the quality of the "tinies" in our ring nowadays. One feels inclined to remark "You've come a long way, baby" in looking at the current contenders in all three varieties and remembering the days when miniatures in this breed were more like dwarfs than the beautiful counterparts of the standards we now take so casually for granted. Careful thought and planning, work, joy, and disappointment have all been included, I am sure, with the progress of the Miniature Dachshund between then and now!

The original purpose in breeding Miniature Dachshunds was to create a very small Dachshund with which to combat the rapid increase in the rabbit population taking place in Eastern Germany during the 1800's. In the attempt to do so, small members of such breeds as Dandie Dinmont Terriers, Miniature Pinschers and Miniature Schnauzers are said to have been bred with standard Dachshunds. The results, as one might assume, were dogs bearing little resemblance to Dachshunds. The Royal gamekeepers were mostly in charge of these efforts, their choice being what they felt would bring fast results. What they wound up with were dogs sadly lacking in both breed type and hunting spirit, thus the efforts were failures.

In later years Dachshunds weighing around 12 pounds were selected for breeding in another attempt by Germany to produce Miniature Dachshunds. This, too, was a failure, for again Dachshund type was sacrificed, these dogs being selected purely for their hunting instincts with the result that we understand they bore little actual resemblance to Dachshunds in appearance.

In 1902 the first Miniature Dachshunds were registered in the German Stud Book. Eleven of them, including two Wire bitches, seven Smooth bitches, and two Smooth dogs. And as the next several years developed, a few kennels started to bring forth recognizable purebred Miniatures.

The first Miniature of whom we've found trace in England was a Smooth by the name of Bitterline imported from Denmark who was an entry at the 1926 Crufts. Miss O.M. New and Lady Blackiston were breeders of them at that time.

In 1935 the Miniature Dachshund Club of England was established. Mrs. Smith-Rewse is generally credited, through her Primrose Patch Kennels, with being responsible for the start of the appearance of quality Miniatures in England, her method having been that of breeding the best of the small Standards to the best at that time available Miniatures. It was a Primrose Patch importation, who came here with his owner, Miss Avis Mary Earle, along with four other Longhair Miniatures when she moved from Great Britain and established her Tinyteckel Kennel in the United States who became the first Longhaired Miniature Dachshund to complete a championship title here, which he did in 1940. This was Champion Primrose Patch Diamond. Miss Earle also gained an obedience dog title with her Tinyteckel Ever Ready, C.D.

It was at the Dachshund Club of America Specialty in 1934 that the first Miniatures were exhibited in the United States, in a combined class for all coats and both sexes. Four exhibitors competed with nine entries. Considerable agitation was created that year when several young puppies whose parents were Standards won over true Miniature Dachshunds in the class for "under nine pounds", with the result that the Miniature age of 12 months was added to the class definition in 1935, the Miniature class made a division of the open class, and making first prize winners in this class eligible to compete against the Standard Dachshunds in the Winners' Class for championship points.

The first decade of Miniature breeding here in America must have been a discouraging time for advocates of this size. Only a very few Miniatures were to be found here, creating great difficulties for those trying to work out and follow a breeding program. Those Miniatures who did exist had both standard size and troublesome faults immediately behind them, presenting many problems for those anxious to breed dogs who were both correctly small and excellent quality. This situation continued until well into the 1940's, by which time the cuteness of tiny Dachshunds had caught the public attention and demand for them was growing rapidly in the pet trade. Grayce Greenburg, a noted breeder and authority on the breed, was among the first to import some from England for her kennel in California. Caroline Clark Roe and Kaye Dore were others to bring over and start breeding them at this same period in California. In June 1947 the first Miniature ever to do so, a Smooth, graced the cover of the *American Dachshund Magazine*. This dog was Webb's Pink Lady, born in 1944, belonging to Mr. and Mrs. Lester Noel Webb.

It was in 1946 that Grayce Greenburg acquired Smooth Miniatures, and the following year she and W.E. Giles, of New York, started work to interest some other Miniature owners in the foundation of the American Miniature Dachshund Association, incorporated in New York during July 1950. A principal purpose of the association was, as quoted from its constitution, "to see changes in the A.K.C. approved standard for the Dachshund so that the Miniature Dachshund will have a separate standard and classification of its own." But this, as we are all aware, was not to be, and to this day Miniature Dachshunds share classification with the Standards, and compete against them in winners classes and for Best of Variety of Breed competition.

It was soon thereafter that Mrs. William Burr Hill and some other Miniature breeders in the East resigned from the American Miniature Dachshund Club and organized the National Miniature Dachshund Club, dedicated to the improvement of the Miniature Dachshund, with no mention of any "separate variety" issue.

For a while after all this took place Miniature entries slumped sharply at the dog shows. But by the late 1950's the results of concentration on breeding a better Miniature rather than seeking separate status for it started to be seen, with some very notable wins at important shows in keen standard competition! The breeders mainly responsible for accomplishing this were Mrs. Hill, Mrs. Lynda Beard (Lincoln, Nebraska), Muriel Glanz (Florida), Mrs. Dwight Garner (Iowa), the Ruffells (Seattle, Washington), Mrs. O'Doud (Ohio), Cordella Jensen and Charlie Mays (both, California).

The movement was on, nationwide, to produce better Miniature Dachshunds and the results impressive.

It is the Wires who have led the way in gaining recognition in the show ring for Miniature Dachshunds. Dr. Lyman R. Fisher was probably the earliest breeder of them here, having imported a pair from Germany in 1931.

These two imports of Dr. Fisher's were Alex Friewaldau and Adda von Swartenbrook. The first American Miniature Dachshund to complete championship was a bitch belonging to Dr. Fisher's Limelight Kennels, who did so in California under the handling of Mrs. Donia Bussey Cline of Crespi Kennels. Actually the first two Wire champions were from Limelight Kennels, Champion Limelight Berlinerlicht and Champion Limelight Breslauerlicht, following which five years elapsed before the next one, Champion Mikosz v Teckeldorf (Limelight Dreamlight-Penelope II) bred by Katharina Lehfeldt and owned by Dr. Hans Lehfeldt, followed one year later by Mikosz's son Champion Misery v Teckeldorf, another from the Lehfeldt's Teckeldorf Kennels. There followed a six-year period with no Miniatures finishing, until the fifth Wire, Champion Ursel v Osterholz, bred and owned by Mr. and Mrs. Fritz Kroeff.

Prominent among Miniature Wire breeders of the 1960's were Tubec Kennels owned by the Neville Stephens, who usually were very much in the winners circle. Best known among their Mini-Wires was American and Canadian Champion Tubec's Wee Johann W, who was the top winning Miniature Dachshund, all coats, for 1958 through 1960. Mary Garner also had a number of Mini-Wire champions to her credit during the 1960's, and Champion Garner's Wee Josh MW, owned by Mrs. Charlie Mays, was the sire of 12 Mini-Wire champions who, like their sire, produced more champions.

The 1960's could well be called the decade of the big breakthrough for Miniature Wires on the United States show scene. During these ten years, 103 Miniature Wires gained title, 11 of them owned by Charlie Mays with the Garners and the Stephens holding their own as well. Champion May's Talleyrand and Champion May's Tyna-Mite MW were the "heavy" individual winners, Tyna-Mite having been the first Miniature to win Best of Variety at a Dachshund Club of America Specialty, after finishing her title in five shows by 11 months of age. Tyna-Mite, shown from 1961-

Ursel v Osterholz, by Strupp v Oster- holz ex the imported Katja v d Jeetzel, an early Miniature Wire- haired winning in 1953. Owned by Osterholz Kennels, Mrs. Fritz Kroeff, New York City.

1967, was then owned by the late Mary Germany and handled throughout her ring career by her later owner Dorothea Metzger. She was Top Winning Dachshund Bitch for two years consecutively.

Another notable Mini-Wire of the 1960's was Champion Elenbusch Jiminy Cricket, born in October 1964 who in the short time of his life (he died in December 1969) racked up a total of four Bests in Show, 166 times Best of Variety, first in Hound Group 20 times, an additional 80 Group placements, three Specialty Bests of Variety, and Best of Variety at Westminster in 1969. Jiminy Cricket was the first Miniature Dachshund to win a Best in Show in the United States. Bred by Ellen Bourgeouis, owned by Beverly and Sherry Snyder.

It was that very great breeder of all coats and varieties in Dachshunds, Mrs. William Burr Hill, who was first to produce an American-bred Longhaired Miniature champion. This was Champion De Sangpur Wee Allene who gained her title in 1954. Gracie Hill was truly a very great lady in the Dachshund world. She was secretary of the Dachshund Club of America for more than two decades, and organizer, in 1959, of the Dachshund Association of Long Island, the famous "DALI" whose Specialties are among the most prestigious to be found anywhere. Additionally she helped to organize the National Miniature Dachshund Club which she has served in several offices. Her De Sangpur Dachshunds are world famous, both as show dogs and as the winners of obedience degrees.

The second Miniature Longhaired to finish was Champion Edmonston's Livin' Doll in 1956. The following year Champion Bayard Chantilly, a black and tan, gained title for breeder-owner Mary Howell. This little bitch began her show career with a bang, taking Reserve Winners at DALI from the puppy class. Chantilly lived to be 15 years old, and was the dam of Champion Bayard le Bistro who gained title in 1965. In total, only nine Miniature Longhairs gained championship between 1954 and 1959.

As had been the case with the Mini-Wires, the Mini-Longs also really took off during the 1960's, with 62 of them becoming champions during this ten year period. Tubac and De Sangpur Kennels, Mary Garner, and others were joined by such outstanding new breeders as Pat Beresford and Paul Tolliver. Pat's Patchwork Miniatures have gained fame, and Best in Show honors for her. Paul Tolliver started his association with Mini-Longs when he purchased the one who became Champion Wee Keli Jean of Wayne from Ruby Arnot, making her his first to gain title in this size and variety. Then came his famous Champion Taunuswald Wee Sakura ML. She had an imposing show career, her honors including four Specialty Best of Opposite Sex to Best of Breed wins; 11 Best of Opposite Sex Longhair wins; three Bests of Breed and eight Bests of Variety at Specialties, and 27 times Best of Variety at all-breed events.

The first Miniature Smooth Dachshund champion did not complete title until 1956, with only 59 gaining title between then and 1972. The first Smooth male champion was Dach's Dan Eric M, owned by Lynda Beard in Lincoln, Nebraska. The second Smooth Miniature champion, also a male, was owned by Mrs. William Burr Hill and gained title in 1958. This was Champion De Sangpur Wee Lancelot. This little dog weighed only eight pounds, yet gained his title in the keenest of competition, taking not less than Best of Winners at five consecutive shows which also brought him two Bests of Variety and a Hound Group placement.

1960 brought forth great Miniature Smooths on both the East Coast and the West Coast. Here in the East it was Champion Johannis Strauss, by Colgo's Black Gamin ex Champion Geam's Wee Trudina MS who was the fourth male to finish and had a host of admiring friends in the dog show world. He was owned by Miss Carolyn Strauss of St. Louis and was presented as a Christmas gift by her to the Hardys. Johannis made his championship in Canada, Bermuda and the United States, and, fortunately, was widely used at stud as a goodly number of his decendants are still to be found in the winning circles of our Miniature Smooth Dachshund rings.

On the West Coast, Champion Garner's Wee Hans M, bred by Mary Garner, by Garner's Little Conquestor ex Garner's Little Tena May, was sold to Jim and Billie Ruffell as a young puppy. He is generally credited with having been the dominant Smooth Miniature stud dog in his part of the country, and, like Johannis, figures in the background of many winning Mini-Smooths still today.

We've talked quite a bit about these good and exciting Mini-Smooth males; but actually it was a bitch who was the first Miniature Smooth champion here in the States, Aldwin's Jewell in 1956, bred and owned by Mr. and Mrs. Richard Farnham. Jewell was an elegant, small and sound black and tan born in August 1952 by Jeetzel von Osterholtz ex Chota Strange Interlude. Shown 61 times she won the Open Miniature Class upon 52 occasions and had 22 points when she finished, that second major having been difficult for a Miniature to come by in those days.

Gracie Hill was the breeder of the second Miniature Smooth bitch who finished, Champion De Sangpur Wee Memmy (Jeetzal von Osterholtz ex De Sangpur Wee Rememberance). She was also the first red Smooth Miniature champion. Her owner was Mrs. James Bell, Jr., her handler Bill Ake.

The first Hound Group 1st award to a Mini-Smooth was to Dach's Dan Eric M in the 1950's. The second was Little Lady of Dachsy Dell who never did complete her title. Third came Champion Tanana's C Candice v Bayard in the 1960's. And in the 1970's Muriel Newhauser's male, Champion Muriel's Mr. Guam M, became the second male and the fourth Mini-Smooth to gain the prestigious honor of taking Best Hound in Show.

We would love to tell you in far more detail about all of the winning Miniatures who helped pave the way for such success stories as those of Champion Spartan's Sloe Gin Fizz, Champion Martini's Fannie Farkle, Champion Chris Harbor's Rhinestone Cowboy, and now the first black and tan Wirehaired Miniature to win Best in Show, Champion Pegden's Fannie Get Your Gun; the many Longhair Miniatures making their presence felt; and the respect with which the Smooth Minis are now being viewed. But, as we have already noted, space is limited and the list is a long one; so for now, we will have to just say "congratulations" and "well done" to all the participants!

Newcomers to the breed sometimes are puzzled by Dappled Dachshunds. These are recognized members of the breed. These dogs should be of a clear brownish or grayish color, or even white, background with dark, irregular patches of dark-gray, brown, red-yellow or black. Large areas of one color are undesirable, and neither the light nor the dark color should predominate.

These pictures of Midachs Nacreous MS, dressed up in sweater, and of Midas Dan Patch MS, described by his owner as a "homozygous dapple mini," are sent to us by Sharon Michael to illustrate what is meant by the description "dapple."

Chapter 8

The Dachshund Club Of America Official Standard

GENERAL FEATURES

GENERAL APPEARANCE - Low to ground, short legged, long bodied, but with compact figure and robust muscular development; with bold and confident carriage of the head and intelligent facial expression. In spite of his shortness of leg, in comparison with his length of trunk, he should appear neither crippled, awkward, cramped in his capacity for movement, nor slim and weasel like.

QUALITIES - He should be clever, lively, and courageous to the point of rashness, persevering in his work both above and below ground; with all the senses well developed. His build and disposition qualify him especially for hunting game below ground. Added to this, his hunting spirit, good nose, loud tongue, and small size render him especially suited for beating the bush. His figure and his fine nose give him an especial advantage over most other breeds of sporting dogs for trailing.

CONFORMATION OF BODY

HEAD - Viewed from above or from the side, it should taper uniformly to the tip of the nose, and should be clean-cut. The skull is only slightly arched, and should slope gradually without stop (the less stop the more typical) into the finely formed slightly arched muzzle (ram's nose). The bridge bones over the eyes should be strongly prominent. The nasal cartilage and tip of the nose are long and narrow; lips tightly stretched, well covering the lower jaw, but neither deep nor pointed; corner of the mouth not very marked. Nostrils well open. Jaws opening wide and hinged well back of the eyes, with strongly developed bones and teeth.

Teeth - Powerful canine teeth should fit closely together, and the outer side of the lower incisors should lightly touch the inner side of the upper. (Scissors bite).

Eyes - Medium size, oval, situated at the sides, with a clean, energetic though pleasant expression; not piercing. Color, lustrous dark reddish-brown to brownish-black for all coats and colors. Wall eyes in the case of dapple dogs are not a very bad fault, but are also not desirable.

Ears - Should be set near the top of the head, and not too far forward, long but not too long, beautifully rounded, not narrow, pointed or folded. Their carriage should be animated, and the forward edge should just touch the cheek.

Neck - Fairly long, muscular, clean-cut, not showing any dewlap on the throat, slightly arched in the nape, extending in a graceful line into the shoulders; carried proudly but not stiffly.

Front - To endure the arduous exertion underground, the front must be correspondingly muscular, compact, deep, long and broad. Forequarters in detail:

Shoulder Blade - Long, broad, obliquely and firmly placed upon the fully developed thorax, furnished with hard and plastic muscles.

Upper Arm - Of the same length as the shoulder blade, and at right angles to the latter, strong of bone and hard of muscle, lying close to the ribs, capable of free movement.

Forearm - This is short in comparison to other breeds, slightly turned inwards; supplied with hard but plastic muscles on the front and outside, with tightly stretched tendons on the inside and at the back.

Joint Between forearm and foot (Wrists) - These are closer together than the shoulder joints, so that the front does not appear absolutely straight.

Paws - Full, broad in front, and a trifle inclined outwards; compact with well arched toes and tough pads.

Toes - There are five of these, though only four are in use. They should be close together, with a pronounced arch; provided on top with strong nails, and underneath with tough toe pads. Dewclaws may be removed.

216

Trunk - The whole trunk in general should be long and fully muscled. The back, with sloping shoulders, and short, rigid pelvis, should lie in the straightest possible line between the withers and the very slightly arched loins, these latter being short, rigid and broad.

Chest - The breastbone should be strong, and so prominent in front that on either side a depression (dimple) appears. When viewed from the front, the thorax should appear oval and should extend downward to the mid-point of the forearm. The enclosing structure of ribs should appear full, and oval when viewed from above or from the side, full volumed, so as to allow by its ample capacity, complete development of heart and lungs. Well ribbed up, and gradually merging into the line of the abdomen. If the length is correct, and also the anatomy of the shoulder and upper arm, the front leg when viewed in profile should cover the lowest point of the breast line.

Abdomen - Slightly drawn up.

Hindquarters - The hindquarters viewed from behind should be of completely equal width.

Croup - Long, round, full, robustly muscled, but plastic, only slightly sinking toward the tail.

Pelvic Bones - Not too short, rather strongly developed, and moderately sloping.

Thigh Bone - Robust and of good length, set at right angles to the pelvic bones.

Hind Legs - Robust and well muscled, with well rounded buttocks.

Knee Joint - Broad and strong.

Calf Bone - In comparison with other breeds, short; it should be perpendicular to the thigh bone, and firmly muscled.

The bones at the base of the foot (tarsus) should present a flat appearance, with a strongly prominent hock and a broad tendon of Achilles.

The central foot bones (metatarsus) should be long, movable toward the calf bone, slightly bent toward the front, but perpendicular (as viewed from behind).

Hind Paws - Four compactly closed and beautifully arched toes, as in the case of the front paws. The whole foot should be posed equally on the ball and not merely on the toes; nails short.

Tail - Set in continuation of the spine, extending without very pronounced curvature, and should not be carried too gaily.

NOTE: Inasmuch as the Dachshund is a hunting dog, scars from honorable wounds shall not be considered a fault.

SPECIAL CHARACTERISTICS OF THE THREE COAT VARIETIES

The Dachshund is bred with three varieties of coat: (1) Shorthaired (or Smooth); (2) Wirehaired; (3) Longhaired. All three varieties should conform to the characteristics already specified. The longhaired and shorthaired are old, well fixed varieties, but into the wirehaired Dachshund, the blood of other breeds has been purposely introduced; nevertheless, in breeding him, the greatest stress must be placed upon conformity to the general Dachshund type. The following specifications are applicable separately to the three coat varieties, respectively:

1) SHORTHAIRED (OR SMOOTH) DACHSHUND

Hair - short, thick, smooth and shining; no bald patches. Special faults are: Too fine or thin hair, leathery ears, bald patches, too coarse or too thick hair in general.

Tail- Gradually tapered to a point, well but not too richly haired, long, sleek bristles on the underside are considered a patch of strong-growing hair, not a fault. A brush tail is a fault, as is also a partly or wholly hairless tail.

Color of hair, nose and nails:

One-Colored Dachshund- This group includes red (often called tan), red-yellow, yellow, and brindle, with or without a shading of interspersed black hairs. Nevertheless a clean color is preferable, and red is to be considered more desirable than red-yellow or yellow. Dogs strongly shaded with interspersed black hairs belong to this class, and not to the other color groups. A small, white spot is admissible, but not desirable. Nose and nails - Black; brown is admissable, but not desirable.

Two-Colored Dachshund - These comprise deep black, chocolate, gray (blue), and white; each with tan markings over the eyes, on the sides of the jaw and underlip, on the inner edge of the ear, front, breast, inside and behind the front legs, on the paws and around the anus, and from there to about one-third to one-half of the length of the tail on the under side. The most common two-color Dachshund is usually called black-and-tan. A small white spot is admissible but not desirable. Absence, undue prominence or extreme lightness of tan markings is undesirable. Nose and nails - In the case of black dogs, black; for chocolate, brown (the darker the better); for gray (blue) or white dogs, gray or even flesh color, but the last named color is not desirable; in the case of white dogs, black nose and nails are to be preferred.

Dappled Dachshund - The color of the dappled Dachshund is a clear brownish or grayish color, or even a white ground, with dark irregular patches of dark-gray, brown, red-yellow or black (large areas of one color not desirable). It is desirable that neither the light nor the dark color should predominate. Nose and nails - As for One- and Two-Colored Dachshund.

(2) WIREHAIRED DACHSHUND

The general appearance is the same as that of the shorthaired, but without being long in the legs, it is permissible for the body to be somewhat higher off the ground.

Hair - With the exception of jaw, eyebrows, and ears, the whole body is covered with a perfectly uniform tight, short, thick, rough, hard coat, but with finer, shorter hairs (undercoat) everywhere distributed between the coarser hairs, resembling the coat of the German Wirehaired Pointer. There should be a beard on the chin. The eyebrows are bushy. On the ears the hair is shorter than on the body; almost smooth, but in any case conforming to the rest of the coat. The general arrangement of the hair should be such that the wirehaired Dachshund, when seen from a distance, should resemble the smooth-haired. Any sort of soft hair in the coat is faulty, whether short or long, or wherever found on the body; the same is true of long, curly, or wavy hair, or hair that sticks out irregularly in all directions; a flag tail is also objectionable.

Tail - Robust, as thickly haired as possible, gradually coming to a point, and without a tuft.

Color of hair, nose and nails - All colors are admissible. White patches on the chest, although allowable, are not desirable.

(3) LONGHAIRED DACHSHUNDS

The distinctive characteristic differentiating this coat from the short-haired or smooth-haired Dachshund is along the rather long, silky coat.

Hair - The soft, sleek, glistening, often slightly wavy hair should be longer under the neck, on the underside of the body, and especially on the ears and behind the legs, becoming there a pronounced feather; the hair should attain its greatest length on the underside of the tail. The hair should fall beyond the lower edge of the ear. Short hair on the ear, so-called "leather" ears, is not desirable. Too luxurious a coat causes the longhaired Dachshund to seem coarse, and masks the type. The coat should remind one of the Irish Setter, and should give the dog an elegant appearance. Too thick hair on the paws, so called "mops," is inelegant, and renders the animal unfit for use. It is faulty for the dog to have equally long hair over all the body, if the coat is too curly, or too scrubby, or if a flag tail or overhanging hair on the ears are lacking; or if there is a very pronounced parting on the back, or a vigorous growth between the toes.

Tail - carried gracefully in prolongation of the spine; the hair attains here its greatest length and forms a veritable flag.

Color of hair, nose the nails - Exactly as for the smoothhaired Dachshund, except that the red with black (heavily sabled) color is permissible and is formally classed as a red.

MINIATURE DACHSHUNDS
NOTE: Miniature Dachshunds are bred in all three coats. Within the limits imposed, symmetrical adherence to the general Dachshund conformation, combined with smallness, and mental and physical vitality, should be the outstanding characteristics of Miniature Dachshunds. They have not been given separate classification but are a division of the Open Class for "under 10 pounds and 12 months old or over."

GENERAL FAULTS
Serious Faults - Over- or undershot jaws, knuckling over, very loose shoulders.

Secondary Faults - A weak, long legged, or dragging figure; body hanging between the shoulders; sluggish, clumsy, or waddling gait; toes turned inwards or too obliquely outwards; splayed paws; sunken back, roach (or carp) back; croup higher than withers; short ribbed or too weak chest; excessively drawn-up flanks like those of a Greyhound; narrow, poorly muscled hindquarters; weak loins; bad angulation in front or hindquarters;

cowhocks; bowed legs; wall eyes, except for dappled dogs; bad coat.

· **Minor Faults** - Ears wrongly set, sticking out, narrow or folded; too marked a stop; too pointed or weak a jaw; pincer teeth; too wide or too short a head; goggle eyes, wall eyes in the case of dappled dogs, insufficiently dark eyes in the case of all other coat-colors; dewlaps; short neck; swan neck; too fine or too thin hair; absence of, or too profuse or too light tan markings in the case of two-colored dogs.

Approved January 12, 1971

THE KENNEL CLUB (GREAT BRITAIN) VARIATION TO STANDARD

All six varieties are given separate championship status by The Kennel Club (GB).

LONG-HAIRED: *Tail:* set on fairly high, not too long, tapering and without too marked curve. Not carried too high. Fully feathered.

WIRE-HAIRED: *Tail:* continues line of the spine; is slightly curved, must not be carried too gaily or reach ground when at rest.

WEIGHT AND SIZE: dogs 20 to 22 pounds; bitches 18 to 20 pounds.

THE DACHSHUND CLUB OF AMERICA

AUTHOR'S NOTE: We are very grateful to John Hart, who compiled the following material regarding the Dachshund Club of America National Specialty Shows, for allowing us to publish it in this book. It gives a record of the 51 Specialty Shows held by this club at the time of writing.

The Dachshund Club of America, as previously mentioned, was founded in 1895. The year 1945 was set aside by Dachshund fanciers as the 50th Anniversary of this event, with numerous special events taking place. It was during this period that the DCA Plaque was commissioned of Miss Katherine Ward Lane and first awarded. As most of you are aware, only the smooth head appeared on the plaques until 1971, when Miss Ward rendered a wire head study and Miss Lee Burnham fashioned the longhaired head study. The Dachshund Club of America's gold-filled pins have been awarded since the first Specialty in 1934.

Left to right: Ch. Arnette v Dachshafen, famous smooth bitch owned by Maude Daniels Smith; L. A. Horswell, judge; and Ch. Gunther v Marienlust owned by Mrs. Jeanette W. Cross. The occasion was the Dachshund Club of America's 50th Year Celebration (mid-1940's). Photo courtesy of Mrs. Cross.

The Roll of Honor, compiled by John R. Hart for the Dachshund Club of America, follows:

ROLL OF HONOR

D.C.A.	Location	Longhaired B.O.V.	Smooth B.O.V.	Wirehaired B.O.V.

D.C.A.	Location	Longhaired B.O.V.	Smooth B.O.V.	Wirehaired B.O.V.
1934	Far Hills, N.J. Somerset Hills, KC		CH. Feri Flottenberg (B) (HG 2)	
1935	Madison, N.J. Morris & Essex, KC		CH. Feri Flottenberg (B)	
1936	Madison, N.J. Morris & Essex, KC		CH. Feri Flottenberg (B) (HG 4)	
1937	Madison, N.J. Morris & Essex, KC		CH. Feri Flottenberg (B) (HG 3)	
1938	Madison, N.J. Morris & Essex, KC	Micky v. Teckelhof	CH. Herman Rinkton (B) (HG 1)	Evechen v. Dachshafen
1939	Madison, N.J. Morris & Essex, KC	CH. Koboldina of Dachshafen	CH. Herman Rinkton (B) (HG 2)	CH. Sunstorms Seven of Diamonds
1940	Madison, N.J. Morris & Essex, KC	Grotonia Doru v. Cram	CH. Leutnant v. Marienlust (B)	Menschenfreund's Dusty
1941	Madison, N.J. Morris & Essex, KC	Robin of Riverbank	Trinket of Windyriver (B)	CH. Menschenfreund's Dusty
1942 No.	Katonah, N.Y. Westchester, KC	CH. Robin of Riverbank	CH. Gunther v. Marienlust (B)	Mitzi v. Konkopt
1943	Rye, N.Y. Westchester, KC	CH. Robin of Riverbank	CH. Günther V. Marienlust (HG 1)	CH. Impudence of Edgemere, CD
1944	Rye, N.Y. Westchester, KC	Vicki V. d. Nidda	Bavarian Joy Win Disallowed - Chap. 7, Sect. 4	Gremlin of Edgemere
1945	New York, N.Y. 50th Anniversary Independent Specialty	CH. Zarky of Gypsy Barn	CH. Gunther v. Marienlust (B)	CH. Vagabond Hubertus

D.C.A.	Location	Longhaired B.O.V.	Smooth B.O.V.	Wirehaired B.O.V.
1946	Rye, N.Y. Westchester, KC	CH. William DeSangpur	CH. Bit O' Black of Tween Hills	CH. Mikosz v. Teckeldorf (MW)
1947	Rye, N.Y. Westchester, KC	CH. Mark Anthony of Northmont	CH. Cynthia v. Jo Rene (HG 1)	Menschenfreund's Dusty II
1948	Rye, N.Y. Westchester, KC	CH. William DeSangpur	CH. Wild Fire of Blue Key (HG 2)	CH. Brentwald Joshua W
1949	Rye, N.Y. Westchester, KC	CH. Hussar v.d. Nidda	CH. Cinderella v. Marienlust (HG 2)	CH. Brentwald Joshua W
1950	Rye, N.Y. Westchester, KC	Siefen Jagenheim Hermann	CH. Aristo v. Marienlust (HG 1)	CH. Grunwald Melody
1951	Rye, N.Y. Westchester, KC	Josephine of Knocknagree	CH. Derbydachs Shatze	CH. Thomanef's Lola
1952	Rye, N.Y. Westchester, KC	CH. Hussar v.d. Nidda	CH. Kleetaf's Congenial (HG 2)	CH. York V Murlake
1953	Rye, N.Y. Westchester, KC	CH. Tytucker of Gypsy Barn	CH. Hardway Welcome Stranger	CH. Thomanef's Lola
1954	Rye, N.Y. Westchester, KC	CH. Glenn Valley's Perfedius	CH. Kleetaf's Rondo	CH. Wylde Sumise
1955	Rye, N.Y. Westchester, KC	CH. Guyman's Long Deal	CH. Kim of Lildon (HG 1)	CH. Fir Trees Coco, CD
1956	Purchase, N.Y. Westchester, KC	CH. DeSangpur Wee Allene (HG 2)	CH. Steve V. Marienlust	CH. Josh v. Teckeldorf
1957	Purchase, N.Y. Westchester, KC	CH. DeSangpur Traveling Man, CD	CH. Venture of Hardway	CH. Tubac's Abner W
1958	Purchase, N.Y. Westchester, KC	CH. Crespi's Happy New Year	CH. Venture of Hardway (HG 2)	CH. Dachscroft's William W
1959	Purchase, N.Y. Westchester, KC	CH. Flori of Knocknagree	CH. Celloyd Daniel (HG 1)	Westphal's Thistle W

D.C.A.	Location	Longhaired B.O.V.	Smooth B.O.V.	Wirehaired B.O.V.
1960	Far Hills, N.J. Somerset Hills, KC	CH. Steele's Jamas	CH. Valient of Maridox (HG 4)	CH. Pepper of the Moat
1961	Chicago, IL	CH. Flori of Knocknagree	CH. Bencelia's Intent (B)	Bismarck v. Tolz
1962	New York, N.Y.	CH Roderick von der Nidda	CH. Willo-Mar's Night and Day (B)	CH. Zipper of Glengary
1963	Pebble Beach, CA	CH. Maxsohn Black Majesty	CH. Lynsulee's Luckibelle (B)	CH. Mays Tyna-Mite MW
1964	New York, N.Y.	CH. DeSangpur Traveler's Trix	Dunkeldorf's Falcon Forester (B)	CH. Vantebe's Draht Timothy
1965	Houston, TX	CH. Pegremos Paragon L	CH. Dunkeldorf's Falcon Fantasy (B)	CH. Vantebe's Draht Timothy
1966	New York, N.Y.	CH. Pegremos Paragon L	Crosswynd's Cracker Jack (B)	CH. Pondwick's Hobgoblin
1967	Cleveland, OH	CH. Bayard le Souvenier	CH. Crosswynd's Cracker Jack (B)	CH. Chartamar's Noah W
1968	New York, N.Y.	CH. Robert de Bayard	CH. Crosswynd's Cracker Jack (B)	CH. Elenbusch Jiminy Cricket MW
1969	Louisville, KY	CH. Midas Fancy Decision (B)	CH. Fleming's Jolly Julie	CH. Wilheen's Knight Wire MW
1970	New York, N.Y.	CH. Robdachs Familiar Stranger	CH. Dunkeldorf's Rittmeister (B)	CH. Westphal's Wandering Wind
1971	Los Angeles, CA	B's Javelin de Bayard	CH. Von Relgib's Beau Brummel (B)	CH. Wagner's Cameo W of Heartacres
1972	New York, N.Y.	Bayard le Fenelon	CH. Sundach's Favorite Fleet	CH. Wag's Springwire (B)
1973	Houston, TX	CH. Von Dyck's Mr. Bojangles L	CH. Sweet Bippy V. Hardaway (B)	CH. Rose Farm's Moon Rockette W
1974	Jacksonville, FL	CH. Kemper Dachs Bjorn (B)	CH. Sandwood Musette	CH. Tharp's Boom-Boom W
1975	Cleveland, OH	CH. Delidachs Rolls Royce L (B)	CH. Karstadt's Lionel	Barhar Minnie's Boy W
1976	Seattle, WA	CH. Delidachs Rolls Royce L (B)	CH. Farmeadow Light Up The Sky	CH. Barhar Minnie's Boy W
1977	Arlington, VA	CH. Delidachs Bentley L (B)	CH. Farmeadow Light Up The Sky	CH. Barhar Pickwick
1978	Kansas City, KS	CH. Han-Jo's Candyman L (B)	CH. Farmeadow Light Up The Sky	CH. Wag's Shadrac
1979	Jacksonville, FL	CH. Van Dyke's Johnny One Note L (B)	CH. Villanof's Gladiator	CH. Saytar Bow Jr. of Joyal
1980	Denver, CO	CH. Blairhaven Star Majesty L (B)	CH. Doxhaus Accolade	CH. Coja Fred Wire
1981	Houston, TX	CH. Robdach's Traminer (B)	Barbadox Jewel	CH. Bristleknoll Brass Buttons
1982	Herndon, VA	CH. Suntura's Blue Max ML (B)	CH. Braaehaus Big Bouy	CH. Lauterdach's Dukat W

D.C.A.	Location	Longhaired B.O.V.	Smooth B.O.V.	Wirehaired B.O.V.
1983	Nashville, TN	CH. Sleepy Hollow's Lion Hearted (B)	CH. Choo Choo Sweetheart	CH. Maraldachs Heinzelman W
1984	Trerose, PA	CH. Bayard le Maximilien (B)	CH. Barbadox Andi	CH. Be Patient Buccaneer W

224

Chapter 9

On Owning a Dachshund

The Dachshund is one of the world's most versatile breeds of dog, having many features to please many people. Originally created as a working dog with strong terrier tendencies, these characteristics remain today if one chooses to encourage and develop them. Your Dachshund is as well adapted as any terrier to "go to ground," plus the added advantage of the keen sense of smell associated with the scent-hound.

Although in many ways a dog who loves the outdoors, a Dachshund also loves his comforts, and will slip very easily into a "family dog" routine if that is what fits your way of life. A soft spot by the fire, or beside you on the sofa, or even on your lap is well appreciated by any of the Dachshunds I have ever met.

Where else can you find a breed of dog who comes in three different coats and two different sizes? Such diversity is an added advantage in looking for "the" dog! We understand that the Minis are every bit as hardy and well able to work as the Standards, and both come within my "handy home size" designation. But, depending on your plans for the dog, there are some situations in which each size is preferable. For example, if you are "on the go" a lot, and like to take your dog along, a Miniature is a cinch for that purpose; light enough to be carried easily; small enough to fit into a carrier beneath or on your plane seat; kept well, happy and satisfied with only a minimal amount of exercise; thus ideal if you live in a small apartment. A Standard, on the other hand, is great for suburban or country living yet still easy to handle, and I feel is the better of the two for young children as the dog is less likely to be hurt if played with too roughly.

To many people, the Smooth Dachshund is the *real* Dachshund—the one whose picture comes to mind immediately the

Miniature Dachshunds and kids get on well together. Here is Dorothy Poole's grandson, Christopher C. Poole, with two of his Grandmother's noted winners. The Wire is Ch. Wilheen's Schon of Doracher MW. The Longhair is Ch. Patchwork Stage Door Johnny.

breed is mentioned. They are beautiful dogs and the easiest of the three coat types to handle, needing little in the line of daily coat care. The Longhairs are usually considered to be the most glamorous, which they very likely are, in full coat with fringes in abundance. They do demand coat-care in the form of frequent brushing, but it is almost worth the trouble because the dog is so elegant when finished. As for the Wire, the comical expression provided by his whiskering, and his sturdy coat type, are instantly endearing to practically everyone who looks at one of these dogs.

226

He is the most "different" of the three, very much an individual, with probably a stronger instinct towards his terrier heritage than the others.

As a former city dweller, my choice for this purpose would be a Smooth or a Wire in whichever size appeals most to you for life in one of the big cities. A full coated Longhair fairly sweeps the ground and can be pretty constantly in need of bathing and grooming to remove from his coat soot and dirt from the streets. The neatness of the smooth coat is ideal in these circumstances; and the wirehair coat is not flowing, nor are the legs normally so short on a wire as on a long, thus he does not "sweep the streets."

Dachshunds are great with children, love them, and get on well. One word of caution—if your kids are young and might possibly be rough with a puppy, take the larger size as being better able to withstand this without injury.

Dachshunds get on well with other household pets, especially when the introductions are made while one or the other is still a baby. They are marvelous watch dogs, too, having throaty "hound voices" that sound very impressive from behind a door.

If you are interested in starting with a breed which is fun to show, here again the Dachshund shines. They are an easy size for the average owner to handle and can be handled and gaited beautifully without tremendous exertion. A moderate walking speed on your part usually fits in with just the right gait for their short legs; you stack them (set them in show position) on the table for the judge's examination which for many people is easier than doing so on the ground. And you can make grooming as easy or as challenging as you wish, depending on which coat type you select--ranging from least work, Smooth; moderate, Longhair; and most difficult to do correctly, Wire.

If you have a young prospective Junior Showmanship star in your family, here again, any of the Dachshunds are extremely manageable and easily controlled by a youngster.

Their alertness and intelligence make Dachshunds great dogs for obedience work, and very easily trainable. Note the many C.D. and more advanced obedience degrees that have been earned by Dachshunds pictured or written of in this book!

You will love your Dachshund's comical ways and sense of humor. They are never a bore and have many amusing and endearing behavior characteristics.

Chapter 10

The Purchase of Your Dachshund

Careful consideration should be given to what breed of dog you wish to own prior to your purchase of one. If several breeds are attractive to you, and you are undecided as to which you prefer, learn all you can about the characteristics of each before making your decision. As you do so, you are thus preparing yourself to make an intelligent choice; and this is very important when buying a dog who will be, with reasonable luck, a member of your household for at least a dozen years or more. Obviously since you are reading this book, you have decided on the breed—so now all that remains is to make a good choice.

It is never wise to just rush out and buy the first cute puppy who catches your eye. Whether you wish a dog to show, one with whom to compete in obedience, or one as a family dog purely for his (or her) companionship, the more time and thought you invest as you plan the purchase, the more likely you are to meet with complete satisfaction. The background and early care behind your pet will reflect in the dog's future health and temperament. Even if you are planning the purchase purely as a pet, with no thoughts of showing or breeding in the dog's or puppy's future, it is essential that if the dog is to enjoy a trouble-free future you assure yourself of a healthy, properly raised puppy or adult from sturdy, well-bred stock.

Throughout the pages of this book you will find the names and locations of many well-known and well-established kennels in various areas. Another source of information is the American Kennel Club (51 Madison Avenue, New York, New York 10010) from whom you can obtain a list of recognized breeders in the vicinity of your home. If you plan to have your dog campaigned by a professional handler, by all means let the handler help you locate and select a good dog. Through their numerous clients, handlers have access to a variety of interesting show prospects; and the usual arrangement is that the handler re-sells the dog to you for what his cost has been, with the agreement that the dog be campaigned for you by him throughout the dog's career. It is most strongly recommended that prospective purchasers follow these suggestions, as you thus will be better able to locate and select a satisfactory puppy or dog.

Your first step in searching for your puppy is to make appointments at kennels specializing in your breed, where you can visit and inspect the dogs, both those available for sale and the kennel's basic breeding stock. You are looking for an active, sturdy puppy with bright eyes and intelligent expression and who is friendly and alert; avoid puppies who are hyperactive, dull, or listless. The coat should be clean and thick, with no sign of parasites. The premises on which he was raised should look (and smell) clean and be tidy, making it obvious that the puppies and their surroundings are in capable hands. Should the kennels featuring the breed you intend owning be sparse in your area or not have what you consider attractive, do not hesitate to contact others at a distance and purchase from them if they seem better able to supply a puppy or dog who will please you *so long as it is a recognized breeding kennel of that breed.* Shipping dogs is a regular practice nowadays, with comparatively few problems when one considers the number of dogs shipped each year. A reputable, well-known breeder wants the customer to be satisfied; thus he will represent the puppy fairly. Should you not be pleased with the puppy upon arrival, a breeder such as described will almost certainly permit its return. A conscientious breeder takes real interest and concern in the welfare of the dogs he or she causes to be brought into the world. Such a breeder also is proud of a reputation for integrity. Thus on two counts, for the sake of the dog's future and the breeder's reputation, to such a person a *satisfied* customer takes precedence over a sale at any cost.

If your puppy is to be a pet or "family dog," the earlier the age at which it joins your household the better. Puppies are weaned and ready to start out on their own, under the care of a sensible new owner, at about six weeks old; and if you take a young one, it is often easier to train it to the routine of your household and to your requirements of it than is the case with an older dog which,

229

even though still a puppy technically, may have already started habits you will find difficult to change. The younger puppy is usually less costly, too, as it stands to reason the breeder will not have as much expense invested in it. Obviously, a puppy that has been raised to five or six months old represents more in care and cash expenditure on the breeder's part than one sold earlier and therefore should be and generally is priced accordingly.

There is an enormous amount of truth in the statement that "bargain" puppies seldom turn out to be that. A "cheap" puppy, cheaply raised purely for sale and profit, can and often does lead to great heartbreak including problems and veterinarian's bills which can add up to many times the initial cost of a properly reared dog. On the other hand, just because a puppy is expensive does not assure one that is healthy and well reared. There have been numerous cases where unscrupulous dealers have sold for several hundred dollars puppies that were sickly, in poor condition, and such poor specimens that the breed of which they were supposedly members was barely recognizable. So one cannot always judge a puppy by price alone. Common sense must guide a prospective purchaser, plus the selection of a *reliable*, well-recommended dealer whom you know to have well satisfied customers or, best of all, a specialized breeder. You will probably find the fairest pricing at the kennel of a breeder. Such a person, experienced with the breed in general and with his or her own stock in particular, through extensive association with these dogs has watched enough of them mature to have obviously learned to assess quite accurately each puppy's potential—something impossible where such background is non-existent.

One more word on the subject of pets. Bitches make a fine choice for this purpose as they are usually quieter and more gentle than the males, easier to house train, more affectionate, and less inclined to roam. If you do select a bitch and have no intention of breeding or showing her, by all means have her spayed, for your sake and for hers. The advantages to the owner of a spayed bitch include avoiding the nuisance of "in season" periods which normally occur twice yearly, with the accompanying eager canine swains haunting your premises in an effort to get close to your female, plus the unavoidable messiness and spotting of furniture and rugs at this time, which can be annoying if she is a household companion in the habit of sharing your sofa or bed. As for the spayed bitch, she benefits as she grows older because this simple operation almost entirely eliminates the possibility of breast cancer ever occurring. It is recommended that all bitches eventually be spayed—even those used for show or breeding when their careers have ended—in order that they may enjoy a happier, healthier old age. Please take note, however, that a bitch who has been spayed (or an altered dog) *cannot be shown at American Kennel Club dog shows once this operation has been performed.* Be certain that you are *not* interested in showing her before taking this step.

Also, in selecting a pet, never underestimate the advantages of an older dog, perhaps a retired show dog or a bitch no longer needed for breeding, who may be available quite reasonably priced by a breeder anxious to place such a dog in a loving home. These dogs are settled and can be a delight to own, as they make wonderful companions, especially in a household of adults where raising a puppy can sometimes be a trial.

Everything that has been said about careful selection of your pet puppy and its place of purchase applies, but with many further considerations, when you plan to buy a show dog or foundation stock for a future breeding program. Now is the time for an in-depth study of the breed, starting with every word and every illustration in this book and all others you can find written on the subject. The Standard of the breed now has become your guide, and you must learn not only the words but also how to interpret them and how they are applicable in actual dogs before you are ready to make an intelligent selection of a show dog.

If you are thinking in terms of a dog to show, obviously you must have learned about dog shows and must be in the habit of attending them. This is fine, but now your activity in this direction should be increased, with your attending every single dog show within a reasonable distance from your home. Much can be learned about a breed at ringside at these events. Talk with the breeders who are exhibiting. Study the dogs they are showing. Watch the judging with concentration, noting each decision made, and attempt to follow the reasoning by which the judge has reached it. Note carefully the attributes of the dogs who win and, for your later use, the manner in which each is presented. Close your ears to the ringside know-it-alls, usually novice owners of only a dog or two and very new to the Fancy, who have only derogatory remarks to make about all that is taking place unless they happen to win. This is the type of exhibitor who "comes and goes" through the Fancy and whose interest is usually of very short duration owing to lack of knowledge and dissatisfaction caused by the failure to recognize the need to learn. You, as a fancier it is hoped will last and enjoy our sport over many future years, should develop independent thinking at this stage; you should learn to draw your own conclusions about the merits, or lack of them, seen before you in the ring and, thus, sharpen your own judgement in preparation for choosing wisely and well.

Note carefully which breeders campaign winning dogs, not just an occasional isolated good one but consistent, homebred winners. It is from one of these people that you should select your own future "star."

If you are located in an area where dog shows take place only occasionally or where there are long travel distances involved, you will need to find another testing ground for your ability to select a worthy show dog. Possibly, there are some representative kennels raising this breed within a reasonable distance. If so, by all means ask permission of the owners to visit the kennels and do so when permission is granted. You may not necessarily buy then and there, as they may not have available what you are seeking that very day, but you will be able to see the type of dog being raised there and to discuss the dogs with the breeder. Every time you do this, you add to your knowledge. Should one of these kennels have dogs which especially appeal to you, perhaps you could reserve a show-prospect puppy from a coming litter. This is frequently done, and it is often worth waiting for a puppy, unless you have seen a dog with which you truly are greatly impressed and which is immediately available.

The purchase of a puppy has already been discussed. Obviously this same approach applies in a far greater degree when the purchase involved is a future show dog. The only place at which to purchase a show prospect is from a breeder who raises show-type stock; otherwise, you are almost certainly doomed to disappointment as the puppy matures. Show and breeding kennels obviously cannot keep all of their fine young stock. An active breeder-exhibitor is, therefore, happy to place promising youngsters in the hands of people also interested in showing and winning with them, doing so at a fair price according to the quality and prospects of the dog involved. Here again, if no kennel in your imme-

Ch. Jiridox Jujube with his owner Peggy Westphal in 1970. This lovely dog, by Ch. Kleetal's Raven Wing ex Ch. Ardencaple Royal Sattelite, was bred by Mr. and Mrs. Richard Gotschall, born August 1968.

diate area has what you are seeking, do not hesitate to contact top breeders in other areas and to buy at long distance. Ask for pictures, pedigrees, and a complete description. Heed the breeder's advice and recommendations, after truthfully telling exactly what your expectations are for the dog you purchase. Do you want something with which to win just a few ribbons now and then? Do you want a dog who can complete his championship? Are you thinking of the real "big time" (*i.e.,* seriously campaigning with Best of Breed, Group wins, and possibly even Best in Show as

233

your eventual goal)? Consider it all carefully in advance; then honestly discuss your plans with the breeder. You will be better satisfied with the results if you do this, as the breeder is then in the best position to help you choose the dog who is most likely to come through for you. A breeder selling a show dog is just as anxious as the buyer for the dog to succeed, and the breeder will represent the dog to you with truth and honesty. Also, this type of breeder does not lose interest the moment the sale has been made but when necessary will be right there ready to assist you with beneficial advice and suggestions based on years of experience.

As you make inquiries of at least several kennels, keep in mind that show-prospect puppies are less expensive than mature show dogs, the latter often costing close to four figures, and sometimes more. The reason for this is that, with a puppy, there is always an element of chance, the possibility of its developing unexpected faults as it matures or failing to develop the excellence and quality that earlier had seemed probable. There definitely is a risk factor in buying a show-prospect puppy. Sometimes all goes well, but occasionally the swan becomes an ugly duckling. Reflect on this as you consider available puppies and young adults. It just might be a good idea to go with a more mature, though more costly, dog if one you like is available.

When you buy a mature show dog, "what you see is what you get," and it is not likely to change beyond coat and condition which are dependent on your care. Also advantageous for a novice owner is the fact that a mature dog of show quality almost certainly will have received show-ring training and probably match-show experience, which will make your earliest handling ventures far easier.

Frequently it is possible to purchase a beautiful dog who has completed championship but who, owing to similarity in bloodlines, is not needed for the breeder's future program. Here you have the opportunity of owning a champion, usually in the two-to-five-year-old range, which you can enjoy campaigning as a special (for Best of Breed competition) and which will be a settled, handsome dog for you and your family to enjoy with pride.

If you are planning foundation for a future kennel, concentrate on acquiring one or two really superior bitches. These need not necessarily be top show-quality, but they should represent your breed's finest producing bloodlines from a strain noted for producing quality, generation after generation. A proven matron who is already the dam of show-type puppies is, of course, the ideal selection; but these are usually difficult to obtain, no one being anxious to part with so valuable an asset. You just might strike it lucky, though, in which case you are off to a flying start. If you cannot find such a matron available, select a young bitch of finest background from top-producing lines who is herself of decent type, free of obvious faults, and of good quality.

Great attention should be paid to the pedigree of the bitch from whom you intend to breed. If not already known to you, try to see the sire and dam. It is generally agreed that someone starting with a breed should concentrate on a fine collection of topflight bitches and raise a few litters from these before considering keeping one's own stud dog. The practice of buying a stud and then breeding everything you own or acquire to that dog does not always work out well. It is better to take advantage of the many noted sires who are available to be used at stud, who represent all of the leading strains, and in each case to carefully select the one who in type and pedigree seems most compatible to each of your bitches, at least for your first several litters.

To summarize, if you want a "family dog" as a companion, it is best to buy it young and raise it according to the habits of your household. If you are buying a show dog, the more mature it is, the more certain you can be of its future beauty. If you are buying foundation stock for a kennel, then bitches are better, but they must be from the finest *producing* bloodlines.

When you buy a pure-bred dog that you are told is eligible for registration with the American Kennel Club, you are entitled to receive from the seller an application form which will enable you to register your dog. If the seller cannot give you the application form you should demand and receive an identification of your dog consisting of the name of the breed, the registered names and numbers of the sire and dam, the name of the breeder, and your dog's date of birth. If the litter of which your dog is a part is already recorded with the American Kennel Club, then the litter number is sufficient identification.

Do not be misled by promises of papers at some later date. Demand a registration application form or proper identification as described above. If neither is supplied, do not buy the dog. So warns the American Kennel Club, and this is especially important in the purchase of show or breeding stock.

Chapter 11

The Care of Your Dachshund Puppy

The moment you decide to be the new owner of a puppy is not one second too soon to start planning for the puppy's arrival in your home. Both the new family member and you will find the transition period easier if your home is geared in advance of the arrival.

The first things to be prepared are a bed for the puppy and a place where you can pen him up for rest periods. Every dog should have a crate of its own from the very beginning, so that he will come to know and love it as his special place where he is safe and happy. It is an ideal arrangement, for when you want him to be free, the crate stays open. At other times you can securely latch it and know that the pup is safely out of mischief. If you travel with him, his crate comes along in the car; and, of course, in traveling by plane there is no alternative but to have a carrier for the dog. If you show your dog, you will want him upon occasion to be in a crate a good deal of the day. So from every consideration, a crate is a very sensible and sound investment in your puppy's future safety and happiness and for your own peace of mind.

The crates most desirable are the wooden ones with removable side panels, which are ideal for cold weather (with the panels in place to keep out drafts) and in hot weather (with the panels removed to allow better air circulation). Wire crates are all right in the summer, but they give no protection from cold or drafts. Aluminum crates, due to the manner in which the metal reflects surrounding temperatures, are not recommended. If it is cold, so is the metal of the crate; if it is hot, the crate becomes burning hot.

When you choose the puppy's crate, be certain that it is roomy enough not to become outgrown. The crate should have sufficient height so the dog can stand up in it as a mature dog and sufficient area so that he can stretch out full length when relaxed. When the puppy is young, first give him shredded newspaper as a bed; the papers can be replaced with a mat or turkish towels when the dog is older. Carpet remnants are great for the bottom of the crate, as they are inexpensive and in case of accidents can be quite easily replaced. As the dog matures and is past the chewing age, a pillow or blanket in the crate is an appreciated comfort.

Sharing importance with the crate is a safe area in which the puppy can exercise and play. If you are an apartment dweller, a baby's playpen can work out well. If you have a yard, an area where he can be outside in safety should be fenced in prior to the dog's arrival at your home. This area does not need to be huge, but it does need to be made safe and secure. If you are in a suburban area where there are close neighbors, stockade fencing works out best as then the neighbors are less aware of the dog and the dog cannot see and bark at everything passing by. If you are out in the country where no problems with neighbors are likely to occur, then regular chain-link fencing is fine. For added precaution in both cases, use a row of concrete blocks or railroad ties inside against the entire bottom of the fence; this precludes or at least considerably lessens the chances of your dog digging his way out.

Be advised that if yours is a single dog, it is very unlikely that it will get sufficient exercise just sitting in the fenced area, which is what most of them do when they are there alone. Two or more dogs will play and move themselves around, but one by itself does little more than make a leisurely tour once around the area to check things over and then lie down. You must include a daily walk or two in your plans if your puppy is to be rugged and well. Exercise is extremely important to a puppy's muscular development and to keep a mature dog fit and trim. So make sure that those exercise periods, or walks, a game of ball, and other such activities, are part of your daily program as a dog owner.

If your fenced area has an outside gate, provide a padlock and key and a strong fastening for it, and use them, so that the gate cannot be opened by others and the dog taken or turned free. The ultimate convenience in this regard is, of course, a door (unused for other purposes) from the house around which the fenced area can be enclosed, so that all you have to do is open the door and out into his area he goes. This arrangement is safest of all, as then you need not be using a gate, and it is easier in bad weather since then you can send the dog out without taking him and becoming soaked yourself at the same time. This is not always possible to manage, but if your house is arranged so that you could do it this way, you would never regret it due to the convenience and added safety thus provided. Fencing in the entire yard, with gates to be opened and closed whenever a caller, deliveryman, postman, or some other person comes on your property, really is not safe at all because people not used to gates and their importance are frequently careless about closing and latching gates *securely*. Many heartbreaking incidents have been brought about by someone carelessly only half closing a gate which the owner had thought to be firmly latched and the dog wandering out. For greatest security a fenced *area* definitely takes precedence over a fenced *yard*.

The puppy will need a collar (one that fits now, not one to be grown into) and a lead from the moment you bring him home. Both should be an appropriate weight and type for his size. Also needed are a feeding dish and a water dish, both made preferably of unbreakable material. Your pet supply shop should have an interesting assortment of these and other accessories from which you can choose. Then you will need grooming tools of the type the breeder recommends and some toys. Equally satisfactory is Nylabone®, a nylon bone that does not chip or splinter and that "frizzles" as the puppy chews, providing healthful gum massage. Rawhide chews are safe, too, *if made in the United States*. There was a problem a few years back, owing to the chemicals with which some foreign rawhide toys had been treated. Also avoid plastics and any sort of rubber toys, *particularly those with squeakers* which the puppy may remove and swallow. If you want a ball for the puppy to use when playing with him, select one of very hard construction made for this purpose and do not leave it alone with him because he may chew off and swallow bits of the rubber. Take the ball with you when the game is over. This also applies to some of those "tug of war" type rubber toys which are fun when used with the two of you for that purpose but again should *not* be left behind for the dog to work on with his teeth. Bits of swallowed rubber, squeakers, and other such foreign articles can wreak great havoc in the intestinal tract—do all you can to guard against them.

Too many changes all at once can be difficult for a puppy. For at least the first few days he is with you, keep him on the food and feeding schedule to which he is accustomed. Find out ahead

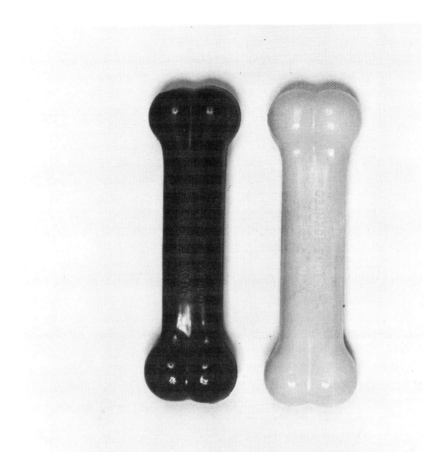

Nylabone® is the safest chewing pacifier you can give your dog, as it is non-abrasive and clean, and the thin nylon shavings pass through the dog's system without effect. Veterinarians and pet shops highly endorse these effective products.

of time from the breeder what he feeds his puppies, how frequently, and at what times of the day. Also find out what, if any, food supplements the breeder has been using and recommends. Then be prepared by getting in a supply of the same food so that you will have it there when you bring the puppy home. Once the puppy is accustomed to his new surroundings, then you can switch the type of food and schedule to fit your convenience, but for the first several days do it as the puppy expects.

Your selection of a veterinarian also should be attended to before the puppy comes home, because you should stop at the vet's office for the puppy to be checked over as soon as you leave the breeder's premises. If the breeder is from your area, ask him for recommendations. Ask you dog-owning friends for their opinions of the local veterinarians, and see what their experiences with those available have been. Choose someone whom several of your friends recommend highly, then contact him about your puppy, perhaps making an appointment to stop in at his office. If the premises are clean, modern, and well equipped, and if you like the veterinarian, make an appointment to bring the puppy in on the day of purchase. Be sure to obtain the puppy's health record from the breeder, including information on such things as shots and worming that the puppy has had.

JOINING THE FAMILY

Remember that, exciting and happy an occasion as it is for you, the puppy's move from his place of birth to your home can be, for him, a traumatic experience. His mother and littermates will be missed. He quite likely will be awed or frightened by the change of surroundings. the person on whom he depended will be gone. Everything should be planned to make his arrival at your home pleasant—to give him confidence and to help him realize that yours is a pretty nice place to be after all.

Never bring a puppy home on a holiday. There just is too much going on with people and gifts and excitement. If he is in honor of an "occasion," work it out so that his arrival will be a few days earlier, or perhaps even better, a few days later than the "occasion." Then your home will be back to it normal routine and the puppy can enjoy your undivided attention. Try not to bring the puppy home in the evening. Early morning is the ideal time, as then he has the opportunity of getting acquainted and the initial strangeness should wear off before bedtime. You will find it a more peaceful night that way. Allow the puppy to investigate as he likes, under your watchful eye. If you already have a pet in the household, keep a careful watch that the relationship between the two gets off to a friendly start or you may quickly find yourself with a lasting problem. Much of the future attitude of each toward the other will depend on what takes place that first day, so keep your mind on what they are doing and let your other activities

Ch. Sheen v Westphalen as a puppy. One of Peggy Westphal's important winning Smooths of the 1960's. By Ch. Dunkeldorf Falcon's Favorite ex Fleet 'n' Lovely v Westphalen. Bred by Janet Koltun.

slide for the moment. Be careful not to let your older pet become jealous by paying more attention to the puppy than to him, as that will start a bad situation immediately.

If you have a child, here again it is important that the relationship start out well. Before the puppy is brought home, you should have a talk with the youngster about puppies so that it will be clearly understood that puppies are fragile and can easily be injured; therefore, they should not be teased, hurt, mauled, or overly rough-housed. A puppy is not an inanimate toy; it is a living thing with a right to be loved and handled respectfully, treatment which will reflect in the dog's attitude toward your child as both mature together. Never permit your children's playmates to mishandle the puppy, tormenting the puppy until it turns on the children in self-defense. Children often do not realize how rough is too rough. You, as a responsible adult, are obligated to assure that your puppy's relationships with children is a pleasant one.

241

Do not start out by spoiling your puppy. A puppy is usually pretty smart and can be quite demanding. What you had considered to be "just for tonight" may be accepted by the puppy as "for keeps." Be firm with him, strike a routine, and stick to it. The puppy will learn more quickly this way, and everyone will be happier at the result. A radio playing softly or a dim night light are often comforting to a puppy as it gets accustomed to new surroundings and should be provided in preference to bring the puppy to bed with you—unless, of course, you intend him to share the bed as a permanent arrangement.

SOCIALIZING AND TRAINING

Socialization and training of your puppy should start the very day of his arrival in your home. Never address him without calling him by name. A short, simple name is the easiest to teach as it catches the dog's attention quickly, so avoid elaborate call names. Always address the dog by the same name, not a whole series of pet names; the latter will only confuse the puppy.

Use his name clearly, and call the puppy over to you when you see him awake and wandering about. When he comes, make a big fuss over him for being such a good dog. He thus will quickly associate the sound of his name with coming to you and a pleasant happening.

Several hours after the puppy's arrival is not too soon to start accustoming him to the feel of a light collar. He may hardly notice it; or he may struggle, roll over, and try to rub it off his neck with his paws. Divert his attention when this occurs by offering a tasty snack or a toy (starting a game with him) or by petting him. Before long he will have accepted the strange feeling around his neck and no longer appear aware of it. Next comes the lead. Attach it and then immediately take the puppy outside or otherwise try to divert his attention with things to see and sniff. He may struggle against the lead at first, biting at it and trying to free himself. Do not pull him with it at this point; just hold the end loosely and try to follow him if he starts off in any direction. Normally his attention will soon turn to investigating his sourroundings if he is outside or you have taken him into an unfamiliar room in your house; curiosity will take over and he will become interested in sniffing around the surroundings. Just follow him with the lead slackly held until he seems to have completely forgotten about it; then try

Old Dominion 1958. Marcia Wheeler showing future Champion Willo-Mar's Lucky Strike at his first show where he took Best of Winners from the puppy class. Barbara Lovering with the Best of Opposite Sex, future Champion Willo-Mar's Queen of Spades. Both sired by Ch. Saber of Gera. Judge is Jerry Cross, a famous Dachshund breeder.

with gentle urging to get him to follow you. Don't be rough or jerk at him; just tug gently on the lead in short quick motions (steady pulling can become a battle of wills), repeating his name or trying to get him to follow your hand which is holding a bite of food or an interesting toy. If you have an older lead-trained dog, then it should be a cinch to get the puppy to follow along after *him*. In any event the average puppy learns quite quickly and will soon be trotting along nicely on the lead. Once that point has been reached, the next step is to teach him to follow on your left side, or heel. Of course this will not likely be accomplished all in one day but should be done with short training periods over the course of several days until you are satisfied with the result.

During the course of house training your puppy, you will need to take him out frequently and at regular intervals: first thing in the morning directly from the crate, immediately after meals, after the puppy has been napping, or when you notice that the puppy is looking for a spot. Choose more or less the same place to take the puppy each time so that a pattern will be established. If he does not go immediately, do not return him to the house as he will probably relieve himself the moment he is inside. Stay out with him until he has finished; then be lavish with your praise for his good behavior. If you catch the puppy having an accident indoors, grab him firmly and rush him outside, sharply saying "No!" as you pick him up. If you do not see the accident occur, there is little point in doing anything except cleaning it up, as once it has happened and been forgotten, the puppy will most likely not even realize why you are scolding him.

Especially if you live in a big city or are away many hours at a time, having a dog that is trained to go on paper has some very definite advantages. To do this, one proceeds pretty much the same way as taking the puppy outdoors, except now you place the puppy on the newspaper at the proper time. The paper should always be kept in the same spot. An easy way to paper train a puppy if you have a playpen for it or an exercise pen is to line the area with newspapers; then gradually, every day or so, remove a section of newspaper until you are down to just one or two. The puppy acquires the habit of using the paper; and as the prepared area grows smaller, in the majority of cases the dog will continue to use whatever paper is still available. It is pleasant, if the dog is alone for an excessive length of time, to be able to feel that if he needs it the paper is there and will be used.

The puppy should form the habit of spending a certain amount of time in his crate, even when you are home. Sometimes the puppy will do this voluntarily, but if not, he should be taught to do so, which is accomplished by leading the puppy over by his collar, gently pushing him inside, and saying firmly, "Down" or "Stay." Whatever expression you use to give a command, stick to the very same one each time for each act. Repetition is the big thing in training—and so is association with what the dog is expected to do. When you mean "Sit" always say exactly that. "Stay" should mean *only* that the dog should remain where he receives the command. "Down" means something else again. Do

Here are four generations of the noted Moffett's Dachshunds, taken at the Mid-West Dachshund Club Specialty Show in 1979. *Left to right:* Ch. Filsheim's Friendly Jester, Ch. Moffett's Georgi, Ch. Cook's Home Brew, and Ch. Moffett's Midas. These important and beautiful dogs have contributed greatly to the quality of Smooth Dachshunds. Mrs. Thelma Moffett, Flint, Michigan.

not confuse the dog by shuffling the commands, as this will create training problems for you.

As soon as he had had his immunization shots, take your puppy with you whenever and wherever possible. There is nothing that will build a self-confident, stable dog like socialization, and it is extremely important that you plan and give the time and energy necessary for this whether your dog is to be a show dog or a pleasant, well-adjusted family member. Take your puppy in the car so that he will learn to enjoy riding and not become carsick as dogs may do if they are infrequent travelers. Take him anywhere you are going where you are certain he will be welcome: visiting friends and relative (if they do not have housepets who may resent the visit), busy shopping centers (keeping him always on lead), or just walking around the streets of your town. If someone admires him (as always seems to happen when one is out with puppies), encourage the stranger to pet and talk with him. Socialization of this type brings out the best in your puppy and helps him to grow up with a friendly outlook, liking the world and its inhabitants. The worst thing that can be done to a puppy's personality is to overly shelter him. By always keeping him at home away from things and people unfamiliar to him you may be creating a personality problem for the mature dog that will be a cross for you to bear later on.

FEEDING YOUR DOG

Time was when providing nourishing food for dogs involved a far more complIcated procedure than people now feel is necessary. The old school of thought was that the daily ration must consist of fresh beef, vegetables, cereal, egg yolks, and cottage cheese as basics with such additions as brewer's yeast and vitamin tablets on a daily basis.

During recent years, however, many minds have changed regarding this procedure. Eggs, cottage cheese, and supplements to the diet are still given, but the basic method of feeding dogs has changed; and the change has been, in the opinion of many authorities, definitely for the better. The school of thought now is that you are doing your dogs a favor when you feed them some of the fine commercially prepared dog foods in preference to your own home-cooked concoctions.

The reason behind this new outlook is easily understandable. The dog food industry has grown to be a major one, participated in by some of the best known and most respected names in America. These trusted firms, it is agreed, turn out excellent products, so people are feeding their dog food preparations with confidence and the dogs are thriving, living longer, happier, and healthier lives than ever before. What more could one want?

There are at least half a dozen absolutely top-grade dry foods to be mixed with broth or water and served to your dog according to directions. There are all sorts of canned meats, and there are several kinds of "convenience foods," those in a packet which you open and dump out into the dog's dish. It is just that simple. The convenience foods are neat and easy to use when you are away from home, but generally speaking a dry food mixed with hot water or soup and meat is preferred. It is the opinion of many that the canned meat, with its added fortifiers, is more beneficial to the dogs than the fresh meat. However, the two can be alternated or, if you prefer and your dog does well on it, by all means use fresh ground beef. A dog enjoys changes in the meat part of his diet, which is easy with the canned food since all sorts of beef are available (chunk, ground, stewed, and so on), plus lamb, chicken, and even such concoctions as liver and egg, just plain liver flavor, and a blend of five meats.

There is also prepared food geared to every age bracket of your dog's life, from puppyhood on through old age, with special additions or modifications to make it particularly nourishing and beneficial. Previous generations never had it so good where the canine dinner is concerned, because these commercially prepared foods are tasty and geared to meeting the dog's gastronomic approval.

Additionally, contents and nutrients are clearly listed on the labels, as are careful instructions for feeding just the right amount for the size, weight, and age of each dog.

With these foods the addition of extra vitamins is not necessary, but if you prefer there are several kinds of those, too, that serve as taste treats as well as being beneficial. Your pet supplier has a full array of them.

Of course there is no reason not to cook up something for your dog if you would feel happier doing so. But it seems unnecessary when such truly satisfactory rations are available with so much less trouble and expense.

How often you feed your dog is a matter of how it works out best for you. Many owners prefer to do it once a day. It is generally agreed that two meals, each of smaller quantity, are better for the digestion and more satisfying to the dog, particularly if yours is a household member who stands around and watches preparations for the family meals. Do not overfeed. This is the shortest route to all sorts of problems. Follow directions and note carefully how your dog is looking. If your dog is overweight, cut back the quantity of food a bit. If the dog looks thin, then increase the amount. Each dog is an individual and the food intake should be adjusted to his requirements to keep him feeling and looking trim and in top condition.

From the time puppies are fully weaned until they are about twelve weeks old, they should be fed four times daily. From three months to six months of age, three meals should suffice. At six months of age the puppies can be fed two meals, and the twice daily feedings can be continued until the puppies are close to one year old, at which time feeding can be changed to once daily if desired. If you do feed just once a day, do so by early afternoon at the latest and give the dog a snack, a biscuit or two, at bedtime.

Remember that plenty of fresh water should always be available to your puppy or dog for drinking. This is of utmost importance to his health.

Chapter 12

Grooming the Dachshund

For those of you who own a Dachshund purely for "the pleasure of his company," grooming is a far simpler matter. He should be bathed only when necessary (brushed first, to remove loose, dead hairs) and brushed frequently to keep his coat healthy and shining. Here again, the Smooth is the easiest of all, since the routine with this variety is minimal.

Special notes on the Longhairs are that the back of the neck and the body should be combed on a regular basis with the Real Stripping Knife mentioned by Mrs. Hutchinson under Show Grooming as it is outstandingly efficient in removing undercoat and dead hair, keeping the coat fresh and in top condition. The hair on the bottom of the feet should be scissored even with the pads for health and comfort. Use thinning shears for shortening the hair on the sides of the neck to neaten the overgrown line on the sides of the neck where the hair of the back of the neck and the front of the neck merge. In bathing a Longhair even though not to be shown, coat condition and appearance will be enhanced by the application of a good creme rinse.

To keep your Wirehaired "family" Dachshund looking trim, you can use a clipper as a short cut. But please remember that the use of a clipper will leave the dog with a softer than desirable coat texture, removing the hard-textured outer hairs on which show texture coat is so dependent. Clippers must *never* be used on the coat of a show Wirehaired Dachshund, lest the damage done to coat texture prove irreparable.

To do your pet Dachshund with a clipper, the same pattern described by Denny Mounce for the show coat should be followed, using a number 10 blade on the head, underside of the neck, and ears; and number 5 on back of neck, body and tail. The eyebrows and beard should be scissored to the shape and length of your preference.

GROOMING THE SMOOTH DACHSHUND
FOR SHOWING

The coat of the Smooth Dachshund is, obviously, by far the easiest of the three varieties to groom. A bit of trimming of whiskers, and tidying up of wispy hairs, plus a touch of baby oil or brilliantine to the coat and he is ready to go, looking his handsome best.

For trimming whiskers, use straight shears with rounded tips to assure no accidents. Cut the whiskers on the muzzle, over the eyes, on the cheeks and on the underside of the jaw, making sure that you do so very close to the skin.

If it is necessary to do so, scissor any stray hairs on the neck where the coat growth back from the front of the neck merge, producing a ridge. Also you may need to trim wispy hairs which may protrude from the front of the breastbone. Use either straight scissors or thinning shears, cutting slowly and carefully to avoid leaving a bare spot or sharp line where you have worked.

Again, if necessary, trim any scraggling or protruding hair from the underside of the tail to give a sleek, tidy and elegant look. Also, any protruding hair from the undersides of the feet should be evened off, bringing the hair even with the pads.

Ravenridge's Royal Falcon and Ravenridge's Winter Gale, a typical study of two Smooth Dachshunds. Michael and Ann Gordon, breeders. Owned by Mandy Cronin.

GROOMING THE LONGHAIRED DACHSHUND
by Dee Hutchinson

The following material was originally written by Mrs. Hutchinson for use in the Dachshund Club of America Handbook. We deeply appreciate permission to include parts of it here.

We shall start with show grooming procedure of the Longhair, whose coat is rather long and silky, reminding one of the Irish Setter. When bathing a Longhaired Dachshund, a good creme rinse should follow each bath to add to the silkiness of the coat. Regular brushing and combing will loosen and remove any dead hair, stimulate the skin, distribute the natural oils throughout the coat, and allow for new coat growth. The bath water should be tepid to cool in temperature; water which is too warm or hot will cause breakage and damage to the coat.

The grooming of the Longhaired Dachshund is done to enhance his elegance and Dachshund body shape. The most difficult of the Longhaired Dachshunds to groom are the reds and chocolates because the undercoat on these dogs is usually lighter in color. With the lighter undercoat, areas that have been recently scissored are very obvious in the show ring. The reds and chocolates should be groomed about six to eight weeks before the dog is to be shown. Finishing touches and neatening can be done during the last week before the show. The dappled Longhaired Dachshund presents a unique challenge in that the silver or white hairs of the dappled areas are generally coarser in texture and give a harsher feel when freshly cut. It is best to do the major part of the grooming of the dappled Dachshund six to eight weeks before the show date, whether they be chocolate, red or black and tan dapples. The black and tan Longhaired Dachshund can be groomed closer to the date of the show since the coat texture and color are uniform all over the body.

HEAD: Use a barber's shears with rounded tips to cut the whiskers on the muzzle, cheek, over the eyes, and under the chin. This should be done the day before the show, and the whiskers should be cut very close to the skin.

Some dogs have longer hairs on the head which give an unkempt appearance. These should be removed either by plucking with the thumb and index finger, or by using a pumice stone in a brushing motion in the direction in which the coat grows.

EARS: The coat on the ears should be long and lie flat against the ears. Some dogs, particularly puppies, have excess hair at the area where the ear joins the skull. This hair gives an overly wide appearance to the head, thus detracting from the elegant appearance. You can pluck out this hair or you can use a thinning shears. In using thinning shears, place the blades under the coat near the top of the ear and cut *only once or twice*. Comb the hair where you have just cut and determine whether or not you should thin the area more. Too many cuts in the same area will create a bald spot! Continue to cut, comb, and evaluate until you achieve the desired effect.

The hair on the inside of the ear at the cheek area and around to the small flap on the inside back of the ear should be cut *very* close to allow the ear to lay flatter against the head, and to outline the ear against the neck.

NECK: The neck should be long, lean and taper into the shoulder area in a very elegant manner. Heavy coat growth tends to make the neck look too short. Thinning shears should be used from the back of the jaw down the front of the neck to a point just above the point of the breastbone. Hold the dog's head up with one hand and place the thinning shears under the coat against the skin and in line with the coat growth (never across the direction of coat growth). Cut once or twice, comb, and see if you need to cut again. Thin the hair from the underside of the jaw down into a long, full coat beginning just above the breastbone. Thin the total neck area to the point where the coat growth coming from the back of the neck joins the hair on the front of the neck on each side.

To groom the back of the neck, I prefer to begin with a Real Stripping Knife. This gem of a tool has a very fine serrated edge and, when used like a comb, will remove an amazing amount of dead hair and undercoat without affecting the longer outercoat. Because of the very fine edge of this tool, use it slowly, and keep the skin taut in the area in which you are using it. It is possible to have the tiny "teeth" catch in a small fold of skin unless great care is taken.

Comb with the Real Stripping Knife in a combing motion down the length of the body and down the sides to remove dead hair and undercoat. The body coat should lay flat and taper into a flowing coat on the sides and underside of the body. Thinning

A family of longcoat winners at the Dachshund Club of California 1970 Specialty Show. *Center,* Best of Breed, Ch. Wayt-A-While Parade, bred by the Wayts in North Carolina, owned by Ethel Bigler. *Left,* Best of Opposite Sex to Best of Breed, his daughter, Ch. Von Relgib's Red Witch, bred and owned by Herbert and Elaine Holtzman, West Lake Island, California. *Right,* Best Puppy in Sweepstakes, Winners Dog and Best of Winners, Von Relgib's Grand Marshal, also bred by the Holtzmans.

shears can be used judiciously on the body to enhance the topline and sleekness of the dog.

LEGS: The hair behind the front legs should form a pronounced feather. Heavy coat growth on the front legs can give the appearance that the elbows point outward. To correct this, use the thinning shears on the outer sides of the front legs, particularly at the elbow area. This will give a close fitting look to the legs. The long hair on the back of the front legs should be combed toward the back of the body. If this coat is too profuse and tends to protrude to the sides, use thinning shears until the coat does comb back. It is also helpful to frequently dampen this hair and comb it back in order to train the coat growth.

The hair on the back of the thighs should also be long and full, but not protruding outward to the side of the back legs. Use the thinning shears to blend this coat into the upper thigh area.

FEET: Cut the hair on the bottom of the feet even with the pads. With the foot placed securely on a firm surface, trim the foot with a straight scissors. The desired foot is a rounded, compact one. You may have to scissor the top of the foot in the area of the nails to remove the wispy hairs which stick up over the nails. *DO NOT* cut the hair in an outline around the toenails. Rather cut so as to blend this hair into a fully coated rounded appearance.

TAIL: The coat of a Longhaired Dachshund should reach its greatest length on the underside of the tail; therefore little is done to the tail other than combing and brushing to maintain the condition.

The authors recommend that owners of show prospect Longhaired Dachshunds have the dogs' coat done for them at least once by an expert, if possible with the owner watching, prior to undertaking the job personally. That way the directions Mrs. Hutchinson has given will be more fully understood, and thus the owner will be more fully prepared to do a creditable job.

GROOMING THE WIREHAIRED DACHSHUND
by Denny Mounce

In this section, we will be discussing the grooming of the Wirehaired Dachshund. Of the three coats, it is by far the most diverse. Within one coat variety, there are several different types of coats. What is intended here is to describe the basic grooming techniques for the average harsh-coated Wire Dachshund. We will begin with a dog which is grown out, and groom it to be shown in approximately 6-8 weeks.

You must first assemble the proper grooming equipment. Always buy quality equipment, for you get what you pay for. You will need the following:

Small grooming table, with a grooming arm and noose;
2″ pair of blunt-nosed scissors (sometimes called ear and nose scissors);
Nail clippers and septic powder;
Ear oil, cotton swabs, cotton balls;
Tooth scraper;
Metal comb (the type made in England is best);
Natural bristle brush;
Set of stripping knives (medium and fine).

When choosing knives, buy a set that feels good in your hand and does not have sharp edges. By all means, do not buy one with a razor blade in it. You do not want to cut the hair, you want to pull it out.

Now, we can begin. Place your grooming table in a well-lighted area where there will be little or no distractions to the dog. First, put three or four drops of ear oil in each ear; we will let that soak in the ear while we cut the toenails. The toenails should be trimmed short enough so that they do not touch the floor when your dog is gaiting. You will need to stop any bleeding with your septic powder. If this is objectionable to you, ask your veterinarian for assistance in cutting the toenails.

Next, you need to remove any excess wax from the ears with cotton swabs or cotton balls. You may want to pull any excess hair out of the ear canal.

Next, check your dog's teeth and scrape away any build-up of tartar. You may polish the teeth by making a paste of baking soda and water, and rubbing the paste over the teeth, either with your fingers or with a damp wash cloth. You should clean the ears and teeth on a weekly basis.

Thoroughly brush the coat on the back (or "jacket") with your natural bristle brush. Then, using your comb, completely and thoroughly comb any mats or tangles out of the legs, chest and beard. You cannot properly trim a dog that has mats. Please make note at this time: *Do not bathe your dog.* Although you want the dog as clean as possible for grooming, bathing will only soften the coat and make it harder to remove.

The object of "stripping" is to remove the dead hair by pulling it out, either with your fingers or with the assistance of a stripping knife. If you use a knife improperly, you will cut the hair and therefore defeat your purpose. To strip the hair out, catch the hair between your thumb and the blade of the knife, a few strands at a time, then pull the hair out. The pulling motion comes from the elbow, not the wrist. If you use wrist action, you will be more likely to cut the hair. Pull the hair out as evenly as possible. If you take too much hair at a time, you will pull "chunks" out of the coat; however, you do want to go deep enough to remove the top coat. Hand stripping is a time-consuming process, and should not be attempted hurriedly.

Now, you are ready to strip your dog. You will begin with the head. Remove any matter from under the eyes first. Then comb the beard and eyebrows forward. Comb the hair on the top of the head backward. *Note:* Always strip the hair in the direction in which it grows. Clean off the top of the head to the undercoat, leaving eyebrows and beard, using your fine stripping knife. You will want to shorten the hair on the ears, and will use either your thumb and forefinger, or the tip of your stripping knife and your thumb to remove the fringes off the ears. Also, you will need to strip clean the inside of the ears. Remember, you are using your fine knife, and removing the hair as close to the skin as possible. Next, take the cheeks down as short as possible. You want to leave the beard from the corner of the mouth forward. Even up the beard with your thumb and forefinger, or the tip of your knife and your thumb, in the same fashion as you did the ear fringes. Now remove the hair from between the eyes and the ridge just in front of the eyes. After you have done that, comb the eyebrows forward again, and starting with the outside corner, pull the hair as close to the eye as possible, working your way toward the inside corner, leaving the hair gradually longer as you work your way toward the inside corner. This will give the eyebrows a pointed effect.

Still using the fine stripping knife, now strip the underside of the neck down to the breastbone, following the contour of the natural "V." Begin at one corner of the mouth, and work your way to the other corner; then work your way down to the breastbone, always remembering to stay inside the "V" formed by the two ridges on either side of the neck. Now remove those ridges, using the tip of your knife and your thumb, as you did the ear fringes. Do not pull any hair below the breastbone at this time. You will do that when you do the leg furnishings.

The next step will be to work on the top and sides of the neck, and down the back. For this you will use your medium stripping knife. Remove the hair down the back of the neck, and on both sides of the neck. Then work your way down the back of the dog, and down both sides of the dog, including the belly, removing all of the topcoat and leaving the undercoat. Do not remove any hair from legs below a line from the elbow to where the flank meets the stifle. Everything below this line will be considered leg furnishing, and will be dealt with later. After you have removed the

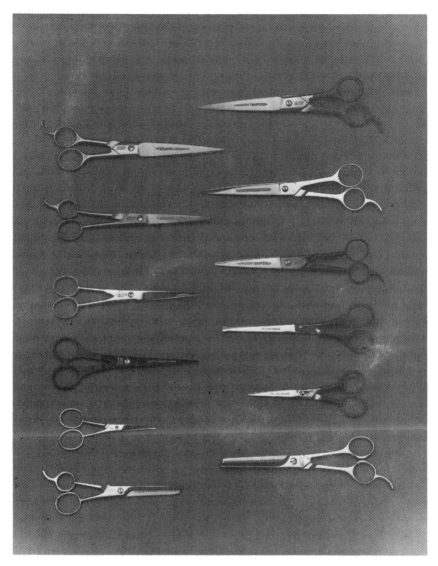

There are scissors of all types, depending on your grooming needs. Check with your local pet shop or with a professional dog groomer for the scissors you will need to keep your Dachshund looking his best. Photo courtesy of Millers Forge, Inc. of Texas.

body coat, strip the tail down to the undercoat, top and bottom.

Using your 2″ blunt-nosed scissors, cut the hair surrounding the rectum, and the testicles (or vulva). Using your fine stripping knife, strip the hair between the rectum and the genital area, including the ridges on the back of the hips, but not past them.

You are now ready to start to trim and shape the leg hair (or "furnishings"). Once again, make sure that the legs are thoroughly combed out, as well as the chest hair. You cannot trim them properly if they are matted or have debris in them. Now, comb the hair straight out from the leg, and using your thumb and the tip of your knife, in a straight line, shorten the hair by about one third. Repeat this step on all four sides of the leg. (On extremely harsh coated dogs, you will want to remove only the tips of the furnishings). The trimming should go all the way to, and include, the foot. Next, using the thumb and forefinger, or thumb and edge of the knife, trim the edges of the foot so you will have a nice, neat foot. Now take the scissors and trim the hair between the pads of the foot. *Never* use the scissors on the edge of the foot.

With the dog facing you, smooth out the shoulders and all of the stray hairs between the breastbone and shoulder. This will be done with the medium knife, stripping this area down to the undercoat. Now, on the breastbone itself, you will want only to shorten it by the same one third you shortened the leg furnishings. Do this using the thumb and forefinger.

Now that the dog is stripped, brush it daily with your natural bristle brush to encourage hair growth. The head, face and neck will need to be stripped again before showtime, as will the ridges on the neck and the butt-piece. How far ahead of showtime will depend on how fast your individual dog's coat grows. The faster it grows, the closer to showtime you can wait (average is 2-3 weeks). You should always clean the teeth, clean the ears and cut the nails a day or so before the show.

Chapter 13

The Making of a Show Dog

If you have decided to become a show dog exhibitor, you have accepted a very real and very exciting challenge. The groundwork has been accomplished with the selection of your future show prospect. If you have purchased a puppy, it is assumed that you have gone through all the proper preliminaries concerning good care, which should be the same if the puppy is a pet or future show dog with a few added precautions for the latter.

GENERAL CONSIDERATIONS

Remember the importance of keeping your future winner in trim, top condition. Since you want him neither too fat nor too thin, his appetite for his proper diet should be guarded, and children and guests should not be permitted to constantly feed him "goodies." The best treat of all is a small wad of raw ground beef or a packaged dog treat. To be avoided are ice cream, cake, cookies, potato chips, and other fattening items which will cause the dog to put on weight and may additionally spoil his appetite for the proper, nourishing, well-balanced diet so essential to good health and condition.

The importance of temperament and showmanship cannot possibly be overestimated. They have put many a mediocre dog across while lack of them can ruin the career of an otherwise outstanding specimen. From the day your dog joins your family, socialize him. Keep him accustomed to being with people and to being handled by people. Encourage your friends and relatives to "go over" him as the judges will in the ring so this will not seem a strange and upsetting experience. Practice showing his "bite" (the manner in which his teeth meet) quickly and deftly. It is quite simple to slip the lips apart with your fingers, and the puppy

Champion Jessell's Seaway, a Standard Longhair, is handled by the late Mrs. Winifred Heckmann, who was a Dachshund breeder, professional handler, and a well-respected all-breed judge.

should be willing to accept this from you or the judge without struggle.

Some judges prefer that the exhibitors display the dog's bite and other mouth features themselves. These are the considerate ones, who do not wish to chance the spreading of possible infection from dog to dog with their hands on each one's mouth—a courtesy particularly appreciated in these days of virus epidemics. But the old-fashioned judges still insist in doing it themselves, so the dog should be ready for either possibility.

Take your future show dog with you in the car, thus accustoming him to riding so that he will not become carsick on the day of a dog show. He should associate pleasure and attention with going in the car, van, or motor home. Take him where it is crowded: downtown, to the shops, everywhere you go that dogs are permitted. Make the expeditions fun for him by frequent petting and words of praise; do not just ignore him as you go about your errands.

Do not overly shelter your future show dog. Instinctively you may want to keep him at home where he is safe from germs or danger. This can be foolish on two counts. The first reason is that a puppy kept away from other dogs builds up no natural immunity against all the things with which he will come in contact at dog shows, so it is wiser actually to keep him well up to date on all protective shots and then let him become accustomed to being among dogs and dog owners. Also, a dog who never is among strange people, in strange places, or among strange dogs, may grow up with a shyness or timidity of spirit that will cause you real problems as his show career draws near.

Keep your show prospect's coat in immaculate condition with frequent grooming and daily brushing. When bathing is necessary, use a mild dog shampoo or whatever the breeder of your puppy may suggest. Several of the brand-name products do an excellent job. Be sure to rinse thoroughly so as not to risk skin irritation by traces of soap left behind and protect against soap entering the eyes by a drop of castor oil in each before you lather up. Use warm water (be sure it is not uncomfortably hot or chillingly cold) and a good spray. Make certain you allow your dog to dry thoroughly in a warm, draft-free area (or outdoors, if it is warm and sunny) so that he doesn't catch cold. Then proceed to groom him to perfection.

Toenails should be watched and trimmed every few weeks. It is important not to permit nails to grow excessively long, as they will ruin the appearance of both the feet and pasterns.

A show dog's teeth must be kept clean and free of tartar. Hard dog biscuits can help toward this, but if tartar accumulates, see that it is removed promptly by your veterinarian. Bones for chewing are not suitable for show dogs as they tend to damage and wear down the tooth enamel.

Assuming that you will be handling the dog yourself, or even if he will be professionally handled, a few moments each day of dog show routine is important. Practice setting him up as you have seen the exhibitors do at the shows you've attended, and teach him to hold this position once you have him stacked to your satisfaction. Make the learning period pleasant by being firm but lavish in your praise when he responds correctly. Teach him to gait at your side at a moderate rate on a loose lead. When you have mastered the basic essentials at home, then hunt out and join a training class for future work. Training classes are sponsored by show-giving clubs in many areas, and their popularity is steadily increasing. If you have no other way of locating one, perhaps your veterinarian would know of one through some of his other clients; but if you are sufficiently aware of the dog show world to want a show dog, you will probably be personally acquainted with other people who will share information of this type with you.

Accustom your show dog to being in a crate (which you should be doing with a pet dog as well). He should relax in his crate at the shows "between times" for his own well being and safety.

MATCH SHOWS

Your show dog's initial experience in the ring should be in match show competition for several reasons. First, this type of event is intended as a learning experience for both the dog and the exhibitor. You will not feel embarrassed or out of place no matter how poorly your puppy may behave or how inept your attempts at handling may be, as you will find others there with the same type of problems. The important thing is that you get the puppy out and into a show ring where the two of you can practice together and learn the ropes.

Only on rare occasions is it necessary to make match show entries in advance, and even those with a pre-entry policy will usually accept entries at the door as well. Thus you need not plan several weeks ahead, as is the case with point shows, but can go when the mood strikes you. Also there is a vast difference in the cost, as match show entries only cost a few dollars while entry fees for the point shows may be over ten dollars, an amount none of us needs to waste until we have some idea of how the puppy will behave or how much more pre-show training is needed.

Match shows very frequently are judged by professional handlers who, in addition to making the awards, are happy to help new exhibitors with comments and advice on their puppies and their presentation of them. Avail yourself of all these opportunities before heading out to the sophisticated world of the point shows.

POINT SHOWS

As previously mentioned, entries for American Kennel Club point shows must be made in advance. This must be done on an official entry blank of the show-giving club. The entry must then

Ch. Jandelo's Don Juan in 1953. Owned by Helen Hill, bred by Jandelo Kennels, Fairview, North Carolina.

Ch. Willo-Mar's Firebrand who in 1958 was the Top Winning Smooth Dachshund in the West, was a Best in Show and Group winner of the late 1950's. Owned by Mrs. Dora Faville, handled by Woody Dorward. Photo courtesy of Mrs. Catherine Berg.

be filed either personally or by mail with the show superintendent or the show secretary (if the event is being run by the club members alone and a superintendent has not been hired, this information will appear on the premium list) in time to reach its destination prior to the published closing date or filling of the quota. These entries must be made carefully, must be signed by the owner of the dog or the owner's agent (your professional handler), and must be accompanied by the entry fee; otherwise they will not be accepted. Remember that it is not when the entry leaves your hands that counts but the date of arrival at its destination. If you are relying on the mails, which are not always dependable, get the entry off well before the deadline to avoid disappointment.

A dog must be entered at a dog show in the name of the actual owner at the time of the entry closing date of that specific show. If a registered dog has been acquired by a new owner, it must be entered in the name of the new owner in any show for which entries close after the date of acquirement, regardless of whether the new owner has or has not actually received the registration certificate indicating that the dog is recorded in his name. State on the entry form whether or not transfer application has been mailed to the American Kennel Club, and it goes without saying that the latter should be attended to promptly when you purchase a registered dog.

In filling out your entry blank, type, print, or write clearly, paying particular attention to the spelling of names, correct registration numbers, and so on. Also, if there is more than one variety in your breed, be sure to indicate into which category your dog is being entered.

The Puppy Class is for dogs or bitches who are six months of age and under twelve months, were whelped in the United States, and are not champions. The age of a dog shall be calculated up to and inclusive of the first day of a show. For example, the first day a dog whelped on January 1st is eligible to compete in a Puppy Class at a show is July 1st of the same year; and he may continue to compete in Puppy Classes up to and including a show on December 31st of the same year, but he is *not* eligible to compete in a Puppy Class at a show held on or after January 1st of the following year.

The Puppy Class is the first one in which you should enter your puppy. In it a certain allowance will be made for the fact that they *are* puppies, thus an immature dog or one displaying less than perfect showmanship will be less severely penalized than, for instance, would be the case in Open. It is also quite likely that others in the class will be suffering from these problems, too. When you enter a puppy, be sure to check the classification with care, as some shows divide their Puppy Class into a 6-9 months old section and a 9-12 months old section.

The Novice Class is for dogs six months of age and over, whelped in the United States or Canada, who *prior to the official closing date for entries* have *not* won three first prizes in the Novice Class, any first prize at all in the Bred-by-Exhibitor, American-bred, or Open Classes, or one or more points toward championship. The provisions for this class are confusing to many people, which is probably the reason exhibitors do not enter in it more frequently. A dog may win any number of first prizes in the Puppy Class and still retain his eligibility for Novice. He may place second, third, or fourth not only in Novice on an unlimited number of occasions but also in Bred-by-Exhibitor, American-bred and Open and still remain eligible for Novice. But he may no longer be shown in Novice when he has won three blue ribbons in that class, when he has won even one blue ribbon in either Bred-by-Exhibitor, American-bred, or Open, or when he has won a single championship point.

In determining whether or not a dog is eligible for the Novice Class, keep in mind the fact that previous wins are calculated according to the official published date for closing of entries, not by the date on which you may actually have made the entry. So if in the interim, between the time you made the entry and the official closing date, your dog makes a win causing him to become ineligible for Novice, change your class *immediately* to another for which he will be eligible, preferably either Bred-by-Exhibitor or American-bred. To do this, you must contact the show's superintendent or secretary, at first by telephone to save time and at the same time confirm it in writing. The Novice Class always seems to have the fewest entries of any class, and therefore it is a splendid "practice ground" for you and your young dog while you are getting the "feel" of being in the ring.

Bred-by-Exhibitor Class is for dogs whelped in the United States or, if individually registered in the American Kennel Club Stud Book, for dogs whelped in Canada who are six months of age

This was one of the very first Dachshunds owned at Knolland Farm by Edward Jenner, Richmond, Illinois. Ch. Kleetal's Jolly Cookie, winning at Tuxedo Park in September 1972. Handled by Howard Atlee.

Ch. Nixon's Forest Sprite taking Winners Bitch at Westminster in 1967. Howard Atlee handled for Dr. C. William Nixon.

or older, are not champions, and are owned wholly or in part by the person or by the spouse of the person who was the breeder or one of the breeders of record. Dogs entered in this class must be handled in the class by an owner or by a member of the immediate family of the owner. Members of an immediate family for this purpose are husband, wife, father, mother, son, daughter, brother, or sister. This is the class which is really the "breeders' showcase," and the one which breeders should enter with particular pride to show off their achievements.

The American-bred Class is for all dogs excepting champions, six months of age or older, who were whelped in the United States by reason of a mating which took place in the United States.

Ch. Groff-Nix Tiny M, owned by Herman and Muriel Newhauser, finished between June and October in 1962. The fifth Miniature Smooth male to attain championship in the United States.

Am. and Can. Ch. Ravenridge's Big Red, by Ch. Dresel's Allegro ex Willo-Mar's Ruby of Ravenridge. Bred and owned by Michael and Ann Gordon, Pittsburgh, Pennsylvania.

Mrs. Jeanette W. Cross shows Kruschina to win her Bermudian championship. The judge, James Walker Trullinger, noted all-breed authority, started in dogs as a Dachshund fancier. Kruschina was bred by Peggy and Wallace Alford of North Carolina.

Ch. Sandwood Musette, by Ch. Kudach's Mark of Lancelot ex Sandwood Oona, handled by David Bolus for Mrs. Dorothy A. Muse, Mountain City, Tennessee.

The Open Class is for any dog six months of age or older (this is the only restriction for this class). Dogs with championship points compete in it, dogs who are already champions are eligible to do so, dogs who are imported can be entered, and, of course, American-bred dogs compete in it. This class is, for some strange reason, the favorite of exhibitors who are "out to win." They rush to enter their pointed dogs in it, under the false impression that by doing so they assure themselves of greater attention from the judges. This really is not so, and some people feel that to enter in one of the less competitive classes, with a better chance of winning it and thus earning a second opportunity of gaining the judge's approval by returning to the ring in the Winners Class, can often be a more effective strategy.

One does not enter the Winners Class. One earns the right to compete in it by winning first prize in Puppy, Novice, Bred-by-Exhibitor, American-bred, or Open. No dog who has been defeated on the same day in one of these classes is eligible to compete for Winners, and every dog who has been a blue-ribbon winner in one of them and not defeated in another, should he have been entered in more than one class (as occasionally happens), *must* do so. Following the selection of the Winners Dog or the Winners Bitch, the dog or bitch receiving that award leaves the ring. Then the dog or bitch who placed second in that class, unless previously beaten by another dog or bitch in another class at the same show, re-enters the ring to compete against the remaining first-prize winners for Reserve. The latter award indicates that the dog or bitch selected for it is standing "in reserve" should the one who received Winners be disqualified or declared ineligible through any technicality when the awards are checked at the American Kennel Club. In that case, the one who placed Reserve is moved up to Winners, at the same time receiving the appropriate championship points.

Winners Dog and Winners Bitch are the awards which carry points toward championship with them. The points are based on the number of dogs or bitches actually in competition, and the points are scaled one through five, the latter being the greatest number available to any one dog or bitch at any one show. Three-, four-, or five-point wins are considered majors. In order to become a champion, a dog or bitch must have won two majors under two different judges, plus at least one point from a third judge, and the additional points necessary to bring the total to fifteen. When your dog has gained fifteen points as described above, a championship certificate will be issued to you, and your dog's name will be published in the champions of record list in the *Pure-Bred Dogs/American Kennel Gazette*, the official publication of the American Kennel Club.

The scale of championship points for each breed is worked out by the American Kennel Club and reviewed annually, at which time the number required in competition may be either changed (raised or lowered) or remain the same. The scale of championship points for all breeds is published annually in the May issue of the *Gazette*, and the current ratings for each breed within that area are published in every show catalog.

When a dog or bitch is adjudged Best of Winners, its championship points are, for that show, compiled on the basis of which sex had the greater number of points. If there are two points in dogs

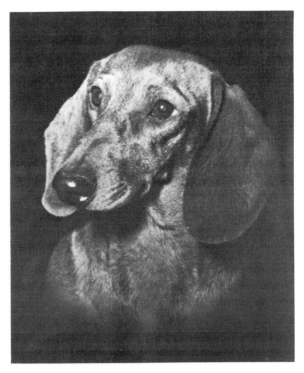

An exquisite head-study of Am. and Can. Ch. Fiddlers Hill Dubonnet, outstanding Smooth bitch owned by Mrs. Catherine (Katay) Burg, Fiddlers Hill Kennels, Portland, Oregon.

and four in bitches and the dog goes Best of Winners, then *both* the dog and the bitch are awarded an equal number of points, in this case four. Should the Winners Dog or the Winners Bitch go on to win Best of Breed or Best of Variety, additional points are accorded for the additional dogs and bitches defeated by so doing, provided, of course, that there were entries specifically for Best of Breed competition or Specials, as these specific entries are generally called.

If your dog or bitch takes Best of Opposite Sex after going Winners, points are credited according to the number of the same sex defeated in both the regular classes and Specials competition. If Best of Winners is also won, then whatever additional points for each of these awards are available will be credited. Many a one- or two-point win has grown into a major in this manner.

Moving further along, should your dog win its Variety Group from the classes (in other words, if it has taken either Winners Dog or Winners Bitch), you then receive points based on the greatest number of points awarded to any member of any breed included within that Group during that show's competition. Should the day's winning also include Best in Show, the same rule of thumb applies, and your dog or bitch receives the highest number of points awarded to any other dog of any breed at that event.

Best of Breed competition consists of the Winners Dog and the Winners Bitch, who automatically compete on the strength of those awards, in addition to whatever dogs and bitches have been entered specifically for this class for which champions of record are eligible. Since July 1980, dogs who, according to their owner's records, have completed the requirements for a championship after the closing of entries for the show, but whose championships are unconfirmed, may be transferred from one of the regular classes to the Best of Breed competition, provided this transfer is made by the show superintendent or show secretary *prior to the start of any judging at the show.*

This has proved an extremely popular new rule, as under it a dog can finish on Saturday and then be transferred and compete as a Special on Sunday. It must be emphasized that *the change must be made prior to the start of any part of the day's judging, not for just your individual breed.*

In the United States, Best of Breed winners are entitled to compete in the Variety Group which includes them. This is not mandatory; it is a privilege which exhibitors value. (In Canada, Best of Breed winners *must* compete in the Variety Group, or they lose any points already won.) The dogs winning *first* in each of the seven Variety Groups *must* compete for Best in Show. Missing the opportunity of taking your dog in for competition in its Group is foolish as it is there where the general public is most likely to notice your breed and become interested in learning about it.

Non-regular classes are sometimes included at the all-breed shows, and they are almost invariably included at Specialty shows. These include Stud Dog Class and Brood Bitch Class, which are judged on the basis of the quality of the two offspring accompanying the sire or dam. The quality of the latter two is beside the point and should not be considered by the judge; it is the youngsters who count, and the quality of *both* are to be averaged to decide which sire or dam is the best and most consistent producer. Then there is the Brace Class (which, at all-breed shows, moves up to Best Brace in each Variety Group and then Best Brace in Show), which is judged on the similarity and evenness of appear-

Ch. Villanol's Troubedour and Villanol's Deacon, by Dark Deacon of Wingalore ex Villanol's Lady Belle, bred, owned and handled by Gordon H. Carvill, winning Best Hound Brace at Albany K.C. in 1963.

ance of the two members of the brace. In other words, the two dogs should look like identical twins in size, color, and conformation and should move together almost as a single dog, one person handling with precision and ease. The same applies to the Team Class competition, except that four dogs are involved and, if necessary, two handlers.

The Veterans Class is for the older dogs, the minimum age of whom is seven years. This class is judged on the quality of the dogs, as the winner competes in Best of Breed competition and has, on a respectable number of occasions, been known to take that top award. So the point is *not* to pick out the oldest dog, as some judges seem to believe, but the best specimen of the breed, exactly as in the regular classes.

Then there are Sweepstakes and Futurity Stakes sponsored by many Specialty clubs, sometimes as part of their regular Specialty shows and sometimes as separate events on an entirely different occasion. The difference between the two stakes is that Sweep-

Georgette Fanelle, Grace Hill's first wirehair Dachshund, a Standard brindle, shown here in the Brood Bitch Class at DALI at nine years of age in 1956.

stakes entries usually include dogs from six to eighteen months age with entries made at the same time as the others for the show, while for a Futurity the entries are bitches nominated when bred and the individual puppies entered at or shortly following their birth.

JUNIOR SHOWMANSHIP COMPETITION

If there is a youngster in your family between the ages of ten and sixteen there is no better or more rewarding hobby than becoming an active participant in Junior Showmanship. This is a marvelous activity for young people. It teaches responsibility, good sportsmanship, the fun of competition where one's own skills are the deciding factor of success, proper care of a pet, and how to socialize with other young folks. Any youngster may experience the thrill of emerging from the ring a winner and the satisfaction of a good job well done.

Entry in Junior Showmanshiop Classes is open to any boy or girl who is at least ten years old and under seventeen years old on the day of the show. The Novice Junior Showmanship Class is open to youngsters who have not already won, at the time the entries close, three firsts in this class. Youngsters who have won three firsts in Novice may compete in the Open Junior Showmanship Class. Any junior handler who wins his third first-place award in Novice may participate in the Open Class at the same show, provided that the Open Class has at least one other junior handler entered and competing in it that day. The Novice and Open Classes may be divided into Junior and Senior Classes. Youngsters between the ages of ten and twelve, inclusively, are eligible for the Junior division; and youngsters between thirteen and seventeen, inclusively, are eligible for the Senior division.

Any of the foregoing classes may be separated into individual classes for boys and for girls. If such a division is made, it must be so indicated on the premium list. The premium list also indicates the prize for Best Junior Handler, if such a prize is being offered at the show. Any youngster who wins a first in any of the regular classes may enter the competition for this prize, provided the youngster has been undefeated in any other Junior Showmanship Class at that show.

Junior Showmanship Classes, unlike regular conformation classes in which the quality of the dog is judged, are judged solely on the skill and ability of the junior handling the dog. Which dog is best is not the point—it is which youngster does the best job with the dog that is under consideration. Eligibility requirements for the dog being shown in Junior Showmanship, and other detailed information, can be found in *Regulations for Junior Showmanship*, available from the American Kennel Club.

A junior who has a dog that he or she can enter in both Junior Showmanship and conformation classes has twice the opportunity for success and twice the opportunity to get into the ring and work with the dog, a combination which can lead to not only awards for expert handling, but also, if the dog is of sufficient quality, for making a conformation champion.

PRE-SHOW PREPARATIONS

Preparations of the items you will need as a dog show exhibitor should not be left until the last moment. They should be planned and arranged for at least several days in advance of the show in order for you to remain calm and relaxed as the countdown starts.

The importance of the crate has already been mentioned, and should already be part of your equipment. Of equal importance is the grooming table, which very likely you have also already acquired for use at home. You should take it along with you to the shows, as your dog will need last minute touches before entering the ring. Should you have not yet made this purchase, folding tables with rubber tops are made specifically for this purpose and can be purchased at most dog shows, where concession booths with marvelous assortments of "doggy" necessities are to be found, or at your pet supplier. You will also need a sturdy tack box (also available at the dog show concessions) in which to carry your grooming tools and equipment. The latter should include brushes, comb, scissors, nail clippers, whatever you use for last minute clean-up jobs, cotton swabs, first-aid equipment, and anything you are in the habit of using on the dog, including a leash or two of the type you prefer, some well-cooked and dried-out liver or any of the small packaged "dog treats" for use as bait in the ring, an atomizer in case you wish to dampen your dog's coat when you are preparing him for the ring, and so on. A large turkish towel to spread under the dog on the grooming table is also useful.

Take a large thermos or cooler of ice, the biggest one you can accommodate in your vehicle, for use by "man and beast." Take a jug of water (there are lightweight, inexpensive ones available at all sporting goods shops) and a water dish. If you plan to feed the dog at the show, or if you and the dog will be away from home more than one day, bring food for him from home so that he will have the type to which he is accustomed.

You may or may not have an exercise pen. While the shows do provide areas for exercise of the dogs, these are among the most likely places to have your dog come in contact with any illnesses which may be going around, and having a pen of your own for your dog's use is excellent protection. Such a pen can be used in other ways, too, such as a place other than the crate in which to put the dog to relax (that is roomier than the crate) and a place in which the dog can exercise at motels and rest stops. These pens are available at the show concession stands and come in a variety of heights and sizes. A set of "pooper scoopers" should also be part of your equipment, along with a package of plastic bags for cleaning up after your dog.

Bring along folding chairs for the members of your party, unless all of you are fond of standing, as these are almost never provided anymore by the clubs. Have your name stamped on the chairs so that there will be no doubt as to whom the chairs belong. Bring whatever you and your family enjoy for drinks or snacks in a picnic basket or cooler, as show food, in general, is expensive and usually not great. You should always have a pair of boots, a raincoat, and a rain hat with you (they should remain permanently in your vehicle if you plan to attend shows regularly), as well as a sweater, a warm coat, and a change of shoes. A smock or big cover-up apron will assure that you remain tidy as you prepare the dog for the ring. Your overnight case should include a small sewing kit for emergency repairs, bandaids, headache and indigestion remedies, and any personal products or medications you normally use.

In your car you should always carry maps of the area where you are headed and an assortment of motel directories. Generally speaking, Holiday Inns have been found to be the nicest about taking dogs. Ramadas and Howard Johnsons generally do so cheerfully (with a few exceptions). Best Western generally frowns on pets (not always, but often enough to make it necessary to find out which do). Some of the smaller chains welcome pets; the majority of privately owned motels do not.

Have everything prepared the night before the show to expedite your departure. Be sure that the dog's identification and your judging program and other show information are in your purse or briefcase. If you are taking sandwiches, have them ready. Anything that goes into the car the night before the show will be one thing less to remember in the morning. Decide upon what you will wear and have it out and ready. If there is any question in your mind about what to wear, try on the possibilities before the day of the show; don't risk feeling you may want to change when you see yourself dressed a few moments prior to departure time!

In planning your outfit, make it something simple that will not detract from your dog. Remember that a dark dog silhouettes attractively against a light background and vice-versa. Sport clothes always seem to look best at dog shows, preferably conservative in type and not overly "loud" as you do not want to detract from your dog, who should be the focus of interest at this point. What you wear on your feet is important. Many types of flooring can be hazardously slippery, as can wet grass. Make it a habit to wear rubber soles and low or flat heels in the ring for your own safety, especially if you are showing a dog that likes to move out smartly.

Your final step in pre-show preparation is to leave yourself plenty of time to reach the show that morning. Traffic can get amazingly heavy as one nears the immediate area of the show, finding a parking place can be difficult, and other delays may occur. You'll be in better humor to enjoy the day if your trip to the show is not fraught with panic over fear of not arriving in time!

ENJOYING THE DOG SHOW

From the moment of your arrival at the show until after your dog has been judged, keep foremost in your mind the fact that he is your reason for being there and that he should therefore be the center of your attention. Arrive early enough to have time for those last-minute touches that can make a great difference when he enters the ring. Be sure that he has ample time to exercise and that he attends to personal matters. A dog arriving in the ring and immediately using it as an exercise pen hardly makes a favorable impression on the judge.

When you reach ringside, ask the steward for your arm-card and anchor it firmly into place on your arm. Make sure that you are where you should be when your class is called. The fact that you have picked up your arm-card does not guarantee, as some seem to think, that the judge will wait for you. The judge has a full schedule which he wishes to complete on time. Even though you may be nervous, assume an air of calm self-confidence. Remember that this is a hobby to be enjoyed, so approach it in that state of mind. The dog will do better, too, as he will be quick to reflect your attitude.

Always show your dog with an air of pride. If you make mistakes in presenting him, don't worry about it. Next time you will do better. Do not permit the presence of more experienced exhibitors to intimidate you. After all, they, too, once were newcomers.

The judging routine usually starts when the judge asks that the dogs be gaited in a circle around the ring. During this period the judge is watching each dog as it moves, noting style, topline, reach and drive, head and tail carriage, and general balance. Keep your mind and your eye on your dog, moving him at his most becoming gait and keeping your place in line without coming too close to the exhibitor ahead of you. Always keep your dog on the inside of the circle, between yourself and the judge, so that the judge's view of the dog is unobstructed.

Calmly pose the dog when requested to set up for examination. If you are at the head of the line and many dogs are in the class, go all the way to the end of the ring before starting to stack the dog, leaving sufficient space for those behind you to line theirs up as well, as requested by the judge. If you are not at the head of the line but between other exhibitors, leave sufficient space ahead of your dog for the judge to examine him. The dogs should be spaced so that the judge is able to move among them to see them from all angles. In practicing to "set up" or "stack" your dog for the judge's examination, bear in mind the importance of doing so quickly and with dexterity. The judge has a schedule to meet and only a few moments in which to evaluate each dog. You will immeasurably help yours to make a favorable impression if you are able to "get it all together" in a minimum amount of time. Practice at home before a mirror can be a great help toward bringing this about, facing the dog so that you see him from the same side that the judge will and working to make him look right in the shortest length of time.

Listen carefully as the judge describes the manner in which the dog is to be gaited, whether it is straight down and straight back; down the ring, across, and back; or in a triangle. The latter has become the most popular pattern with the majority of judges. "In a triangle" means the dog should move down the outer side of the ring to the first corner, across that end of the ring to the second corner, and then back to the judge from the second corner, using the center of the ring in a diagonal line. Please learn to do this pattern without breaking at each corner to twirl the dog around you, a senseless maneuver that has been noticed on occasion. Judges like to see the dog in an uninterrupted triangle, as they are thus able to get a better idea of the dog's gait.

It is impossible to overemphasize that the gait at which you move your dog is tremendously important and considerable study and thought should be given to the matter. At home, have someone move the dog for you at different speeds so that you can tell which shows him off to best advantage. The most becoming action almost invariably is seen at a moderate gait, head up and topline holding. Do not gallop your dog around the ring or hurry him into a speed atypical of his breed. Nothing being rushed appears at its best; give your dog a chance to move along at his (and the breed's) natural gait. For a dog's action to be judged accurately, that dog should move with strength and power, but not excessive speed, holding a straight line as he goes to and from the judge.

As you bring the dog back to the judge, stop him a few feet away and be sure that he is standing in a becoming position. Bait him to show the judge an alert expression, using whatever tasty morsel he has been trained to expect for this purpose or, if that works better for you, use a small squeak-toy in your hand. A reminder, please, to those using liver or treats. Take them with you when you leave the ring. Do not just drop them on the ground where they will be found by another dog.

When the awards have been made, accept yours graciously, no matter how you actually may feel about it. What's done is done, and arguing with a judge or stomping out of the ring is useless and a reflection on your sportsmanship. Be courteous, congratulate the winner if your dog was defeated, and try not to show your disappointment. By the same token, please be a gracious winner; this, surprisingly, sometimes seems to be still more difficult.

Chapter 14

Obedience and Field Trials

For its own protection and safety, every dog should be taught, at the very least, to recognize and obey the commands "Come," "Heel," "Down," "Sit," and "Stay." Doing so at some time might save the dog's life and in less extreme circumstances will certainly make him a better behaved, more pleasant member of society. If you are patient and enjoy working with your dog, study some of the excellent books available on the subject of obedience and then teach your canine friend these basic manners. If you need the stimulus of working with a group, find out where obedience training classes are held (usually your veterinarian, your dog's breeder, or a dog-owning friend can tell you) and you and your dog can join up. Alternatively, you could let someone else do the training by sending the dog to class, but this is not very rewarding because you lose the opportunity of working with your dog and the pleasure of the rapport thus established.

If you are going to do it yourself, there are some basic rules which you should follow. You must remain calm and confident in attitude. Never lose your temper and frighten or punish your dog unjustly. Be quick and lavish with praise each time a command is correctly followed. Make it fun for the dog and he will be eager to please you by responding correctly. Repetition is the keynote, but it should not be continued without recess to the point of tedium. Limit the training sessions to ten- or fifteen-minute periods at a time.

Formal obedience training can be followed, and very frequently is, by entering the dog in obedience competition to work toward an obedience degree, or several of them, depending on the dog's aptitude and your own enjoyment. Obedience trials are held in conjunction with the majority of all-breed conformation dog shows, with Specialty shows, and frequently as separate Specialty events. If you are working alone with your dog, a list of trial dates might be obtained from your dog's veterinarian, your dog breeder, or a dog-owning friend; the AKC *Gazette* lists shows and trials to be scheduled in the coming months; and if you are a member of a training class, you will find the information readily available.

The goals for which one works in the formal AKC Member or Licensed Trials are the following titles: Companion Dog (C.D.), Companion Dog Excellent (C.D.X.), and Utility Dog (U.D.). These degrees are earned by receiving three "legs," or qualifying scores, at each level of competition. The degrees must be earned in order, with one completed prior to starting work on the next. For example, a dog must have earned C.D. prior to starting work on C.D.X.; then C.D.X. must be completed before U.D. work begins. The ultimate title attainable in obedience work is Obedience Trial Champion (O.T.Ch.)

When you see the letters C.D. following a dog's name, you will know that this dog has satisfactorily completed the following exercises: heel on leash and figure eight, heel free, stand for examination, recall, long sit, and long down. C.D.X. means that tests have been passed on all of those just mentioned plus heel free and figure eight, drop on recall, retrieve on flat, retrieve over high jump, broad jump, long sit, and long down. U.D. indicates that the dog has additionally passed tests in scent discrimination (leather article), scent discrimination (metal article), signal exercise, directed retrieve, directed jumping, and group stand for examination. The letters O.T.Ch. are the abbreviation for the only obedience title which precedes rather than follows a dog's name. To gain an obedience trial championship, a dog who already holds a Utility Dog degree must win a total of one hundred points and must win three firsts, under three different judges, in Utility and Open B Classes.

There is also a Tracking Dog title (T.D.) which can be earned at tracking trials. In order to pass the tracking tests the dog must follow the trail of a stranger along a path on which the trail was laid between thirty minutes and two hours previously. Along this track there must be more than two right-angle turns, at least two of which are well out in the open where no fences or other boundaries exist for the guidance of the dog or the handler. The dog wears a harness and is connected to the handler by a lead twenty to forty feet in length. Inconspicuously dropped at the end of the track is an article to be retrieved, usually a glove or wallet, which the dog is expected to locate and the handler to pick up. The letters T.D.X. is the abbreviation for Tracking Dog Excellent, a more difficult version of the Tracking Dog test with a longer track and more turns to be worked through.

Champion Dachsborough Nedrum, C.D.X., is a very distinguished obedience dog who has brought proud honors to his owners, his breed and himself. A son of Champion Close Call v Westphal ex Ch. Nedra of Dachsborough, Ned started his obedience career in July 1983, scoring consistently in the 190s in his obedience trials. He was High in Trial at the Golden 50th Show of the Dachshund Club of America at Nashville; the following month, on the Astro Hall Circuit, at Baytown he took a 1st placement in a class of 89 entries; and a fourth at Houston in a class of 110.

Ned is the first obedience dog ever trained by his owner-handler Candy Holder. She found him to be intelligent, willing to learn, and wanting to please. He is now being trained, by Candy, for Utility in hopes of adding UD to his titles in the very near future.

Ned's owners are Carl and Candy Holder, owners of the Candachs Kennels at Lumberton, Texas.

DACHSHUND FIELD TRIALS

by Patricia Nance

The Dachshund is a hunter. So many times these words are repeated, both orally and written. This factual reminder is taken steps further by some—many steps during hours spent in the fields and woods with their Dachshunds. Tales of hunting dog's performances are always enthusiastically recounted. Interested listeners are soon bound to request a demonstration or two so they can see and judge for themselves. Perhaps the work of one man's dog is sized up against that of another's in a friendly, yet purposeful competition. As this is true today, so it was true in the days long past when the sport of field trialing was born.

What are Field Trials? Field trials are competitions in which judges assess the abilities of gundogs and hounds to perform specified tasks afield. Demonstrations based on practical use, stamina and obedience are the core around which field trials developed. It has long been true that the fate of many of the hunting breeds of dogs lie in the hands of generally non-hunting fanciers. Field trials offer the means by which a sample of the distinctive capabilities of members of these breeds can be brought to light and examined.

The Dachshund! Speaking of distinctive! Think of some of the genuine needs of the early German foresters and sportsmen in their molding of an all-round hunting companion. A small dog for badger and fox den; some even smaller for hare warren. But not to underestimate strength—how about short legs to help with den size, while maintaining a larger and stronger head and body? Body length for flexibility? Three differently coated varieties to suit job, locality and hunter preference? Lots of courage and enthusiasm for hunting? Intelligence, quickness, co-operation? A terrific nose for locating and trailing game, and a loud voice to inform the hunter of progress?

All of these details add up to something of a description of the Dachshund as he has been known as a breed for over one hundred years. Americans have been quite familiar with him for a large part of that time. We've seen him popular in the show ring; the bench has helped serve the important need for evaluation of physical make-up. Additionally, the Dachshund has been much appreciated as a family companion. In themselves, these things speak very well for the breed. But, by and large, the Dachshund in America has a long history of absence in the most telling and fundamental arena of all—the field.

Early promotion of Dachshund field activity was not totally without success, however. In 1933, in an effort to encourage a working concept of the breed, the Dachshund Club of America appointed a committee to study possibilities in the way of field trials. Details examined by the committee included German field tests, limitations of American game laws, regulations of Humane Societies, rules of the American Kennel Club, and the trials of other breeds. The committee, with George McKay Schieffelin as Chairman, gave its report to the Dachshund Club of America and the American Kennel Club in the summer of 1935. Shortly afterward, on September 22, the first field trial of Dachshunds in America was held in New Jersey. A second trial was held in Pennsylvania later that fall, and fall field trials of the Dachshund Club of America have been conducted regularly ever since.

Many years went by before other, regional Dachshund clubs jumped on the field trial bandwagon. The Dachshund Club of New Jersey led the way, staging its first licensed trial in April of

1967. Several more clubs have followed and now, in addition to New Jersey, trials are being held in California, Connecticut, New York, Ohio and Pennsylvania for an average of about twelve licensed trials in the U.S. each year.

The regular classes offered at Dachshund field trials are the Open All-Age Stake for Dogs and the Open All-Age Stake for Bitches. As the names suggest, these classes are open to any dog or bitch registered, or eligible for registration, with the American Kennel Club, regardless of age or experience. These classes provide championship points to the Dachshunds placing first through fourth, on the following scale. First place winner earns a number of points equal to the number of actual starters in that stake. Second place earns one-half the number of points awarded the first place winner. Third and fourth placing dogs receive one-third and one-fourth, respectively, the number of points earned by the dog placing first in that stake. For example; if there were 16 bitches started in an Open All-Age Bitch stake, the bitch placing first would earn 16 points toward her Field Championship. Those bitches placing second, third and fourth would be awarded Field Championship points of the numbers eight, five and one-third, and four, respectively. The term "starters" refers to those Dachshunds actually judged in competition, not absent, disqualified, or otherwise ineligible. In all classes, after first through fourth placings have been awarded, the judges designate the next best qualified Dachshund as "N.B.Q." N.B.Q. is not a placing and in case of disqualification of a placed Dachshund, the N.B.Q. Dachshund is not moved up.

The rules state that if fewer than six are entered in either of the regular stakes, the two shall be combined and run as a single stake. Also, a club may be approved to hold additional, non-regular classes provided that descriptions of the eligibility requirements appear in the premium list. Many trials include the non-regular stakes "Field Champions Only;" "Best of Winners" in which the winners of the two Open All-Age stakes compete against each other; and "Best in Trial." Best in Trial may be determined either of two ways. One is where the dog or bitch declared Best of Winners competes with the winner of the Field Champion stake. By the other method, the winner of the Field Champion class and the winners of the two regular stakes compete as a trio for Best in Trial, if there is no Best of Winners stake.

Non-regular classes do not award Field Championship points.

The total number of championship points that a Dachshund must win to be declared a Field Champion of Record by the American Kennel Club is 35. These points must be acquired in Open All-Age classes at three or more trials. Some of a dog's championship points must have been earned by a placing of first in an Open All-Age stake.

Judging of field trial classes is done by two persons who work together in evaluating the dogs' performances. Judges are not required to obtain licenses. However, they must be in good standing with the American Kennel Club, must be 18 years of age or older, and not be officers or Field Trial Committeemen of the trial-giving club. Judges are required to sign a statement saying that they are familiar with trial rules and procedures and that they agree to judge in accordance with them.

Dachshund field trials are conducted on wild rabbits, or hare, and are located on grounds with enough space, cover and game to allow the dogs to show what they can do. Firearms are not present at the trials; game is not shot. The rabbits or hare are simply roused to flee from their places. To pursue the game, the Dachshunds use their noses to "work" the scent trail left behind. The dogs in each stake are worked in competitive pairs or "braces." The order of pairing and running in each stake is determined by a drawing done before the trial, after entries have closed. At the end of the pairing, if there is a dog left over, a "bye dog," his competitor is selected after all the braces have run.

Field Trial Champions

1936	Amsel v Holzgarten	George McKay Schieffelin
1938	Stine v Schwarlenbrook Adolph v Ernst	Thomas H. Andrews Fred Ernst
1939	Amsels Truffles	George McKay Schieffelin
1940	Alfreda v Kargollheim	Gerald M. Livingston
1943	Vagabund v Paulinenberg	George C. White
1944	Truffles Trigamous Trixie	Earl Cutler
1956	Teufelin mit Honig	Mrs. George S. Goodspeed

1957	Baskerville of Greenfield	Mrs. George S. Goodspeed
1958	Rock City Ricky	Paul J. Taylor
1959	Augusta of Willow Creek, CD	Mrs. Katharine Buckmaster
1961	Die Liebe Hussarin	Mrs. George S. Goodspeed
1963	Rock City Rocco	Paul J. Taylor
	Rock City Tess	Paul J. Taylor
1964	Cyrano's Plume of Greenfield	Mrs. George S. Goodspeed
1965	Red Mist of Da-Dor	Mrs. Dorothy M. Mullen
1967	Carla vom Rode	Dr. John Jeanneney
	Kookie of Da-Dor	Mrs. Dorothy M. Mullen
1968	CH. Uta v Moosbach	Dr. John Jeanneney and James Swyler
1969	Quarta von der Lonsheide	Dr. John Jeanneney
	Baron von Haussen	George R. Magee
1971	Klara v Wald Wind	Martha-Ann H. Lamberson
	Holmdach's Constant Avenger	J. David Lamberson and Mrs. Elisabeth Holmberg
	Ric-Ran's Wee Waggie Maggie	Robert Stephenson
1972	CH. Nobles Carpetbagger	Nancy L. Nolan
	Helia v Wald Wind	Martha-Ann H. Lamberson
	Gabrielle v Wald Wind	Martha-Ann H. Lamberson
1973	Clary von Moosbach	Dr. John Jeanneney
	Nantschi von der Rotmainquelle	Herta E. Schofield
1975	Liesele von Wald Wind, CD	Martha-Ann H. Lamberson
	Magee's Little Haussen	George Magee
	CH. Wald Wind's Constant Electra	Martha-Ann H. Lamberson
1976	Gretchen v Blutenwinkel, UD, TD	Albert L. and Gertrude Scheaffer
1977	Axel von der Grenedier Halde	Alexander Sangal
	Juliana v Blutenwinkel	Albert L. and Gertrude Scheaffer
	Wald Wind's Best Bet	Martha-Ann H. Lamberson

1978	Drossel von Moosbach, CG	Dr. John Jeanneney
	Kassandra of Da-Dor	Burt R. Kennedy Jr.
	Markeelyn's Heathcliff	Steven Cox
	Tanja vom Muthsam	Robert L. Reynolds
1979	Cognac von der Schofielden	Dr. Klaus H. and Deborah I. Jander
1980	Dachsie von Waldes Ruh	Adel and Gabrielle Hakki
	Elsa von Moosbach	Hans A. Klein
	Mt. Mansfield's Foolish Fun	Rosamond A. Chambers
	Oslo du Bellerstein	Dr. John Jeanneney
	CH. Westerly Petit Beurre, CG	Gwen Wexler
1981	Axel von Spurlaut	Hans A. Klein
	Eda von Moosbach	Paul M. Jeanneney
	CH. I Spy Wiretap, UDT, VC	Selma Sholes
	CH. Mt. Mansfield's Capt. Bangbang	Darby A. Chambers
1982	Adelheid von Spurlaut	Donald A. and Penny A. Hickman
	Gustav Schnapps Patch	Sue McClelland
	CH. Han-Jo's Cassius, L	Robert Stephenson
	Ima Little Bit Country, MW	Wanda L. Wilkes and Lance E. Bellomy
	Natasha of Badgerbane, CD, CG	Diane E. and Gordon P. Heldebrant
	Roach o Rio von Williams	Bonejean Shinn Williams
1983	Ahab von dem Jaegerheim, CG	Dr. John Jeanneney
	Augustus von dem Jaegerheim	Donald A. and Penny A. Hickman
	Gertruda of Bittersweet	Joan M. Malley and Dorothea F. Metzger
	Gertrude von Moosbach	Sydney A. Baker
1984	Badgerbane's Wonderful Woman	Diane E. and Gordon P. Heldebrant
	Berta von dem Jaegerheim	Robert F. Pultz
	Doxmans Jo Jo, MW	Paul V. and Cathern A. Essman
	Gisela von Moosbach	Donald A. and Penny A. Hickman
	Jesse von dem Jaegerheim	Robert E. Chapman
	Sherif du Bellerstien	Dr. John Jeanneney
	CH. Valona's Heaven Help Us	Ruth T. and Richard W. Martucci

Chapter 15

Breeding Your Dachshund

An earlier chapter discussed selection of a bitch you plan to use for breeding. In making this important purchase, you will be choosing a bitch who you hope will become the foundation of your kennel. Thus she must be of the finest producing bloodlines, excellent in temperament, of good type, and free of major faults or unsoundness. If you are offered a "bargain" brood bitch, be wary, as for this purchase you should not settle for less than the best and the price will be in accordance with the quality.

Conscientious breeders feel quite strongly that the only possible reason for producing puppies is the ambition to improve and uphold quality and temperament within the breed—definitely *not* because one hopes to make a quick cash profit on a mediocre litter, which never seems to work out that way in the long run and which accomplishes little beyond perhaps adding to the nation's heartbreaking number of unwanted canines. The only reason ever for breeding a litter is, with conscientious people, a desire to improve the quality of dogs in their own kennel or, as pet owners, to add to the number of dogs they themselves own with a puppy or two from their present favorites. In either case breeding should not take place unless one definitely has prospective owners for as many puppies as the litter may contain, lest you find yourself with several fast-growing young dogs and no homes in which to place them.

THE DACHSHUND BROOD BITCH

Bitches should not be mated earlier than their second season, by which time they should be from fifteen to eighteen months old. Many breeders prefer to wait and first finish the championships of their show bitches before breeding them, as pregnancy can be a disaster to a show coat and getting the bitch back in shape again takes time. When you have decided what will be the proper time, start watching at least several months ahead for what you feel would be the perfect mate to best complement your bitch's quality and bloodlines. Subscribe to the magazines which feature your breed exclusively and to some which cover all breeds in order to familiarize yourself with outstanding stud dogs in areas other than your own for there is no necessity nowadays to limit your choice to a local dog unless you truly like him and feel that he is the most suitable. It is quite usual to ship a bitch to a stud dog a distance away, and this generally works out with no ill effects. The important thing is that you need a stud dog strong in those features where your bitch is weak or lacking, a dog whose bloodlines are compatible with hers. Compare the background of both your bitch and the stud dog under consideration, paying particular attention to the quality of the puppies from bitches with backgrounds similar to your bitch's. If the puppies have been of the type and quality you admire, then this dog would seem a sensible choice for yours, too.

Jandelo's Patrician Knepper at eight and a half years old. The dam of nine champions, an important bitch in Jandelo Kennel history. The Van Valens, Fairview, North Carolina.

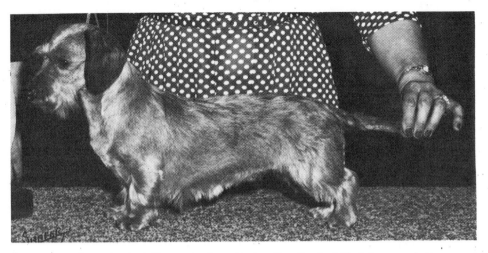

Ch. Bonnie MW of Sharondachs winning the Best of Variety award, Nor Port Dachshund Club, 1962.

Stud fees may be a few hundred dollars, sometimes even more under special situations for a particularly successful sire. It is money well spent, however. *Do not* ever breed to a dog because he is less expensive than the others unless you honestly believe that he can sire the kind of puppies who will be a credit to your kennel and your breed.

Contacting the owners of the stud dogs you find interesting will bring you pedigrees and pictures which you can then study in relation to your bitch's pedigree and conformation. Discuss your plans with other breeders who are knowledgeable (including the one who bred your own bitch). You may not always receive an entirely unbiased opinion (particularly if the person giving it also has an available stud dog), but one learns by discussion so listen to what they say, consider their opinions, and then you may be better qualified to form your own opinion.

As soon as you have made a choice, phone the owner of the stud dog you wish to use to find out if this will be agreeable. You will be asked about the bitch's health, soundness, temperament, and freedom from serious faults. A copy of her pedigree may be requested, as might a picture of her. A discussion of her background over the telephone may be sufficient to assure the stud's owner that she is suitable for the stud dog and of type, breeding, and quality herself to produce puppies of the quality for which the dog

291

is noted. The owner of a top-quality stud is often extremely selective in the bitches permitted to be bred to his dog, in an effort to keep the standard of his puppies high. The owner of a stud dog may require that the bitch be tested for brucellosis, which should be attended to not more than a month previous to the breeding.

Check out which airport will be most convenient for the person meeting and returning the bitch if she is to be shipped and also what airlines use that airport. You will find that the airlines are also apt to have special requirements concerning acceptance of animals for shipping. These include weather limitations and types of crates which are acceptable. The weather limits have to do with extreme heat and extreme cold at the point of destination, as some airlines will not fly dogs into temperatures above or below certain levels, fearing for their safety. The crate problem is a simple one, since, if your own crate is not suitable, most of the airlines have specially designed crates available for purchase at a fair and moderate price. It is a good plan to purchase one of these if you intend to be shipping dogs with any sort of frequency. They are made of fiberglass and are the safest type to use for shipping.

Normally you must notify the airline several days in advance to make a reservation, as they are able to accommodate only a certain number of dogs on each flight. Plan on shipping the bitch on about her eighth or ninth day of season, but be careful to avoid shipping her on a weekend when schedules often vary and freight offices are apt to be closed. Whenever you can, ship your bitch on a direct flight. Changing planes always carries a certain amount of risk of a dog being overlooked or wrongly routed at the middle stop, so avoid this danger if at all possible. The bitch must be accompanied by a health certificate which you must obtain from your veterinarian before taking her to the airport. Usually it will be necessary to have the bitch at the airport about two hours prior to flight time. Before finalizing arrangements, find out from the stud's owner at what time of day it will be most convenient to have the bitch picked up promptly upon arrival.

It is simpler if you can plan to bring the bitch to the stud dog yourself. Some people feel that the trauma of the flight may cause the bitch to not conceive; and, of course, undeniably there is a slight risk in shipping which can be avoided if you are able to drive the bitch to her destination. Be sure to leave yourself sufficient time to assure your arrival at the right time for her for breeding (normally the tenth to fourteenth day following the first signs of color); and remember that if you want the bitch bred twice, you should allow a day to elapse between the two matings. Do not expect the stud's owner to house you while you are there. Locate a nearby motel that takes dogs and make that your headquarters.

Just prior to the time your bitch is due in season, you should take her to visit your veterinarian. She should be checked for worms and should receive all the booster shots for which she is due plus one for parvovirus, unless she has had the latter shot fairly recently. The brucellosis test can also be done then, and the health certificate can be obtained for shipping if she is to travel by air. Should the bitch be at all overweight, now is the time to get the surplus off. She should be in good condition, neither underweight nor overweight, at the time of breeding.

The moment you notice the swelling of the vulva, for which you should be checking daily as the time for her season approaches, and the appearance of color, immediately contact the stud's owner and settle on the day for shipping or make the appointment for your arrival with the bitch for breeding. If you are shipping the bitch, the stud fee check should be mailed immediately, leaving ample time for it to have been received when the bitch arrives and the mating takes place. Be sure to call the airline, making her reservation at that time, too.

Do not feed the bitch within a few hours before shipping her. Be certain that she has had a drink of water and been well exercised before closing her in the crate. Several layers of newspapers, topped with some shredded newspaper, make a good bed and can be discarded when she arrives at her destination; these can be replaced with fresh newspapers for her return home. Remember that the bitch should be brought to the airport about two hours before flight time as sometimes the airlines refuse to accept late arrivals.

If you are taking your bitch by car, be certain that you will arrive at a reasonable time of day. Do not appear late in the evening. If your arrival in town is not until late, get a good night's sleep at your motel and contact the stud's owner first thing in the morning. If possible, leave children and relatives at home, as they will only be in the way and perhaps unwelcome by the stud's owner. Most stud dog owners prefer not to have any unnecessary people on hand during the actual mating.

Ch. Rose Farm's Merrakesh Express owned by Dee Hutchinson, Pound Ridge, New York.

After the breeding has taken place, if you wish to sit and visit for awhile and the stud's owner has the time, return the bitch to her crate in your car (first ascertaining, of course, that the temperature is comfortable for her and that there is proper ventilation). She should not be permitted to urinate for at least one hour following the breeding. This is the time when you get the business part of the transaction attended to. Pay the stud fee, upon which you should receive your breeding certificate and, if you do not already have it, a copy of the stud dog's pedigree. The owner of the stud dog does not sign or furnish a litter registration application until the puppies have been born.

Upon your return home, you can settle down and plan in happy anticipation a wonderful litter of puppies. A word of caution! Remember that although she has been bred, your bitch is still an interesting target for all male dogs, so guard her carefully for the next week or until you are absolutely certain that her season has entirely ended. This would be no time to have any unfortunate incident with another dog.

294

THE DACHSHUND STUD DOG

Choosing the best stud dog to complement your bitch is often very difficult. The two principal factors to be considered should be the stud's conformation and his pedigree. Conformation is fairly obvious; you want a dog that is typical of the breed in the words of the Standard of perfection. Understanding pedigrees is a bit more subtle since the pedigree lists the ancestry of the dog and involves individuals and bloodlines with which you may not be entirely familiar.

To a novice in the breed, then, the correct interpretation of a pedigree may at first be difficult to grasp. Study the pictures and text of this book and you will find many names of important bloodlines and members of the breed. Also make an effort to discuss the various dogs behind the proposed stud with some of the more experienced breeders, starting with the breeder of your own bitch. Frequently these folks will be personally familiar with many of the dogs in question, can offer opinions of them, and may have access to additional pictures which you would benefit by seeing. It is very important that the stud's pedigree be harmonious with

Ch. Pondwick's Hobgoblin, the great wire English import brought to the United States by Nancy Onthank who became sire of the amazing total of 89 champions. Owned by Dee Hutchinson, Rose Farm Kennels, Pound Ridge, New York.

that of the bitch you plan on breeding to him. Do not rush out and breed to the latest winner with no thought of whether or not he can produce true quality. By no means are all great show dogs great producers. It is the producing record of the dog in question and the dogs and bitches from which he has come that should be the basis on which you make your choice.

Breeding dogs is never a money-making operation. By the time you pay a stud fee, care for the bitch during pregnancy, whelp the litter, and rear the puppies through their early shots, worming, and so on, you will be fortunate to break even financially once the puppies have been sold. Your chances of doing this are greater if you are breeding for a show-quality litter which will bring you higher prices, as the pups are sold as show prospects. Therefore, your wisest investment is to use the best dog available for your bitch regardless of the cost; then you should wind up with more valuable puppies. Remember that it is equally costly to raise mediocre puppies as it is top ones, and your chances of financial return are better on the latter. To breed to the most excellent, most suitable stud dog you can find is the only sensible thing to do, and it is poor economy to quibble over the amount you are paying in a stud fee.

It will be your decision which course you decide to follow when you breed your bitch, as there are three options: linebreeding, inbreeding, and outcrossing. Each of these methods has its supporters and its detractors! Linebreeding is breeding a bitch to a dog belonging originally to the same canine family, being descended from the same ancestors, such as half brother to half sister, grandsire to granddaughter, niece to uncle (and vice-versa) or cousin to cousin. Inbreeding is breeding father to daughter, mother to son, or full brother to sister. Outcross breeding is breeding a dog and a bitch with no or only a few mutual ancestors.

Linebreeding is probably the safest course, and the one most likely to bring results, for the novice breeder. The more sophisticated inbreeding should be left to the experienced, longtime breeders who throroughly know and understand the risks and the possibilities involved with a particular line. It is usually done in an effort to intensify some ideal feature in that strain. Outcrossing is the reverse of inbreeding, an effort to introduce improvement in a specific feature needing correction, such as a shorter back, better movement, more correct head or coat, and so on.

Am. and Can. Ch. Jolly Dachs George, by Ch. Falcon of Heying-Teckel ex Georgette of Heying-Teckel. Bred by Joy and Al Levy. Owned by Ann Gordon, Pittsburgh, Pennsylvania.

It is the serious breeder's ambition to develop a strain or bloodline of their own, one strong in qualities for which their dogs will become distinguished. However, it must be realized that this will involve time, patience, and at least several generations before the achievement can be claimed. The safest way to embark on this plan, as we have mentioned, is by the selection and breeding of one or two bitches, the best you can buy and from top-producing kennels. In the beginning you do *not* really have to own a stud dog. In the long run it is less expensive and sounder judgement to pay a stud fee when you are ready to breed a bitch than to purchase a stud dog and feed him all year; a stud dog does not win any popularity contests with owners of bitches to be bred until he becomes a champion, has been successfully Specialed for a while, and has been at least moderately advertised, all of which adds up to quite a healthy expenditure.

One of the very outstanding dogs in the background of our modern winners, Ch. Leutnant v Marienlust, the most important sire of the early 1940's. Mr. and Mrs. Joseph Mehrer, owners, West Hempstead, New York.

The wisest course for the inexperienced breeder just starting out in dogs is as outlined above. Keep the best bitch puppy from the first several litters. After that you may wish to consider keeping your own stud dog if there has been a particularly handsome male in one of your litters that you feel has great potential or if you know where there is one available that you are interested in, with the feeling that he would work in nicely with the breeding program on which you have embarked. By this time, with several litters already born, your eye should have developed to a point enabling you to make a wise choice, either from one of your own litters or from among dogs you have seen that appear suitable.

The greatest care should be taken in the selection of your own stud dog. He must be of true type and highest quality as he may be responsible for siring many puppies each year, and he should come from a line of excellent dogs on both sides of his pedigree which themselves are, and which are descended from, successful producers. This dog should have no glaring faults in conformation; he should be of such a quality that he can hold his own in keenest competition within his breed. He should be in good health, be virile and be a keen stud dog, a proven sire able to transmit his correct qualities to his puppies. Need I say that such a dog will be enormously expensive unless you have the good fortune to produce him in one of your own litters? To buy and use a lesser stud dog, however, is downgrading your breeding program unnecessarily since there are so many dogs fitting the description of a fine stud whose services can be used on payment of a stud fee.

You should *never* breed to an unsound dog or one with any serious disqualifying faults according to the breed's standard. Not all champions by any means pass along their best features; and by the same token, occasionally you will find a great one who can pass along his best features but never gained his championship title due to some unusual circumstances. The information you need about a stud dog is what type of puppies he has produced and with what bloodlines and whether or not he possesses the bloodlines and attributes considered characteristic of the best in your breed.

If you go out to buy a stud dog, obviously he will not be a puppy but rather a fully mature and proven male with as many of the best attributes as possible. True, he will be an expensive investment, but if you choose and make his selection with care and forethought, he may well prove to be one of the best investments you have ever made.

Of course, the most exciting of all is when a young male you have decided to keep from one of your litters due to his tremendous show potential turns out to be a stud dog such as we have described. In this case he should be managed with care, for he is a valuable property that can contribute inestimably to this breed as a whole and to your own kennel specifically.

Do not permit your stud dog to be used until he is about a year old, and even then he should be bred to mature, proven matron accustomed to breeding who will make his first experience pleasant and easy. A young dog can be put off forever by a maiden bitch who fights and resists his advances. Never allow this to happen. Always start a stud dog out with a bitch who is mature, has been bred previously, and is of even temperament. The first breeding should be performed in quiet surroundings with only you and one other person to hold the bitch. Do not make it a circus, as the experience will determine the dog's outlook about future stud work. If he does not enjoy the first experience or associates it with any unpleasantness, you may well have a problem in the future.

Your young stud must permit help with the breeding, as later there will be bitches who will not be cooperative. If right from the beginning you are there helping him and praising him, whether or not your assistance is actually needed, he will expect and accept this as a matter of course when a difficult bitch comes along.

Things to have handy before introducing your dog and the bitch are K-Y jelly (the only lubricant which should be used) and a length of gauze with which to muzzle the bitch should it be necessary to keep her from biting you or the dog. Some bitches put up a fight; others are calm. It is best to be prepared.

At the time of the breeding, the stud fee comes due, and it is expected that it will be paid promptly. Normally a return service is offered in case the bitch misses or fails to produce one live puppy. Conditions of the service are what the stud dog's owner makes them, and there are no standard rules covering this. The stud fee is paid for the act, not the result. If the bitch fails to conceive, it is customary for the owner to offer a free return service; but this is a courtesy and not to be considered a right, particularly in the case of a proven stud who is siring consistently and whose fault the failure obviously is *not*. Stud dog owners are always anxious to see their clients get good value and to have in the ring winning young stock by their dog; therefore, very few refuse to mate the second time. It is wise, however, for both parties to have the terms of the transaction clearly understood at the time of the breeding.

If the return service has been provided and the bitch has missed a second time, that is considered to be the end of the matter and the owner would be expected to pay a further fee if it is felt that the bitch should be given a third chance with the stud dog. The management of a stud dog and his visiting bitches is quite a task, and a stud fee has usually been well earned when one service has been achieved, let alone by repeated visits from the same bitch.

The accepted litter is one live puppy. It is wise to have printed a breeding certificate which the owner of the stud dog and the owner of the bitch both sign. This should list in detail the conditions of the breeding as well as the dates of the mating.

Upon occasion, arrangements other than a stud fee in cash are made for a breeding, such as the owner of the stud taking a pick-of-the-litter puppy in lieu of money. This should be clearly specified on the breeding certificate along with the terms of the age at which the stud's owner will select the puppy, whether it is to be a specific sex, or whether it is to be the pick of the entire litter.

The price of a stud fee varies according to circumstances. Usually, to prove a young stud dog, his owner will allow the first breeding to be quite inexpensive. Then, once a bitch has become pregnant by him, he becomes a "proven stud" and the fee rises accordingly for bitches that follow. The sire of championship quality puppies will bring a stud fee of at least the purchase price of one show puppy as the accepted "rule-of-thumb." Until at least one champion by your stud dog has finished, the fee will remain equal to the price of one pet puppy. When his list of champions starts to grow, so does the amount of the stud fee. For a top-producing sire of champions, the stud fee will rise accordingly.

Almost invariably it is the bitch who comes to the stud dog for the breeding. Immediately upon having selected the stud dog you wish to use, discuss the possibility with the owner of that dog. It is the stud dog owner's perogative to refuse to breed any bitch deemed unsuitable for this dog. Stud fee and method of payment should be stated at this time and a decision reached on whether it is to be a full cash transaction at the time of the mating or a pick-of-the-litter puppy, usually at eight weeks of age.

If the owner of the stud dog must travel to an airport to meet the bitch and ship her for the flight home, an additional charge will be made for time, tolls, and gasoline based on the stud owner's proximity to the airport. The stud fee includes board for the day on the bitch's arrival through two days for breeding, with a day in between. If it is necessary that the bitch remain longer, it is very likely that additional board will be charged at the normal per-day rate for the breed.

Be sure to advise the stud's owner as soon as you know that your bitch is in season so that the stud dog will be available. This is especially important because if he is a dog being shown, he and his owner may be unavailable, owing to the dog's absence from home.

As the owner of a stud dog being offered to the public, it is essential that you have proper facilities for the care of visiting bitches. Nothing can be worse than a bitch being insecurely housed and slipping out to become lost or bred by the wrong dog. If you are taking people's valued bitches into your kennel or home, it is imperative that you provide them with comfortable, secure housing and good care while they are your responsibility.

There is no dog more valuable than the proven sire of champions, Group winners, and Best in Show dogs. Once you have such an animal, guard his reputation well and do *not* permit him to be bred to just any bitch that comes along. It takes two to make the puppies; even the most dominant stud cannot do it all himself, so never permit him to breed a bitch you consider unworthy. Remember that when the puppies arrive, it will be your stud dog who will be blamed for any lack of quality, while the bitch's shortcomings will be quickly and conveniently overlooked.

Going into the actual management of the mating is a bit superfluous here. If you have had previous experience in breeding a dog and bitch you will know how the mating is done. If you do not have such experience, you should not attempt to follow direction given in a book but should have a veterinarian, breeder friend, or handler there to help you with the first few times. You do not just turn the dog and bitch loose together and await developments, as too many things can go wrong and you may altogether miss getting the bitch bred. Someone should hold the dog and the bitch (one person each) until the "tie" is made and these two people should stay with them during the entire act.

If you get a complete tie, probably only the one mating is absolutely necessary. However, especially with a maiden bitch or one that has come a long distance for this breeding, we prefer following up with a second breeding, leaving one day in between the two matings. In this way there will be little or no chance of the bitch missing.

Once the tie has been completed and the dogs release, be certain that the male's penis goes completely back within its sheath. He should be allowed a drink of water and a short walk, and then he should be put into his crate or somewhere alone where he can settle down. Do not allow him to be with other dogs for a while as they will notice the odor of the bitch on him, and, particularly with other males present, he may become involved in a fight.

PREGNANCY, WHELPING, AND THE LITTER

Once the bitch has been bred and is back at home, remember to keep an ever watchful eye that no other males get to her until at least the twenty-second day of her season has passed. Until then, it will still be possible for an unwanted breeding to take place, which at this point would be catastrophic. Remember that she actually can have two separate litters by two different dogs, so take care.

In other ways, she should be treated normally. Controlled exercise is good, and necessary for the bitch throughout her pregnancy, tapering it off to just several short walks daily, preferably on lead, as she reaches about her seventh week. As her time grows close, be careful about her jumping or playing too roughly.

The theory that a bitch should be overstuffed with food when pregnant is a poor one. A fat bitch is never an easy whelper, so the overfeeding you consider good for her may well turn out to be a hindrance later on. During the first few weeks of pregnancy,

Who could possibly resist a Dachshund puppy? These charmers, owned by Peggy Westphal, von Westphalen Kennels, New Milford, Connecticut.

your bitch should be fed her normal diet. At four to five weeks along, calcium should be added to her food. At seven weeks her food may be increased if she seems to crave more than she is getting, and a meal of canned milk (mixed with an equal amount of water) should be introduced. If she is fed just once a day, add another meal rather than overload her with too much at one time. If twice a day is her schedule, then a bit more food can be added to each feeding.

A week before the pups are due, your bitch should be introduced to her whelping box so that she will be accustomed to it and feel at home there when the puppies arrive. She should be encouraged to sleep there but permitted to come and go as she wishes. The box should be roomy enough for her to lie down and stretch out in but not too large, lest the pups have more room than is needed in which to roam and possibly get chilled by going too far away from their mother. Be sure that the box has a "pig rail"; this will prevent the puppies from being crushed against the sides. The room in which the box is placed, either in your home or in the kennel, should be kept at about 70 degrees Fahrenheit. In winter it may be necessary to have an infrared lamp over the whelping box, in which case be careful not to place it too low or close to the puppies.

Newspapers will become a very important commodity, so start collecting them well in advance to have a big pile handy for the whelping box. With a litter of puppies, one never seems to have papers enough, so the higher pile to start with, the better off you will be. Other necessities for whelping time are clean, soft turkish towels, scissors, and a bottle of alcohol.

You will know that her time is very near when your bitch becomes restless, wandering in and out of her box and of the room. She may refuse food, and at that point her temperature will start to drop. She will dig at and tear up the newspapers in her box, shiver, and generally look uncomfortable. Only you should be with your bitch at this time. She does not need spectators; and several people, even though they may be family members whom she knows, hanging over her may upset her to the point where she may harm the puppies. You should remain nearby, quietly watching, not fussing or hovering; speak calmly and frequently to her to instill confidence. Eventually she will settle down in her box and begin panting; contractions will follow. Soon thereafter a

Can. Ch. Tori-Jarice's Wee Angus MS, August 11, 1970-May 25, 1982. Co-holder of the title All-Time Top Producing Smooth Miniature in the United States and sire of record-setting miniatures. By Verdon's Vice M ex Am. and Can. Ch. Tori Russet Princess. Breeder, Thomas A. Rice. Owner, Jeanne A. Rice, Valley Stream, New York.

puppy will start to emerge, sliding out with the contractions. The mother immediately should open the sac, sever the cord with her teeth, and then clean up the puppy. She will also eat the placenta, which you should permit. Once the puppy is cleaned, it should be placed next to the bitch unless she is showing signs of having the next one immediately. Almost at once the puppy will start looking for a nipple on which to nurse, and you should ascertain that it is able to latch on successfully.

If the puppy is a breech (*i.e.*, born feet first), you must watch carefully for it to be completely delivered as quickly as possible and for the sac to be removed quickly so that the puppy does not drown. Sometimes even a normally positioned birth will seem extremely slow in coming. Should this occur, you might take a clean towel, and as the bitch contracts, pull the puppy out, doing so gently and with utmost care. If, once the puppy is delivered, it shows little signs of life, take a rough turkish towel and massage the puppy's chest by rubbing quite briskly back and forth. Continue this for about fifteen minutes, and be sure that the mouth is free of liquid. It may be necessary to try mouth-to-mouth breathing, which is done by pressing the puppy's jaws open and, using a finger, depressing the tongue which may be stuck to the roof of the mouth. Then place your mouth against the puppy's and blow hard down the puppy's throat. Rub the puppy's chest with the towel again and try artificial respiration, pressing the sides of the chest together slowly and rhythmically—in and out, in and out. Keep trying one method or the other for at least twenty minutes before giving up. You may be rewarded with a live puppy who otherwise would not have made it.

If you are successful in bringing the puppy around, do not immediately put it back with the mother as it should be kept extra warm. Put it in a cardboard box on an electric heating pad or, if it is the time of year when your heat is running, near a radiator or near the fireplace or stove. As soon as the rest of the litter has been born, it then can join the others.

An hour or more may elapse between puppies, which is fine so long as the bitch seems comfortable and is neither straining nor contracting. She should not be permitted to remain unassisted for more than an hour if she does continue to contract. This is when you should get her to your veterinarian, whom you should already have alerted to the possibility of a problem existing. He should examine her and perhaps give her a shot of Pituitrin. In some cases the veterinarian may find that a Caesarean section is necessary due to a puppy being lodged in a manner making normal delivery impossible. Sometimes this is caused by an abnormally large puppy, or it may just be that the puppy is simply turned in the wrong position. If the bitch does require a Caesarean section, the puppies already born must be kept warm in their cardboard box with a heating pad under the box.

Once the section is done, get the bitch and the puppies home. Do not attempt to put the puppies in with the bitch until she has regained consciousness as she may unknowingly hurt them. But do get them back to her as soon as possible for them to start nursing.

Should the mother lack milk at this time, the puppies must be fed by hand, kept very warm, and held onto the mother's teats several times a day in order to stimulate and encourage the secretion of milk, which should start shortly.

Assuming that there has been no problem and that the bitch has whelped naturally, you should insist that she go out to exercise, staying just long enough to make herself comfortable. She can be offered a bowl of milk and a biscuit, but then she should settle down with her family. Freshen the whelping box for her with fresh newspapers while she is taking this respite so that she and the puppies will have a clean bed.

Unless some problem arises, there is little you must do about the puppies until they become three to four weeks old. Keep the box clean and supplied with fresh newspapers the first few days, but then turkish towels should be tacked down to the bottom of the box so that the puppies will have traction as they move about.

If the bitch has difficulties with her milk supply, or if you should be so unfortunate as to lose her, then you must be prepared to either hand-feed or tube-feed the puppies if they are to survive. Tube-feeding is so much faster and easier. If the bitch is available, it is best that she continues to clean and care for the puppies in the normal manner excepting for the food supplements you will provide. If it is impossible for her to do this, then after every feeding you must gently rub each puppy's abdomen with wet cotton to make it urinate, and the rectum should be gently rubbed to open the bowels.

Newborn puppies must be fed every three to four hours around the clock. The puppies must be kept warm during this time. Have your veterinarian teach you how to tube-feed. You will find that it is really quite simple.

After a normal whelping, the bitch will require additional food to enable her to produce sufficient milk. In addition to being fed twice daily, she should be given some canned milk several times each day.

When the puppies are two weeks old, their nails should be clipped, as they are needle sharp at this age and can hurt or damage the mother's teats and stomach as the pups hold on to nurse.

Between three and four weeks of age, the puppies should begin to be weaned. Scraped beef (prepared by scraping it off slices of beef with a spoon so that none of the gristle is included) may be offered in very small quantities a couple of times daily for the first few days. Then by the third day you can mix puppy chow with warm water as directed on the package, offering it four times daily. By now the mother should be kept away from the puppies and out of the box for several hours at a time so that when they have reached five weeks of age she is left in with them only overnight. By the time the puppies are six weeks old, they should be entirely weaned and receiving only occasional visits from their mother.

Most veterinarians recommend a temporary DHL (distemper, hepatitis, leptospirosis) shot when the puppies are six weeks of age. This remains effective for about two weeks. Then at eight weeks of age, the puppies should receive the series of permanent shots for DHL protection. It is also a good idea to discuss with your vet the advisability of having your puppies inoculated against the dreaded parvovirus at the same time. Each time the pups go to the vet for shots, you should bring stool samples so that they can be examined for worms. Worms go through various stages of development and may be present in a stool sample even though the sample does not test positive in every checkup. So do not neglect to keep careful watch on this.

Ch. Rose Farm's Moon Rockette at DALI in October 1971, here taking Best of Variety. Bred by Nancy Onthank.

The great Ch. Roderick von der Nidda winning one of his Bests in Show, at Harford County K.C. in 1959. A very great and influential longhair! Jerry Rigden handling.

The puppies should be fed four times daily until they are three months old. Then you can cut back to three feedings daily. By the time the puppies are six months of age, two meals daily are sufficient. Some people feed their dogs twice daily throughout their lifetime; others go to one meal daily when the puppy becomes one year of age.

The ideal age for puppies to go to their new homes is between eight and twelve weeks, although some puppies successfully adjust to a new home when they are six weeks old. Be sure that they go to their new owners accompanied by a description of the diet you've been feeding them and a schedule of the shots they have already received and those they still need. These should be included with the registration application and a copy of the pedigree.

Another of Jerry Rigden's important winners of the 1950's, Ch. Dachscroft's William W.W. winning Best Wirehair at the Dachshund Club of New Jersey, May 1959.

Ch. Dresel's Allegro at eight and a half years of age. Owned by Ann and Michael Gordon, Pittsburgh, Pennsylvania.

Chapter 16

Traveling with Your Dachshund

When you travel with your dog, to shows or on vacation or wherever, remember that everyone does not share your enthusiasm or love for dogs and that those who do not, strange creatures though they seem to us, have their rights, too. These rights, on which your should not encroach, include not being disturbed, annoyed, or made uncomfortable by the presence and behavior of other people's pets. Your dog should be kept on lead in public places and should recognize and promptly obey the commands "Down," "Come," "Sit," and "Stay."

Take along his crate if you are going any distance with your dog. And keep him in it when riding in the car. A crated dog has a far better chance of escaping injury than one riding loose in the car, should an accident occur or an emergency arise. If you do permit your dog to ride loose, never allow him to hang out a window, ears blowing in the breeze. An injury to his eyes could occur in this manner. He could also become overly excited by something he sees and jump out, or he could lose his balance and fall out.

Never, ever, under any circumstances, should a dog be permitted to ride loose in the back of a pick-up truck. Some people do transport dogs in this manner, which is cruel and shocking. How easily such a dog can be thrown out of the truck by sudden jolts or an impact! Doubtless many dogs have jumped out at the sight of something exciting along the way. Some unthinking individuals tie the dog, probably not realizing that were he to jump under those circumstances, his neck would be broken, he could be dragged alongside the vehicle, or he could be hit by another vehicle. If you are for any reason taking your dog in an an open-back truck, please have sufficient regard for that dog to at least provide a crate for him; and then remember that, in or out of a

311

Ch. Vantebe's Draht Timothy, one of the most famous and influential Standard Wire Dachshunds of all time, was an important sire and leading show dog for Peggy and Allen Westphal, von Westphalen Kennels, during the 1960's.

crate, a dog riding under the direct rays of the sun in hot weather can suffer and have his life endangered by the heat.

If you are staying at a hotel or motel with your dog, exercise him somewhere other than in the flower beds and parking lot of the property. People walking to and from their cars really are not thrilled at "stepping in something" left by your dog. Should an accident occur, pick it up with a tissue or paper towel and deposit it in a proper receptacle; do not just walk off leaving it to remain there. Usually there are grassy areas on the sides of and behind motels where dogs can be exercised. Use them rather than the more conspicuous, usually carefully tended, front areas or those close to the rooms. If you are becoming a dog show enthusiast, you will eventually need an exercise pen to take with you to the show. Exercise pens are ideal to use when staying at motels, too, as they permit you to limit the dog's roaming space and to pick up after him more easily.

Never leave your dog unattended in the room of a motel unless you are absolutely, positively certain that he will stay there quietly and not damage or destroy anything. You do not want a long list of complaints from irate guests, caused by the annoying barking or whining of a lonesome dog in strange surroundings or an over-zealous watch dog barking furiously each time a footstep passes the door or he hears a sound from an adjoining room. And you certainly do not want to return to torn curtains or bedspreads, soiled rugs, or other embarrassing evidence of the fact that your dog is not really house-reliable after all.

If yours is a dog accustomed to traveling with you and you are positive that his behavior will be acceptable when left alone, that is fine. But if the slightest uncertainty exists, the wise course is to leave him in the car while you go to dinner or elsewhere; then bring him into the room when you are ready to retire for the night.

When you travel with a dog, it is often simpler to take along from home the food and water he will need rather than to buy food and look for water while you travel. In this way he will have the rations to which he is accustomed and which you know agree with him, and there will be no fear of problems due to different drinking water. Feeding on the road is quite easy now, at least for short trips, with all the splendid dry prepared foods and high-quality canned meats available. A variety of lightweight, refillable water containers can be bought at many types of stores.

Be careful always to leave sufficient openings to ventilate your car when the dog will be alone in it. Remember that during the summer, the rays of the sun can make an inferno of a closed car within only a few minutes, so leave enough window space open to provide air circulation. Again, if your dog is in a crate, this can be done quite safely. The fact that you have left the car in a shady spot is not always a guarantee that you will find conditions the same when you return. Don't forget that the position of the sun changes in a matter of minutes, and the car you left nicely shaded half an hour ago can be getting full sunlight far more quickly than you may realize. So, if you leave a dog in the car, make sure there is sufficient ventilation and check back frequently to ascertain that all is well.

If you are going to another country, you will need a health certificate from your veterinarian for each dog you are taking with you, certifying that each has had rabies shots within the required time preceding your visit.

Chapter 17

Responsibilities of Breeders and Owners

The first responsibility of any person breeding dogs is to do so with care, forethought, and deliberation. It is inexcusable to breed more litters than you need to carry on your show program or to perpetuate your bloodlines. A responsible breeder should not cause a litter to be born without definite plans for the safe and happy disposition of the puppies.

A responsible dog breeder makes absolutely certain, so far as is humanly possible, that the home to which one of his puppies will go is a good home, one that offers proper care and an enthusiastic owner. To be admired are those breeders who insist on visiting (although doing so is not always feasible) the prospective owners of their puppies to see if they have suitable facilities for keeping a dog and to find out if they understand the responsibility involved, and if all members of the household are in accord regarding the desirability of owning one. All breeders should carefully check out the credentials of prospective purchasers to be sure that the puppy is being placed in responsible hands.

No breeder ever wants a puppy or grown dog he has raised to wind up in an animal shelter, in an experimental laboratory, or as a victim of a speeding car. While complete control of such a situation may be impossible, it is as important to make every effort to turn over dogs to responsible people. When selling a puppy, it is a good idea to do so with the understanding that should it become necessary to place the dog in other hands, the purchaser will first contact you, the breeder. You may want to help in some way, possibly by buying back or taking back the dog or placing it elsewhere. It is not fair to just sell puppies and then never again give a thought to their welfare. Family problems arise, people may be forced to move where dogs are prohibited, or people just plain

A touch of nostalgia from 1962. *Left,* the late Gracie (Mrs. William Burr) Hill presenting trophy; *center,* Lorraine Heichal (now Masely) the judge; *right,* Dorothy Hardy, at the final of the DALI Specialty Show, judged by Lorraine with Ch. Herthwood's Mark of Rose Farm which Mrs. Hardy is winning Best of Breed for Mrs. Nancy Onthank.

grow bored with a dog and its care. Thus the dog becomes a victim. You, as the dog's breeder, should concern yourself with the welfare of each of your dogs and see to it that the dog remains in good hands.

The final obligation every dog owner shares, be there just one dog or an entire kennel involved, is that of making detailed, explicit plans for the future of these dearly loved animals in the event of the owner's death. Far too many of people are apt to procrastinate and leave this very important matter unattended to, feeling that everything will work out or that "someone will see to them." The latter is not too likely, at least not to the benefit of the dogs, unless you have done some advance planning which will assure their future well-being.

Life is filled with the unexpected, and even the youngest, healthiest, most robust of us may be the victim of a fatal accident or sudden illness. The fate of your dogs, so entirely in our hands, should never be left to chance. If you have not already done so, please get together with your lawyer and set up a clause in your will specifying what you want done with each of your dogs, to whom they will be entrusted (after first making absolutely certain that the person selected is willing and able to assume the responsibility), and telling the locations of all registration papers, pedigrees, and kennel records. Just think of the possibilities which might happen otherwise! If there is another family member who shares your love of the dogs, that is good and you have less to worry about. But if your heirs are not dog-oriented, they will hardly know how to proceed or how to cope with the dogs themselves, and they may wind up disposing of or caring for your dogs in a manner that would break your heart were you around to know about it.

It is advisable to have in your will specific instructions concerning each of your dogs. A friend, also a dog person who regards her own dogs with the same concern and esteem as we do, may agree to take over their care until they can be placed accordingly and will make certain that all will work out as you have planned. This person's name and phone number can be prominently displayed in your van or car and in your wallet. Your lawyer can be made aware of this fact. This can be spelled out in your will. The friend can have a signed check of yours to be used in case of an emergency or accident when you are traveling with the dogs; this check can be used to cover her expense to come and take over the care of your dogs should anything happen to make it impossible for us to do so. This is the least any dog owner should do in preparation for the time their dogs suddenly find themselves alone. There have been so many sad cases of dogs unprovided for by their loving owners, left to heirs who couldn't care less and who disposed of them in any way at all to get rid of them, or left to heirs who kept and neglected them under the misguided idea that they were providing them "a fine home with lots of freedom." These misfortunes must be prevented from befalling your own dogs who have meant so much you!

Index